Java
Foundations

Java™ Foundations

Todd Greanier

SYBEX

San Francisco ◆ London

Associate Publisher: Neil Edde
Acquisitions and Developmental Editor: Maureen Adams
Production Editor: Mae Lum
Technical Editor: Jerome Goodman
Copyeditor: Pat Coleman
Compositor: Maureen Forys, Happenstance Type-O-Rama
Graphic Illustrator: Jeff Wilson, Happenstance Type-O-Rama
Proofreaders: Laurie O'Connell, Nancy Riddiough
Indexer: Ted Laux
Book Designer: Judy Fung
Cover Designer: Ingalls + Associates
Cover Illustrator/Photographer: Jerry Driendl, Taxi

An earlier version of this book was published under the title *Java Certification JumpStart* © 2003 SYBEX Inc.

Library of Congress Card Number: 2004109314

ISBN: 0-7821-4373-3

Manufactured in the United States of America

10 9 8 7 6 5 4 3 2 1

For my son, Maximilian Arthur

Acknowledgments

Without my wife, Stacey Ann, this book could never have been written. Her patience and support are seemingly endless, and I am eternally grateful to her. As an author, I have to make certain sacrifices, but as a wife, she has to make those same sacrifices and then some. Sore fingers and tired eyes don't seem such a bother when she walks into the room.

Other friends also deserve a bit of thanks, including Don Holt, Bill Mulligan, Kelby and Beth Zorgdrager, Sean and Heather Lahman, Randy Bonferraro, Cara Lynch, Paul Eberhardt, Lee and Judy Bruder, Kwai Chang Caine, and Dan Millman.

Of course, I also want to thank several of the fine folks at Sybex who helped get this book into your hands. Maureen Adams first brought the idea to me and helped me get the ball rolling. Pat Coleman and Mae Lum helped me to turn the chaos of my thoughts into coherent sentences and made the entire writing process extremely pleasant. Thanks also to Maureen Forys of Happenstance Type-O-Rama for the book layout and to Ted Laux for the index.

Contents

Introduction

When you're learning any new topic or technology, it's important to have all the basics at your disposal. The Sybex Foundations series provides the building blocks of specific technologies that help you establish yourself in IT.

Java is one of the most popular languages in the world and can be used to develop everything from web applications to cell-phone tools to space vehicles. Although it has enormous flexibility and power, it is not a difficult language to learn. *Java Foundations* assumes no prior knowledge of Java programming and provides a solid introduction to this language, explaining the fundamentals in simple terms with plenty of examples.

My goal with *Java Foundations* is to introduce you to the core Java concepts so that you'll come away with an intermediate understanding of the language. This book isn't boringly technical; each topic is covered to sufficient depth, but not to an extreme.

As a software architect and instructor, I have several years' experience working in the computer industry and specifically with Java. Drawing from this experience, I've tried to present the relevant material in an interesting way, and I've included what I have found to be the most important concepts. The book is filled with several simple examples, diagrams, and screen captures in an effort to make the Java language more tangible.

This book is neither operating system–specific nor software-specific. Concepts are presented so that you can gain an understanding of the topic without being tied to a particular platform.

NOTE

Who Should Read This Book?

Java Foundations is designed to teach the fundamentals of the Java programming language to people who are fairly new to the topic. This book will be useful for:

- People interested in learning more about Java
- Decision-makers who need to know the fundamentals in order to make valid, informed choices around Java
- Administrators who feel they are missing some of the foundational information about Java
- Small-business owners interested in a language they can use for their applications
- Instructors teaching a Java fundamentals course
- Students enrolled in a Java fundamentals course

What This Book Covers

Working with Java has been an interesting, exciting, and rewarding experience. As I continue to learn about today's applications and Java, the more I see the need to continue learning. No matter what sector of the computer industry you're employed in (or even if you're not employed in IT yet), Java is an important foundational topic that you must understand.

Java Foundations contains many drawings and charts that help create a comfortable learning environment. It provides many real-world analogies that you will be able to relate to and through which the Java language will become tangible. The analogies provide a simple way to understand the technical knowledge required to successfully use Java.

This book builds your understanding about Java progressively, like climbing a ladder. Here's how the information is presented:

> **Chapter 1**   This chapter provides an overview of where Java came from and why it is an important language.
>
> **Chapters 2–5**   These chapters describe the fundamentals of the Java language, including all the keywords, the flow-control syntax, and arrays.
>
> **Chapters 6–7**   These two chapters introduce you to the world of object-oriented programming and show you how to master the techniques with Java.
>
> **Chapter 8**   This chapter discusses the exception-handling mechanism that aids in creating robust Java applications.
>
> **Chapter 9**   This chapter contains some of the common Java classes that you will use over and over again as you learn more about the language.
>
> **Chapter 10**   This chapter introduces the collection classes provided by the Java language to allow more complex forms of data structuring.

Making the Most of This Book

At the beginning of each chapter of *Java Foundations*, you'll find a list of the topics that I'll cover within the chapter.

To help you soak up new material easily, I've highlighted new terms, such as *flow control*, in italics and defined them in the page margins.

In addition, several special elements highlight important information:

flow control
Special constructs in a language that allow simple or complex algorithms to be defined. Essentially, these form the intelligence of your code.

NOTE   Notes provide extra information and references to related information.

Tips are insights that help you perform tasks more easily and effectively.

TIP

Warnings let you know about things you should—or shouldn't—do as you learn more about Java.

WARNING

At the end of each chapter, you can test your knowledge of the chapter's relevant topics by answering the review questions. (You'll find the answers to the review questions in Appendix A.)

Chapter 1

The History of Java

Way back in 1995, Sun Microsystems released the first version of the Java programming language to the public. Since then, Java technology has become an extremely popular language and has been adopted by millions of developers to create robust applications. Though Java applications can be executed in practically any environment, they are most commonly used in networked environments such as an intranet or the Internet.

Java technology can be seen as both a language and a platform. The language is simple, secure, and powerful. Using it, you can write applications that can run on practically any device, including a PC, a personal digital assistant (PDA), a cellular phone, or a television.

Where Java Technology Came From

Back in 1991, some folks at Sun Microsystems were thinking about the future of computing. Their research indicated the "next big thing" would be intelligent consumer devices. A small group was formed under the code name "Green Project" to create a prototype for a consumer device to try to get a jump on the market. The Green Project was essentially a secret project inside Sun, and the members of the group cut themselves off from the rest of the company to pursue their goals.

The Green Project

After 18 months of hard work, the Green Project team emerged with a device that they called Star7. Essentially, it worked like today's PDA (though it was a lot bigger) and had an animated, color touchscreen. It ran an application that featured a character named Duke who reacted to user prompts to perform various tasks. The Star7 device was only meant as a demonstration platform, however. The Green Team expected that the software running on the Star7 could be deployed on dozens of platforms such as televisions, kiosks, and "smart" home appliances. In other words, the real power of the Star7 was the programming language that made it work.

One of the team members, James Gosling, created the language that made the demo work. He called this language Oak after a large oak tree outside his office window. The language was completely processor-independent so it could easily be used on all the available consumer devices. A primary feature of this software was that it could function nicely in a networked environment. The Green Project team tried to convince some new industries, including digital cable companies, that their creation was ideal. Unfortunately, at that time those industries were young and had murky visions of the future, so the entire Green Project was nearly dashed.

Enter the Web

In 1993, however, the World Wide Web exploded, something that proved to be good fortune for the Green Project team and Sun. Because the language that they created was designed to work over networks and provide dynamic content, the Internet suddenly seemed like the perfect environment in which the language could live. They immediately realized they had created a programming language that had possibilities much larger than just the consumer devices market. In fact, they had something that would change the way we use the Internet altogether.

In 1994, the Green Project began promoting their new programming language as a language-based operating system and targeted the online multimedia aspects of the Internet. They soon discovered that an obscure, existing programming language was called Oak, so they had to change the name. Among others, Neon, Pepper, Silk, and Lyric were suggested before Java finally became the official name. Sun Microsystems began giving the language away on the Internet and finally officially announced the language in May 1995.

Since that time, Java technology has become incredibly popular. We use it to provide dynamic content on the Internet, but it also has become a powerful language for developing large-scale enterprise applications and e-commerce applications. Java has even come full circle and is now embedded in many consumer devices such as cellular phones, PDAs, and smart cards.

Remember Duke, the character on the original Star7 device? The Green Project team so loved the little guy that they kept him around, and he has been the mascot for the Java programming language all along. Hey, it isn't every programming language that has a mascot!

NOTE

The Features of Java Technology

A long list of features makes Java an excellent programming language. Java can be described as simple, object oriented, interpreted, portable, robust, secure, multithreaded, and high performance. Beyond this, it also saves time and money and solves some important problems.

Those are all excellent traits for a language, so it is no surprise that so many people are excited about Java and that it has become adopted worldwide. The next few sections discuss each of these features of the language and show you why many people are so excited about programming with Java.

The Java platform is formed from two components:

- The Java application programming interface (Java API)
- The Java Virtual Machine (JVM)

The Java API is a set of libraries that you can use to accomplish tasks such as creating graphical user interfaces (GUIs), performing file input/output (I/O), and establishing network communication. The JVM is in charge of executing your code in a specific environment.

The father of Java technology, James Gosling, along with Henry McGilton, wrote the official white paper on Java upon its original release in 1996. This paper discusses the features of the language in detail. You can check it out at `http://java.sun` `.com/docs/white/langenv/index.html`**.**

NOTE

Java Is Simple

Learning a new programming language is often a lot of hard work. I am not about to tell you that you won't face challenges in learning Java, but I can say that because of the stylistic simplicity of the language, many people learn it quickly. Java does not have a lot of clutter to get in the way, and because it was built from the ground up with modern programming concepts in mind, those who have worked with other languages will notice a degree of familiarity.

One of the primary goals of the Java language developers was to remove any aspects of languages such as C and C++ that were determined to be overly complicated and extraneous. Java does not have a large number of constructs, and thus it is small and simple to understand. However, do not equate simplicity with inferiority; Java is a powerful language indeed—much like English. After all, even though the English alphabet has only 26 letters, those letters can be combined in virtually limitless ways!

Part of ensuring Java's simplicity involved creating the syntax of the language itself. Java looks much like C++, a language with which many developers are familiar. If you are a JavaScript programmer, you will be comfortable writing Java code because the syntax is similar. Don't think for a minute that this simplicity somehow results in a trivial language, though. Java is powerful, but its simplicity makes for straightforward access. After all, programmers want to produce solid code without having to twist their mind into knots trying to understand what they are doing. Java programs are easier to create than programs in a comparable language such as C++, but the results can be equally robust. You might even find yourself with a smile on your face once in a while when working with Java!

Java Is Object Oriented

The *object-oriented* paradigm has risen in popularity and has become the de facto standard for today's software development. An *object* is a model in software and contains qualities of both state and behavior. In a program, you can use objects to represent anything you want.

For example, an object such as an airplane has qualities of *state*, such as the number of seats in first class and coach, the amount of fuel the airplane holds, and the movie that will be shown. The airplane also has qualities of *behavior*, such as taking off, flying, turning, and landing. Object-oriented programming focuses on the state and behavior of individual objects. These objects can communicate with one another to form the complex logic necessary in most of today's programs.

---

object

A distinct unit of code in memory that, when combined with other objects, can form complete applications. Most programs will be composed of multiple objects that communicate with one another via methods.

object-oriented

A programming methodology that organizes programs following a real-world model. In the real world, objects are often composed of smaller components. In object-oriented development, this same concept is applied, which leads to flexible, reusable code.

state

The data of a program or an application. For example, the balance of a bank account is a state. Subsequent functions can operate on that state. For example, a method can calculate the interest on the balance passed to the method.

behavior

The collection of methods for a particular class. The behavior of objects typically manipulates their state.

procedural code

This code is composed of a series of functions that perform distinct units of work on data passed to them. Procedural code is often difficult to manage and extend, though it is also generally easier to grasp initially than object-oriented code.

Earlier programming languages often used more *procedural code*, meaning that the focus was on the behavior and not so much on the state. In other words, the state existed only to support the behavior. To model an airplane with procedural code, *methods* control the plane, making it take off, fly, turn, and land instead of the plane doing these things on its own. The object-oriented approach is much closer to how things work in the real world.

If you have worked only with procedural programming before your venture into the world of Java, you will probably find learning the object-oriented concepts the most challenging aspect of your studies. Once your mind makes the paradigm shift to objects, though, you will see a whole new world of power and possibilities.

If the concepts of objects and object-oriented programming are confusing, don't worry. You will learn more about this powerful methodology in Chapter 6, "Introduction to Object-Oriented Programming."

method
A unit of code that performs one or more actions. For example, an object can have a method named `print` that sends a document to a printer. In other languages, methods are sometimes called functions, procedures, and operations.

bytecode
The platform-independent format of compiled Java code that executes in the Java Virtual Machine.

NOTE

Java Is Interpreted

Java source code is passed to a compiler that generates the *bytecode*. The bytecode is not targeted at any specific platform. Instead, a *Java Virtual Machine (JVM)* interprets the bytecode at runtime and executes it. This means that only the JVM itself is platform-dependent; the bytecode of your Java programs remains platform-independent.

This approach is different from that of a truly compiled language such as C or C++. In a compiled language, platform-dependent information must be linked into the compiled code, forcing one compiled version for every target platform. For example, if you write a program to calculate the distances of stars from each other and want it to run on Microsoft Windows, Linux, Sun Solaris, and Macintosh, you would have to compile it four times, once for each system.

The significant drawback with an interpreted language like Java is that code being dynamically interpreted executes more slowly than code that is compiled and native to a particular platform. Although this fundamental fact may be true, the JVM has been augmented over the years to become the *Java HotSpot Virtual Machine (Java HotSpot VM)*. The HotSpot VM contains an adaptive compiler that allows performance hot spots to be detected at runtime and optimized while your code is executing. This results in faster running code that still gains the benefits of being interpreted. Nowadays, properly designed Java programs execute at speeds comparable to similar programs written in C++. In essence, the one black mark of being interpreted has been removed completely.

Java Virtual Machine (JVM)
An abstract computing machine in which all Java programs execute. The JVM is the key to Java's cross-platform nature because it provides the same environment on any platform on which it actually runs. The JVM is the intermediary between your Java code and the actual system on which the code executes.

Java HotSpot Virtual Machine (Java HotSpot VM)
The Java HotSpot Virtual Machine is specially tuned to provide optimum performance. It incorporates an adaptive compiler that allows code to be optimized as it executes. This means faster, more efficient code at runtime than past virtual machines have been able to achieve.

Java Is Portable

applets
Executable modules that are automatically downloaded to a user's web browser over a network such as the Internet. Applets allow deployment to be simple and provide a mechanism to add advanced functionality to web pages.

In the past, portability was not as much of a concern as it has become today. Most applications were fairly static in the sense that they were deployed on a consistent platform and did not require a lot of changes and tinkering to keep them running. However, in today's systems it is not at all uncommon for many components to be distributed across various hardware, operating systems, and networks. This heterogeneousness would pose great problems for many languages, but not Java!

Java applications can run practically anywhere, which makes Java quite revolutionary. Essentially anything that has some kind of processor can be Java-enabled, from mainframes to personal computers to telephones and beyond. Java programs are flexible enough to be local applications, web-based *applets*, server-side applications, and embedded software. The application code does not usually have to be changed to run on these different devices, either. This means you can truly write the code once and run it anywhere you want.

The key to this portability is the interpreted nature of the language. Because code does not have to be compiled to specific platforms, your Java programs can run anywhere that a JVM exists. The world does not run on one type of platform alone, and new platforms are constantly being introduced. By being portable, Java programs written today can still be viable tomorrow.

strongly typed
When a language is strongly typed, it imposes strict rules on the declarations made in the code itself. Some languages allow a variable to represent an unknown data type, but languages such as Java force you to declare all variables to be a specific type before they can be used.

You can achieve this portability for your Java code only if you follow the rules, though. Believe me, it is entirely possible to write some very nonportable code if you are not careful. For this reason, Sun has introduced the 100% Pure Java initiative, which allows you to ensure that your code is portable by running it through a variety of test suites. Obviously, maintaining portability is considered extremely valuable; Java was designed with this important consideration in mind. It is nice to know that the engineers at Sun are always working to make your life a bit easier!

Java Is Robust

pointers
In languages such as C and C++, a pointer represents a specific location in memory that the code itself controls. Pointers can lead to dangerous problems, including data corruption, if they are not used correctly. Java removes the whole notion of managing your own pointers, which removes this often unnecessary complexity.

Robust code is reliable code. Java has a few features that tend to make it more robust than many other languages, thus easing the burden on developers attempting to avoid pitfalls. Specifically, Java is strongly typed, includes automatic memory management, utilizes garbage collection, and provides an exception-handling mechanism. Let's take a look at what these qualities mean.

Java is considered a *strongly typed* language. This means that many checks are made against the code to ensure that it correctly follows the rules of the language. Java is strict about what is considered legal in code, and the compiler simply does not allow you to make many of the mistakes that have plagued developers working in other languages for years. Essentially, the compiler enforces the rule that all declarations in your code are explicitly given. You cannot use a variable called *fred* without declaring what type *fred* actually is (perhaps an integer, a byte, or an image). Similarly, you cannot invoke a method unless you have already defined that method, and you cannot pass any parameters to that method unless you have explicitly listed them.

The compiler is only half the solution, however. The JVM also plays a part in ensuring robustness. All memory is managed for you automatically, and it is impossible for Java code to stomp on your system memory, potentially corrupting parts of your data. The interpreted nature of the language allows the JVM to take full control of memory management, freeing developers from having to handle these complex details on their own. Java developers do not work with *pointers* at all, thus immediately removing the possibility of many complex bugs.

The runtime also includes the *garbage collection* mechanism. This is a part of the JVM that monitors memory and determines if there is any "garbage" to clean up. With C++, for example, you have to ensure that all objects you used were removed from memory or risk the nasty business of a memory leak. With Java, all this potentially complex memory cleanup and maintenance is handled for you automatically.

Java also includes an extensible mechanism for *exception handling*, similar to the system used in C++. Instead of creating simple error codes and passing these around your programs, Java allows you to define exception types that signify specific error conditions. For example, you might want to signify that a network port is unavailable or that there are not enough items in an inventory to fulfill an order. These possible error conditions can then be handled within the programs that are attempting to perform these actions. These errors can even be overcome without any user intervention whatsoever; the code can correct these errors while it is running. In other words, the exception-handling aspect of the language allows you to maintain robustness in your specific programs.

Java Is Secure

One of the top features for end users of a Java application is that it can be dynamically downloaded from a remote location. Although this is indeed a powerful, desirable feature, a lot of risk is inherent in the process. It does not seem wise to download code from someone on the Internet and then just let it run at will on your system, does it? This is how things such as viruses and other maliciousness can invade your otherwise happy computer. Luckily, Java recognized these potential threats and incorporated a multiphase approach to ensure a high level of security.

To begin with, you just learned about the robustness of the language in regard to its memory management and compile-time checking. These two features also contribute significantly to Java's security. Because the JVM is "in charge," it is impossible for normal Java code to cause a problem with system memory that could lead to insecure or corrupted data. It also means that pure Java code is

garbage collection
Part of the Java Virtual Machine's responsibility is managing memory on your behalf. When memory space you have used in your code is no longer needed, the garbage collection mechanism kicks in and eventually clears that memory automatically. Because of this automatic procedure, there isn't a standard way to manually clear memory from within Java programs. The garbage collection process is a great benefit because it reduces both the amount of code you need to create and, more important, dangerous bugs that can creep into your code if you could otherwise mismanage memory.

exception handling
A form of flow control that handles program errors. In many other languages, errors are reported as a code number of some kind that is often cryptic and difficult to work with. Java uses exception handling, which provides a more robust method for trapping and recovering from logical errors.

unable to install a virus or worm on your system because it cannot "touch" memory directly.

Java security also extends to so-called foreign code. Foreign code is not written in another country, of course, but executes across a network. If you access code over a network (as would be the case with a Java applet), the natural reaction of Java is to not trust the code whatsoever. This does not mean that the code cannot execute, but it does mean that the code cannot access your local file system or devices such as printers and modems. The end user can override this security, but the default behavior is to protect their systems from potential harm. This is the type of security most users are immediately concerned with because it prevents an invasion of their privacy.

Because Java technology is so prevalent on networks and in today's enterprise systems, its security aspects are absolutely vital. Because Java provides such excellent security inherently, it is the perfect language to be used in these environments and can be trusted not to cause more harm than good.

WARNING   Security is never perfect. It is unwise to ever consider anything on a network completely secure. If hackers have enough motivation, they can defeat any security. The true goal of any security scheme is to make it so difficult to breech that it becomes practically pointless to continue trying. In all my years of working with security, I have found the best way to thwart attacks is to force the miscreants to just give up and go away. The Java language has established itself as being extremely secure, but this does not mean that just because you use the language your programs are totally protected from attack.

Java Is Multithreaded

multithreaded
An application that can control individual threads to perform specific actions is considered multithreaded. By divvying up the processing across these threads, an application can appear to be performing multiple actions simultaneously. Java is inherently multithreaded, making the creation of these advanced programs simpler than other languages.

threads
Lightweight processes contained within an actual process. Threads are the building blocks of multithreaded programs and provide separate distinct processing.

If a program is *multithreaded*, it can do more than one thing at a time. Most applications that you use are multithreaded, such as your web browser, for instance. Imagine visiting a website that allows you to play a music clip while you are scrolling through information on a page. Because you are probably working on a machine with a single processor, only one thing can be done at a time. However, when an application is multithreaded, "lightweight processes" can execute concurrently. These lightweight processes are still only executing one at a time, but they are swapped out so quickly that it appears as if several things are happening simultaneously.

These lightweight processes are called *threads*, and each thread can be assigned a specific operation to perform for the master application. Because the Java language is natively a multithreaded language, utilizing threads in your programs is a straightforward task.

NOTE   Threads are an advanced concept and are not discussed further in this book. If you are interested in learning more about threads and multithreading, I recommend *Java Threads* by Scott Oaks and Henry Wong.

Java Is High Performance

In the past, some performance issues generated concerns for Java's viability, but recent versions have performed at the speed that developers demand. The perception that Java programs were slow was mainly because it is an interpreted language. An interpreted language has to read every individual instruction and compile it into instructions that are understood by the system on which the code is executing. These added steps tend to slow down programs considerably. With all the other great features the Java language provided, it was unfortunate, but not surprising, that speed was the major drawback. Speed is, after all, usually paramount on anyone's list of importance in an application.

However, advancements in the way that the JVM works have made Java's speed comparable to the speed of C++ code in most situations. This increase in horsepower was achieved without sacrificing any of the other important features too! These improvements have made Java the perfect choice for today's developer, especially when they are developing for the Internet and other networked environments.

An important point to keep in mind about Java is that it performs wonderfully in most applications, including GUI-based solutions and network code. Those types of applications are not constantly executing but spend most of their time waiting for input, processing data, and returning output. Although Java is not a language designed to write low-level device drivers and the like, it is an excellent language for almost every other type of application.

> **NOTE**
>
> You may wonder why Java is not a good choice for writing device drivers. A device driver should be targeted to specific hardware to allow it to take full advantage of speed and free access to video cards, printer ports, and so on. Because Java is a cross-platform language, it is best suited for higher-level applications that do not directly access hardware-specific features. If you were hoping to write a Java video driver, you might want to rethink your plans a bit!

Java Saves Time and Money

By using Java technology, you can often significantly reduce the cost of development. Software development with Java is a much quicker process than with most other languages. This is largely because of the platform independence and familiarity of the language. Because the syntax is similar to popular languages such as C/C++ and JavaScript, it is usually relatively simple for developers to learn how to work with Java technology, and because of the widespread industry support, it is often convenient to incorporate Java applications into an existing infrastructure.

Deployment costs are also lowered and often eliminated altogether. It is common for Java applications to be delivered dynamically over a network without any user intervention whatsoever. This means the end user does not have to install, configure, or otherwise tinker with the application that they want to use.

Java Solves Important Problems

From the beginning, Java was designed for networking and security. Applications used over a public, insecure network such as the Internet pose problems. Who would use online banking software that was not secure? What user wants to install dozens of applications on their system to access online applications? From the business perspective, how can you handle problems such as deployment and version control and also be sure that the code cannot be used in a dangerous fashion to exploit your sensitive corporate information?

Java is perfect for solving many of these problems. Many businesses use the public Internet backbone to deploy websites for their prospective consumers; often these businesses want to provide enhanced functionality. This might include account management at a bank, three-dimensional modeling of automobiles, or even a virtual desktop that allows employees to work from remote locations. All these types of applications—and many more—can be created with Java technology.

How Java Compares with Other Languages

Though Java is a great language, it is one of the newer kids on the block. Other languages such as C++, JavaScript, and Perl are also popular choices. Java has commonality with each of these as well as many differences. In this section, you'll see how Java stacks up head to head with these languages and why Java might be a better choice.

We can group programming languages into three categories. First are the compiled languages such as C and C++ that are bound to each native platform, making them high performance but not very portable. Second are the scripting languages such as JavaScript and Python that are useful for portable processing but have little to offer in the way of performance. Third, and somewhere in between these first two categories, is the Java language itself. It combines the portability and simplicity of the scripting languages, yet it can execute at speeds comparable to the compiled languages. Because of this unique combination of traits, Java can solve many problems in many different situations.

C++
An object-oriented version of the C programming language that gained immense popularity in the early 1990s. C++ can be thought of as a close cousin to the Java programming language.

Java and C++   C++ is another popular, object-oriented language that can be used to create high-performance code. In fact, most enterprise development that is not being written in Java is probably being written in C++. As a language, C++ is syntactically fairly simple, though it is not as user friendly as Java tends to be. C++ is also truly compiled code, so it cannot run on just any platform without a binary executable for the system.

Although both languages are classified as object oriented, Java was designed with those concepts in mind from the beginning. This contributes to Java's flexibility, syntactic simplicity, and overall "friendliness."

Java and JavaScript   It has been said that the only thing that the Java and *JavaScript* languages really have in common are their first four letters. That is not exactly true, but it does indicate that the similarity is not as close as you might think. Sun Microsystems created the Java programming language, and Netscape created JavaScript. JavaScript is a scripting language that is based on object-oriented concepts, but it does not treat objects exactly the same way that a language such as Java does.

Java and Perl   Perl is another scripting language used in a variety of scenarios. Perl really became popular when it became known for extending websites and allowing dynamic processing. Perl is a common implementation language for *Common Gateway Interface (CGI)* solutions and is prevalent on the Internet. Perl is one of those languages that you either love or hate. It is flexible and powerful, but it is also perceived as somewhat complicated. Java can do anything that Perl can do functionally, but it was designed to be more user friendly than Perl seems to those new to the language.

JavaScript
A scripting language developed by Netscape to add interactivity to web documents. JavaScript is a programming language but is simple to learn and use, making it excellent for web content developers who don't have backgrounds in more complex programming languages.

Common Gateway Interface (CGI)
A standard for interfacing external applications with HTTP servers on the Web. CGI solutions are often used to provide functionality to a website such as processing forms, creating images, and generating dynamic HTML.

How to Download and Install Java

Before you actually download and install Java on your system, let's take a look at some of the various available downloads.

The Java 2 Platform Standard Edition (J2SE)   The J2SE is the essential download that you need to both develop and execute Java programs. It contains the API libraries, the compiler used to produce bytecode, the JVM and interpreter, and various other tools.

The Java 2 Runtime Environment, Standard Edition (J2RE)   The J2RE is a trimmed-down version of the J2SE, basically. It does not contain the compiler or other tools, but it still has the API libraries and the interpreter. This download should be installed on a system that needs to execute Java code only. It does not provide the mechanisms needed to create Java applications, only to run them.

Something called the Java Plug-in provides the runtime environment for most users of online Java applications. Essentially, the Java Plug-in is an automatically deployed version of the J2RE. If you download the J2SE, the Java Plug-in is included. You can learn more about the Java Plug-in by going to http://java.sun.com/products/plugin.

NOTE

The Java 2 Platform, Enterprise Edition (J2EE)   J2EE is both a platform and a technology, designed to simplify the creation of highly scalable enterprise applications. J2EE relies on various vendor-provided servers to provide the execution environment. Note that J2EE still requires the standard APIs found in the J2SE to operate.

JavaServer Web Development Kit (JSWDK)   The JSWDK is used for writing and testing servlets or JavaServer Pages (JSP), which let you extend a web server more powerfully than traditional CGI solutions.

The Java 2 Platform, Micro Edition (J2ME)   The J2ME is an optimized and smaller version of the J2SE that is designed to produce programs capable of running on consumer devices such as smart cards, cell phones, and PDAs. It supports networked as well as standalone applications, user interfaces, and security.

There are some other Java technology–related downloads, but these are the five major bundles available. The remainder of this book deals only with the first download, the J2SE itself. The good news is that every one of the other Java downloads is built on the fundamentals you will learn in this book, so you will eventually be able to investigate all of them.

Downloading the J2SE Software

Let's get started! Be sure you are connected to the Internet. Then open your browser and enter the URL **http://java.sun.com/j2se/1.5.0/ download.jsp**. You will find a list of downloads for Windows, Linux, and Solaris, as shown here.

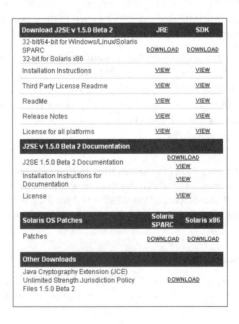

As you can see, there are multiple download options for each platform, including the choice between the Java Runtime Environment (JRE) and the Java 2 Software Development Kit, Standard Edition (J2SDK). We are specifically interested in the SDK choices.

After you select the file to download, you are taken to a license agreement. After reading it, click the Accept button to open a page with a link to the download itself. You can choose to either download the entire installation file or run the installation over the network. Whichever you choose, just click the link and wait until the download completes.

These downloads are rather large, so be sure that your Internet connection is available for the time required.

WARNING

Once you have the download on your system, you are ready to install. I have provided directions for the Windows and Linux platforms in the following sections.

Instructions for installing J2SE on Solaris can be found at `http://java.sun.com/j2se/1.5.0/install-solaris.html`**.**

NOTE

Installing J2SE on Windows

The J2SE is supported on Windows 98, Windows Me, Windows XP, Windows 2000 Professional, and Windows NT 4. Ensure that at least 120 megabytes of space is available in your file system before you begin the following steps.

These directions are specific to Windows XP. The installation procedure is effectively identical on all the supported versions of Windows, but small differences might appear in some screens.

NOTE

1. After the executable extracts the required contents to a temporary folder, another license agreement opens.

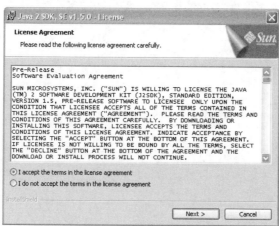

2. After you read the license, select "I accept the terms of the license agreement" and click the Next button to open the first Custom Setup screen.

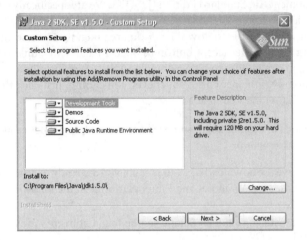

3. The Custom Setup screen lists the optional features that you can install. At this point, all the options are selected, and you can just leave this section alone. Toward the bottom of this window, you'll see the installation folder. If you want to choose your own folder, click the Change button. This will open a window so you can choose a different installation directory.

4. Click Next to open a screen that displays the progress of the installation. This will take some time.

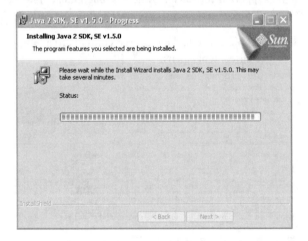

When the next Custom Setup window pops up, continue to step 5.

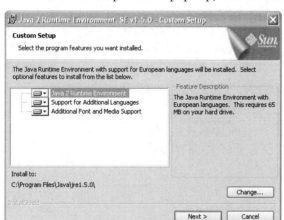

5. This new screen displays the options for the Java Runtime Environment. Once again, just stick with the defaults. You can change the installation folder if you want as before. Once you are satisfied with the choices, click Next to open the Browser Registration screen.

6. On the Browser Registration screen, you see the browser selections available on your system. You can deselect browsers on this screen if you do not want the Java Plug-in to be automatically associated with them. Click Next to begin the installation.

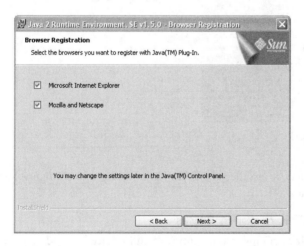

As is typical, you see the progress bar as the files are installed on your system.

7. When all the files are installed, you see the final screen indicating success. Click the Finish button to complete the installation.

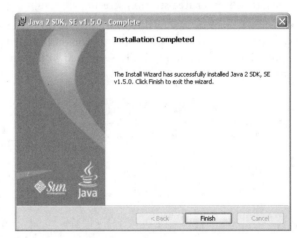

You have now installed the J2SE. Now you have to configure Java for your environment.

Configuring the Installation on Windows

To use the Java compiler and runtime, you first need to update your PATH environment variable. How you do so depends on your specific version of Windows.

NOTE

These configuration steps are specific to Windows XP. If you are using a different version of Windows, you can find specific configuration instructions at `http://java.sun.com/j2se/1.5.0/install-windows.html`.

1. On the Desktop, right-click the My Computer icon and choose Properties from the shortcut menu to open the System Properties dialog box.

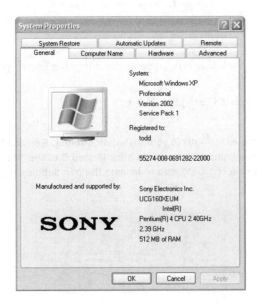

2. Click the Advanced tab, and then click the Environment Variables button to open the Environment Variables dialog box.

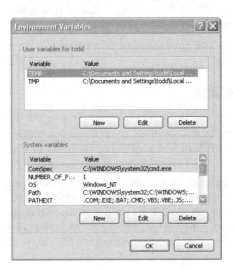

3. In the System Variables section, select the PATH environment variable, and then click the Edit button to open the Edit System Variable dialog box.

4. In the Variable Value box, append the following line to your path statement:

```
C:\Program Files\jdk1.5.0\bin
```

This may not be the exact path to your installation folder. Replace the installation folder with whatever selection you made back in step 3 of the "Installing J2SE on Microsoft Windows" section. Be sure to include the *bin* subdirectory in your path, though.

5. Click OK to close the Edit System Variable dialog box, click OK to close the Environment Variables dialog box, and finally click OK to close the System Properties dialog box.

Congratulations! You have installed Java on your system, and the configuration is now complete.

Installing J2SE on Linux

If you are running the Linux operating system, you do not have the advantage of a wizard-based installation. Even so, the procedure is not difficult, and this section should help you install and configure Java for your system.

These instructions are for the automatic installation provided via the Linux RPM file. This installs Java to the /usr/java directory by default and requires you to become root to complete the installation. If you need more control over which directory Java installs to or you do not have root access, follow the instructions for installing a self-extracting binary at http://java.sun.com/j2se/1.5.0/install-linux.html.

1. Download the Linux RPM in the self-extracting file from the download location discussed at the beginning of the "Downloading the J2SE Software" section. Be sure to select the SDK, not the JRE, because you want the compiler installed as well.

2. Open a terminal window, and change to the directory where the RPM download is located.

3. You need to make the file executable, so type the following command at the prompt in your terminal window:

   ```
   chmod a+x j2sdk-1_4_1_01-linux-i586-rpm.bin
   ```

4. To unpack the downloaded RPM, type the following in the terminal window:

   ```
   ./j2sdk-1_5_0-beta2-linux-i586-rpm.bin
   ```

   This displays a license agreement. After you read the agreement and agree with the terms, the RPM is extracted to the current directory.

5. You need to become the root user to continue, so switch to su now and enter your root password when prompted.

6. To install the download automatically, type the following command in the terminal window:

   ```
   rpm -iv j2sdk-1_5_0-beta2-linux-i586-rpm.bin
   ```

7. You can verify that the installation was successful by checking the version of the Java runtime. Type the following line in the terminal window:

   ```
   /usr/java/j2sdk1.5.0/bin/java -version
   ```

   This should return the version number of the download you installed (in this case, the version will begin with 1.5.0).

Now you're ready to configure your system.

Configuring the Installation on Linux

Now that Java is installed on your Linux system, you need to set your PATH environment variable to include the directory where the Java tools are stored.

1. Open your shell's startup script (for example, the .cshrc or .kshrc file).

2. Set up the JAVA_HOME environment variable. How you do this depends on which Linux shell you are using, but the value of JAVA_HOME should be set similar to the following:

   ```
   /usr/java/j2sdk1.5.0
   ```

——— **WARNING** ——— The value in step 2 may be different if you installed the SDK to a different directory or if you are using a different SDK version. If you are not sure what the exact value should be, consult the online installation instructions.

3. Now add the PATH environment variable. Note that you may already have a PATH set in your startup script. This command adds the required path to the Java tools to your existing PATH environment variable. You might want to check the installation instructions for setting this value, but the value you need to add will be similar to the following:

   ```
   $JAVA_HOME/bin:$PATH
   ```

4. Close your startup script, and restart your system. Once the system is rebooted, your Java installation should be configured and ready to go.

——— **TIP** ——— If you are familiar with your Linux shell, you do not have to reboot the entire system. Instead, you can run your startup script using the specific "source" command for your system. Consult your system documentation for more information on refreshing your startup script.

Terms to Know

applets	method
behavior	multithreaded
bytecode	object
C++	object-oriented
Common Gateway Interface (CGI)	pointers
exception handling	procedural code
garbage collection	state
Java HotSpot Virtual Machine (Java HotSpot VM)	strongly typed
Java Virtual Machine (JVM)	threads
JavaScript	

Review Questions

1. Which two components form the Java platform?

2. What was the name of the internal project at Sun Microsystems that produced the first version of the Java programming language?

3. What are some types of applications for which Java is suited?

4. Who is considered the father of Java technology?

5. What does it mean for a language such as Java to be strongly typed?

6. What does the Java compiler produce from source code?

7. What is the engine that allows Java code to be platform independent?

8. To which of today's development paradigms does the Java language adhere?

9. What is included in the Java 2 SDK Standard Edition?

10. On which language was Java syntax largely based?

Chapter 2

Java Fundamentals

Now that you have learned a little of Java's history and should have
the JDK installed on your system, it is time to start concentrating on writing some code. We'll begin with a simple example of a Java program, but
don't let that simplicity fool you. Everything you learn in this chapter
lays the foundation for creating well-written and functional Java
programs.

In This Chapter

- How to write a simple class and method
- How to compile and execute a Java program
- The types of Java programs
- Which standard primitive types are available

Creating a Java Program

You need to take three distinct steps to create any Java program, and we investigate all three in this chapter. Here are brief descriptions of these three steps:

source code

The "human" language of Java. You write the source code and eventually compile it into the more cryptic bytecode needed by the JVM. Source code is a high-level view of a programming language.

Write the source code.   This is just plain text, but you need to write it following the Java programming language rules. The *source code* is passed to the compiler to produce the bytecode, but it can also be read by human beings. When you can access the source code for a program, you can use it to learn everything that the underlying code is designed to do.

Compile the source code.   After you finish writing the source code, you must *compile* it by passing it to a Java *compiler*, a tool that converts the source code into a class file. Remember that a class file contains bytecode.

compile

The process of converting source code into Java bytecode. The Java compiler creates class files that can be interpreted by any JVM.

Execute the program.   You accomplish this using the Java *interpreter*, which reads the bytecode instructions so that the program can perform its functions. The interpreter reads an entire class file into memory and translates the standard bytecode into the real operating system instructions for the target system.

These are the three stages of all Java programs, from the simplest types to the extremely complex. So, without further delay, let's actually perform all three of these steps with our first program.

The HelloWorld Program

compiler

The tool that converts the source code into class files. The compiler reads each line of source code and makes sure that you have followed all the rules. If the compiler finds any problems, it reports those errors to you on the command line.

Throughout the annals of programming books, one tradition has survived dozens of years and hundreds of languages: the HelloWorld example. Although this example is always a simple program that just prints a greeting to its creator, the tradition exists for good reason. Essentially, it lets new developers get their hands dirty quickly with simple but obvious results, instead of reading a bunch of theory early in the game. In other words, those learning new languages often find that it is more effective to see the working machinery before they learn how to put it together.

interpreter

An interpreter parses and executes each statement as it is found in a class file. When you execute a Java program, you use the java command followed by the class that you want to execute. This java command is the interpreter.

Traditionally, developers start learning a new language by copying code and playing with it, an approach I'm going to heartily advocate in this book. It is probably best to type the code as you see it in the text first, but then you should feel free to alter the code that you see in the following section or anywhere else in the book. I can tell you from experience that the absolute best way to further your knowledge of Java is to *play with it!*

So let's start playing.

Writing the HelloWorld Source Code

Writing code is not easy, especially when you are working with a new programming language. Besides the logic that you need to construct top-notch code, there are a host of other considerations. For instance, how do you terminate lines of code? How do you define a method? Overall, how do you begin writing in the first place?

Thus, the HelloWorld example was born. In a moment, you will find a Java version of HelloWorld. Enter the code exactly as you see it into your editor. Java is a case-sensitive language, so you cannot just type your code haphazardly. Be sure to maintain capitalization throughout your source code because "HelloWorld" is *not* the same as "helloworld," "Helloworld," or "HELLOWORLD." This is especially important if you commonly work on a Windows system, which is not typically concerned with case sensitivity.

NOTE

You can use any text editor to write Java programs. If you are working on a Windows system, you can use the Notepad program. On a UNIX system, you can use the standard text editor. In addition, you will find a lot of Java editors for all platforms available for Internet download; so make sure to find something that you are comfortable with. Try searching for "Java Editor" at www.download.com **if you want something more elaborate than a simple text editor. Although you are free to use any editor you want, all the code examples in this book are based on simple text editors and command-line processing.**

After you complete writing, compiling, and executing this program, you will learn about the various sections of this program in detail as we walk through it line by line.

```
/*
 * The traditional HelloWorld example
 */
public class HelloWorld
{
    public static void main(String[] args)
    {
        System.out.println("Hello World!");
    }
}
```

Not a lot of code, is it? This code results in the message "Hello World!" being printed to your command line, so it is indeed simple. However, we can talk about many things in this code that will help you begin learning the details of writing Java programs. I'll break down every line a bit later in this chapter.

First, though, let's save, compile, and execute this program. It is always better to see something work than to just read about it!

Saving the HelloWorld Source Code

Now that you have the HelloWorld program entered in your chosen editor, you must save it. All Java source code must be saved in files that end in the `.java` extension. You must also name the source file the same as the class name itself. In this case, the class name is what follows the `class` keyword. So, following those rules, the resulting filename must be `HelloWorld.java`. You can save this file to any directory that you want.

TIP

If you are using a text editor such as Window's Notepad that automatically adds an extension to your files, just put quotes around the entire filename when you save it. This prevents extensions such as `.txt` from being added to your Java source code.

Compiling the HelloWorld Source Code

Now that the source code is saved, we must compile the code into Java bytecode. The tool that you use to compile Java code is `javac`. To compile, open a command prompt window (or a terminal window on a UNIX system) and move to the same directory where you saved the source code.

NOTE

To actually compile this code, you need Java downloaded and installed as discussed in Chapter 1, "The History of Java." If you have any problems with this section, be sure you followed all the instructions in Chapter 1 for your particular system.

To actually compile the code, type **javac** and just pass the source code file, including the extension, to this tool. The command looks just like this:

```
javac HelloWorld.java
```

Help! The Code Will Not Compile!

It can be disconcerting to receive an error message after you try to compile the code. However, in almost all cases, you will find that the error is simple to correct.

Essentially, you might receive any of three major error messages. The first occurs when your system cannot find the compiler, `javac`. If you receive this message, your PATH environment variable has not been updated. Check out the installation steps in Chapter 1, specifically the configuration section for either Windows or Linux.

Continues

> The second common error is that the compiler cannot find the `HelloWorld.java` file. This could be simply because you are compiling in a directory that does not contain your saved source code file, so make sure that is not the problem by changing to the correct directory. More likely, though, it is because the name of the source file and the name specified on the command line do not match. Be sure all cases match and try compiling again.
>
> The third error is a syntax error. This might be a missing semicolon, a missing brace, or a misspelled word in the program. You will learn more about these syntax errors a bit later in this chapter. For now, just make sure your source code looks just like the code in this chapter and try compiling again.

Don't forget that Java is a case-sensitive language; be sure to always type names exactly as you see them in print. Although in most Windows environments, the compiler works even without the correct case at all times, get used to case sensitivity right from the beginning because you will have to follow these rules in your own source code.

WARNING

When the compilation completes, control will simply return to the command prompt. If you get there, you have successfully compiled your first Java program!

Executing the HelloWorld Program

Can you hear that drum roll in your head? It is finally time to run your first Java program. If you perform a listing of the directory in which you compiled the source code, you should find a new file called `HelloWorld.class`. This file contains the compiled bytecode, so don't bother trying to read it yourself. It will look like a bunch of nonsense to you, but it is just what the interpreter needs to run your code. This is also the file that the JVM needs to make your program run.

The interpreter is a tool named `java`. All you have to do to run the Hello-World program is type the following command at your prompt:

```
java HelloWorld
```

The interpreter automatically appends the `.class` extension, so do not include it on the command line. If you do, you will receive an error message telling you that the interpreter cannot find the specified class file.

The interpreter reads in the class file and follows the bytecode instructions that the class contains. What you should see is the ever-friendly message, "Hello World!" printed underneath this command.

Congratulations, you have completed your first Java program! Now that you have gone through the process of writing, compiling, and executing this program, it is time to take a closer look at the source code itself.

Help! The Code Will Not Run!

If you receive an error message such as NoClassDefFoundException, the interpreter cannot find the HelloWorld.class file. This could be because it is not in the directory in which you are trying to execute it. Do a directory listing, and ensure that the class file is indeed present in your current directory. If it is not, change to the correct directory.

Examining the Source Code

The source code you created is mainly for the compiler to convert into a class file. However, source code is also an invaluable resource for learning about the Java language. If you think about it, the only part of this process that requires your skill is the source code creation stage. The compiler and interpreter are just tools that you use; the source code is how the programs get told what to do in the first place.

Here is the HelloWorld source code again:

```
1 /*
2  * The traditional HelloWorld example
3  */
4 public class HelloWorld
5 {
6     public static void main(String[] args)
7     {
8        System.out.println("Hello World!");
9     }
10 }
```

WARNING

Do *not* include the line numbers when you type this code into your editor. The line numbers are present only to make referencing specific lines of code easier while you read this book.

Including the four lines that contain just a single brace, the HelloWorld source code is 10 lines long. Although that is a small piece of code, it still contains several items that are found in almost all Java source code. Let's investigate each section of the code and discuss it in more detail.

Using Comments

Including *comments* in your source code is always a good idea. Often these comments can help the developer understand why specific choices were made, who wrote the code, and when it was written. They might also indicate the code's version or any information that explains or helps the developer maintain the code.

The compiler ignores comments, and nothing written in the comments will end up in the class file. In other words, comments are only for the people reading the code and contain information that only they would be interested in.

The first three lines of the HelloWorld source code are a comment:

```
/*
 * The traditional HelloWorld example
 */
```

Of course, only one of these lines actually contains any information, but it is common to format comments like this so that they can be read easily.

It is also common to include comments at the beginning of source code to specify standard information such as the author, contact information, and the code's version number. However, you can place comments throughout your source code, and doing so is often a good idea.

Not long ago, a friend of mine was forced to revisit some Java source code that he had written three years earlier. This code was much lengthier and more complicated than the HelloWorld program, to be sure. However, my friend had not added a single comment to the source code when he wrote it. Hey, at that point, he felt it was just a waste of his time to comment on his own code. After all, he would be the only one reading it. What he quickly discovered was that he did not remember what certain sections of the code did and simply could not make a great deal of sense of many of the lines he had written. Needless to say, he was not happy that he made that decision three years before.

The lesson here is don't fall into this trap. Use comments and use them liberally. It can save you or someone else a lot of headaches in the future. For all I know, my friend may *still* be trying to figure out that code!

comments
A special notation that you can add to your source code to describe or explain sections of code. Using comments is an excellent practice because doing so makes your source code much easier to understand when it is referenced in the future.

Three Styles Of Comments

The Java language allows three styles of comments in your source code. The first two are similar to the comments used in C and C++. The third is a special form of comment that allows for automatic documentation.

The Single Line Comment

If you just need to produce a quick comment that fits on one line in your source code, this is the perfect kind of comment to use. The syntax is //, followed by whatever comment text you want. You can use this style of comment before or after a line of code.

For example, you might add the following to the HelloWorld program to explain what is happening on a particular line:

```
System.out.println("Hello World!");// prints the message
```

The important thing to keep in mind is that this style of comment can be on only one line. You cannot include a carriage return in this kind of comment. If you do, every new line must be prefaced with //.

The Block Comment

This is the style of comment used in the HelloWorld source code we have been working with in this chapter. This is an excellent comment to use when you want a lengthier comment section that usually will include carriage returns.

The syntax for this comment is to start the block with /* and end it with */. The compiler ignores everything between those two symbols. You have already seen this style of comment in use:

```
/*
 * The traditional HelloWorld example
 */
```

Although each line in this example contains an asterisk (*), an asterisk is not required. It needs to be included only with the opening of the comment (/*) and the closing of the comment (*/). Common practice, however, is to include an asterisk before each line of a block comment. This can help readily identify each line as a part of a comment as opposed to an actual line of code.

TIP

You may find that the block comment style is handy to use in your source code. This is a versatile comment to use because it can contain carriage returns. Nothing is wrong with the // style, but you can also use the /* */ pair on one line. Many developers find it much cleaner to stick to the latter style throughout their code. Another plus of the block comment is that you can add new comment information to it whenever you want.

The Documentation Comment

This is a special form of block comment. You use it in conjunction with another tool you received when you downloaded and installed Java—javadoc.

The syntax for the documentation comment is the same as that for the standard block comment, except you use an extra asterisk to open the block:

```
/**
 * This is a documentation comment.
 * @author Todd Greanier
 * @version 1.0
 */
```

The documentation comment also allows you to use special standard tags for information such as the author of the code, the version, and other details. In the preceding code, the `@author` and `@version` tags are read by the `javadoc` command, and the values are included in the output.

So what exactly does `javadoc` output? Essentially, it produces HTML documents that will be part of the documentation for your applications. It provides a series of linked documents that you can view in any web browser. This type of automatic documentation is one of the underrated features of the Java programming language.

You can use this special form of comment to describe the entire program as well as specific portions of the code itself.

NOTE

A complete discussion of using the `javadoc` tool is beyond the scope of this book. However, if you want to learn more about this tool and how to use it with documentation comments, check out `http://java.sun.com/j2se/1.4.1/docs/tooldocs/javadoc/index.html`.

Whichever kind of comment you choose to use, comment your code whenever possible. You do not always need the documentation that you produce by using the documentation comments, but it never hurts to just use them all the time. Essentially, wherever you can use a normal block comment, you can use a documentation comment instead.

Using White Space

The fourth line of the HelloWorld program is just a blank line. When you are writing code, it is always a good idea to format the code so that it is neat and readable. You can make it more legible by inserting spaces, tabs, and completely blank lines between certain elements of the code.

Although adding these extra white-space characters to your source code increases the source code size, they do *not* increase the compiled class file size. The Java compiler ignores all white space surrounding elements of your code. When you compiled this program, the fourth line of the HelloWorld program was ignored. If you go into the source file, remove that blank line, and recompile, the size of the resulting class file is the same as before.

Of course, the only white space that is ignored are those spaces, tabs, and blank lines between elements. For example, in the eighth line of the code, the phrase "Hello World" is being printed. Because that phrase is enclosed in quotation marks, the space separating the two words is preserved.

Defining the Class

The fourth line of this code looks like this:

```
public class HelloWorld
```

class
The fundamental component of all Java programs. A class is a template for a user-defined type. From a single class, several objects can be created.

This line declares a *class* named HelloWorld. Every Java program includes at least one class definition. A class definition contains all the *variables* and methods that make the program work. The class is the fundamental component of all Java programs.

Before we can really continue, we need to define exactly what a class is. Essentially, a class is a template that details how code should execute. Classes are the key components of an object-oriented language such as Java. A class defines a specific set of variables and methods, and eventually *objects* are created from these definitions.

variables
These can be defined in classes and methods and hold values that can often be changed through the course of a program's execution. Variables in Java are either primitive types or reference types.

You probably have a television somewhere in your house. Your television may even be made by the same vendor and be the same model as mine. However, changing your channel obviously does not change the channel on my television, does it? We both have the same make of television, but we do not have the same specific television.

All this talk of televisions is a good analogy for how classes relate to objects. Just as the schematics for a television can be used to create one or more real televisions, a single class can be *instantiated* into one or more objects. These objects are used to communicate with other objects in most cases, forming the logic of your applications.

NOTE

You will learn much more about objects and object-oriented programming in Chapter 6, "Introduction to Object-Oriented Programming."

objects
Objects are the runtime versions of classes. Two objects built from the same class are considered the same type, but they are distinct from each other in memory. Changes to one object do not affect the other. Objects make up the key data structure of the Java language.

A class is composed of variables that hold data for each object and methods that provide functionality. Usually those methods alter the value of the variables in a particular object. For example, if we stick with the television analogy, we might have a variable called poweredOn that can be set to either true or false. To control the state of that variable, you can produce a method named something like togglePower() that contains the steps necessary to turn the television on and off.

With classes, you should follow a certain convention. Whenever you define a class, the name should begin with an uppercase letter, and each new word should start with an uppercase letter. So you could have a class called HelloWorld, Television, or JavaDeveloper.

The *Public* Keyword

instantiate
The process of creating a new object. Instantiation is a relatively expensive process, but it is required for every new object used in a Java program. Once instantiation has completed, the object is accessible and ready for use.

The first word in the HelloWorld class definition is public. We discuss this keyword in more detail in Chapter 3, "Keywords and Operators." However, you are probably curious about that keyword right now, so I will give you a brief explanation.

The `public` keyword is actually an *access modifier*. There are four types of access modification in Java, and they are all used to control the "visibility" of classes, variables, and methods. The `public` modifier indicates a particular class that is designed to be used by anyone, anytime, anywhere. Essentially, the `public` keyword signifies that the entire world can use the code.

The alternative to `public`, as you will learn more about later, is restricting access. Sometimes you want to ensure that specific code can be called by only a controllable set of entities to provide some protection against misuse.

For example, if you are designing a bank account as a class, you might define a variable to hold your current balance. Would you really want that variable to be accessible, and therefore modifiable, by just anyone? Obviously that does not make a great deal of sense. As you will see in Chapter 3, if you used the `private` keyword instead of `public`, the balance can be altered only from *within the account class itself*.

access modifier
A special Java keyword that controls the visibility of classes, variables, and methods. There are four access modifiers in the Java language: `public`, `private`, `protected`, and `default`.

> Remember that a lot of what you learn in this chapter is covered in more detail later. If this discussion of access modifiers is a little confusing right now, hang in there. For now, just use the `public` keyword whenever you see it in the example code.

NOTE

The Braces

The fifth line of this code is a single character, the left brace (`{`). This indicates the beginning of the *class body*, which contains any variables and methods that the class needs. The left brace also indicates the beginning of a method body as well (you can see this on line 7).

Placing the left brace character on its own line was purely a stylistic choice on my part. The brace could also have gone at the end of the fourth line. The reason I choose to place my braces on individual lines is that I think my code looks neater and is more readable that way, and placing it there allows me to handle what can be a frustrating problem in complex code: brace alignment.

For every left brace that opens a class or method, you need a corresponding right brace to close the class or method. In the `HelloWorld` class, the right brace on line 9 matches with the left brace on line 7, and the right brace on line 10 matches with the left brace on line 5. Those two right braces close the method body and class body respectively.

Here is something you should commit to memory as soon as possible: *a right brace always closes its nearest left brace.* That may sound simple, but I assure you from years of developing code, tracking down unaligned braces can sometimes be painful to the point of sobbing!

Which style you choose to use for your braces, whether to put each brace on its own line or whether to put the left brace on the same line as the class or method declaration, is entirely up to you, of course. Neither is correct or incorrect. However, long ago I found my battle with brace alignment drastically less

class body
Everything between the left and right braces is considered part of the class body (except comments). This includes all variables and methods.

severe when I put braces on their own lines every time. Don't forget, the compiler ignores the newline characters, so your class file will be the same size either way.

Defining the Method

In most programming languages, there are sections of code called functions or procedures. These provide a reusable set of instructions that can be "called" whenever applications need them. For example, withdrawing money from the bank is not as simple as debiting your balance and handing you cash. A number of things must be done to fulfill your withdrawal request:

- The amount to withdraw has to be valid (not negative, for example).
- Your balance must be larger than the amount you are withdrawing.
- The withdrawal amount must be deducted from your balance.
- The entire withdrawal must be recorded in your transaction log.

When you go to the bank and request a withdrawal, however, you may not even know that all these things are happening. Nor do you really need to. As far as you're concerned, you make a request (to withdraw money) and receive a response (the money or an explanation of why you cannot withdraw that amount). This request-response system is the basis for all method calls in any programming language.

Java likes to be different, so these functions are called methods in Java code. The definition is exactly the same, however. All methods in Java are composed of the following elements:

- An access modifier (such as `public`)
- A return type (this is the "response" of the method)
- A name (such as `withdraw` or `deposit`)
- A parameter list (zero or more items needed to fulfill the "request")

method signature
That part of a method that must be unique in the scope of a class. Technically, a method signature is the name of the method and its parameter list.

Later in this book, you learn how to create methods and choose return types and parameters for them. For now, just remember that all methods have the four elements in the preceding list. The name and parameter lists combine to form the *method signature*. Every method must have a unique method signature within the same class definition.

The *main()* Method

All Java programs include a special method called `main()`. This is the only method defined in the `HelloWorld` class, and it is the method that makes a Java program go. To execute this code, you typed the following line at your command prompt:

```
java HelloWorld
```

Whenever you invoke a program using `java`, the `main()` method is automatically executed. Whatever you instructed the `main()` method to do is carried out at that time. For that reason, the `main()` method can be called the bootstrap method of all Java applications. It is the method that makes everything else execute.

The following `main()` method is found on line 6:

```
public static void main(String[] args)
```

A lot of information is contained in this method, so let's take a look at each piece.

The *public* Keyword

The `public` keyword is the same access modifier that I discussed when analyzing the class definition. The `main()` method must be public so that the interpreter can invoke the method for you. If you forget to use the `public` modifier, the interpreter will not be able to run the code.

The *static* Keyword

You will learn more about the `static` keyword in Chapter 3, but for now you should know that it is a required part of the `main()` method. In this case, the `static` keyword is needed so that the interpreter can access the method right from the class instead of requiring an object. From the brief discussion of objects so far, you should know that normally a class is just a template for individual objects. A nonstatic method can be called only if an object has been created from a class. A static method can be called without any objects being created.

Because the `main()` method is providing the bootstrap entry point into your code, no objects are present yet. That is why you must always include the `static` keyword in this method.

You can also use `static` with variables and other methods, so it is not solely for use by the `main()` method. You learn how, why, and when to do this in Chapter 3.

NOTE

The *void* Return Type

As you learned before, all methods require a return type. This can be a number, a string of characters, or even another object altogether. However, in some cases, you do not want to return anything at all. This is the case if a method simply performs some task. Think of the return type of all methods as a container that has whatever type you specify inside. So if you say that you are returning an integer, the container is returned with one integer in it. Presumably, that integer would be used by whomever called this method.

When you want to return nothing from a method, you need to do so with the same container concept in mind. The difference is that, in this case, the container has nothing in it! To indicate an empty container as your return type, you use the special keyword `void`. Just remember that there is a difference between an empty container and no container at all. The `void` keyword indicates an empty container.

NOTE All methods must return something, though you now know that can be `void`. You will learn in Chapter 6 about a special method called a constructor that returns nothing at all, not even `void`. In other words, a constructor is the only type of method that returns an "empty container."

If you are familiar with languages such as C, you may be used to returning numbers from methods to indicate error codes. That is not done in Java programming. The `main()` method *always* returns `void` and can never return anything else. If you try to return something other than `void` from the `main()` method, your code will not run at all.

The Method Name, *main*

This method is called the "`main()` method" not just because it is the first method to run in all Java applications. It just so happens that the actual name of the method is `main` as well. All methods have a name, of course. Conventionally, those names always start with a lowercase letter, and each new word in the name begins with an uppercase letter. If you follow convention, you might create methods called `togglePower()`, `orbitPlanet()`, or `learnJavaProgramming()`.

NOTE You may have noticed that whenever I refer to a method, the name ends with a pair of parentheses. This is the syntax for referring to methods in Java. Variables do not have parentheses at the end of their names when you refer to them. So you can always tell that `state` is a variable and `togglePower()` is a method. All methods have a list of parameters that are specified within parentheses. When the parentheses are empty, you are calling a method that requires no parameters.

Don't forget that Java is a case-sensitive language. The `main()` method must be named `main` with all lowercase letters. If you name it `Main` or `MAIN` or use anything besides the lowercase letters m-a-i-n, the interpreter will not be able to execute your code.

WARNING The compiler does not enforce these conventions. If you name the `main()` method `MAIN`, your code *will* compile (assuming you have not made any other mistakes!). This shows you the importance of learning and following the Java conventions. You can find a list of code conventions for the Java language at `http://java.sun.com/docs/codeconv/html/CodeConvTOC.doc.html`.

The Parameter List

All methods have zero or more parameters, separated by commas. These can be any type: numbers, strings of characters, or other objects. If you do not require parameters for a method, you do *not* use the `void` keyword. You use `void` only as a return type, never for anything else. To indicate zero method parameters, you simply leave the parentheses blank. Unlike return types, nothing really means nothing when you are defining parameter lists!

The `main()` method always takes one and only one parameter, an array of strings. Essentially an array is just a collection of "things." In this case, the `main()` method takes an array of strings, so that array will contain zero or more strings of characters.

The strings contained in this array are any arguments that you passed on the command line. Later in this section, I show you how to work with this array to process command-line arguments. Right now, though the interpreter is passing the array automatically to this method when you execute the code, it is completely empty.

Remember that even if you are not accepting any command-line arguments, you **must** have the array of strings as the parameter for this method. Otherwise it is not a valid `main()` method and will not be invoked by the interpreter.

WARNING

You may not be completely clear on how and why the `main()` method is defined as it is, so for now just be sure to include it as you see here in any code that you want the interpreter to invoke. This method will make more sense as you continue your study of the language throughout this book. You will also learn how to create and execute your own methods.

The Method Body

So far, you have learned how to define the method signature for the `main()` method. Of course, it makes little sense to define a method that does not do anything, does it? The method body is composed of a sequence of steps, just like the functions and procedures of other languages. You can have an unlimited number of steps in each method.

The `main()` method in the HelloWorld example has only a single line:

```
System.out.println("Hello World!");
```

This line is called a *statement*. A statement is a line of code that tells the interpreter to perform some action, such as adding two numbers together or turning on the television. This statement tells the interpreter to print the "Hello World!" string to the standard output.

The `System.out` portion of the statement actually refers directly to the standard output and is part of the standard Java class libraries. The standard output on a Windows system is the command prompt. The standard output on a UNIX system is the terminal window.

The `println()` part of the statement is a method that prints the subsequent "Hello World!" parameter to the standard output. The `println()` method automatically adds a newline to whatever it sends to the output. This is why your prompt returns on a separate line after you run this code.

statement
A complete unit of work in a Java program. A statement is always terminated with a semicolon and can span multiple lines in your source code. Every statement is executed in the order in which it is found in the class or method.

terminating character
Whatever character or characters are used in a programming language to indicate the end of a statement. In Java, the terminating character is always the semicolon.

The final part of this statement is the semicolon (;). The end of every statement that you write requires this character. The semicolon is a *terminating character* that lets the interpreter know that it has reached the conclusion of the statement. Without the semicolon, the interpreter would not know when the statement ends, so the compiler enforces semicolons at the end of all statements.

_____ *TIP* _____

It is the semicolon, not a newline, that specifies the end of a statement. This means you can often span multiple lines in your source code with one statement. As long as the compiler finds the semicolon, the statement terminates correctly. Using a semicolon also allows you to format your code nicely so that anyone else who is looking at it (human, that is) can read it easily. Because you will likely be reading your own source code, this is something you should use often!

dot notation
Java uses a system of periods—the dots—to refer to member variables and methods. The syntax `object.method()` is typically how dot notation is used; this denotes that the object "owns" the method.

The entire line `System.out.println("Hello World!")` tells the interpreter to send the string "Hello World!" to the `println()` method of the `System.out` object.

Notice that every element is separated by a period (.). This syntax is known as *dot notation*. To put it simply, what is to the right of the dot is "owned" by what is to the left of the dot. So you can decipher this line as follows: "the `println()` method is owned by the `out` object, which, in turn, is owned by the `System` class."

Dot notation is used constantly in Java code, so it is definitely something we will be investigating throughout this book. The "owned" part—what is to the right of the dot—is called a *member*. So finally, we can say the `println()` method is a *member* of the `out` object, which, in turn, is a *member* of the `System` class.

member
Something "owned" by a class or an object. All variables and methods are called members of their corresponding object or class. Sometimes you will even hear the term *member variable* to differentiate those variables defined directly in the class body from those defined in specific method bodies.

How do you know `System` is a class? This is another convention, and you should always follow it. All classes, as you may recall, start with an uppercase letter, whereas all methods and variables start with a lowercase letter. If you follow the conventions (and the standard Java API, of course, follows them to the letter), it is a simple matter to read code and quickly identify classes, methods, and variables.

Wrapping Up the HelloWorld Program

You have finally written, compiled, and executed your first Java program. Though this is an admittedly simple example, you have learned the key parts of building a class, defining a method, and providing a method body with statements. Everything we do for the remainder of this book stems from the basics you have learned thus far.

Because of the importance of the syntax and process shown to you in this section, be sure to refer to it if you ever find yourself confused. It is a lot to remember, so keep this simple introduction to writing Java code in mind as you progress through this book. The rest of the chapters introduce a lot more code for you to work with and any new features or syntax are thoroughly explained at that time. I assume, however, that you are comfortable with the following:

◆ Writing Java source code, including using comments, white space, and braces that are aligned correctly

◆ Defining classes and methods

◆ Compiling your source code into class files using `javac`

◆ Executing your class files with `java`

Working with Arguments in the *main()* Method

Next, you will learn how to work with parameters in your `main()` method, learn about some Java-predefined types (such as numbers and characters), and finally take a look at the various types of Java programs that can be created.

The `main()` method always takes an array of strings as its sole parameter. The strings contained in this array are any arguments that you passed on the command line. Command-line arguments allow you to pass information to your code at runtime instead of hardcoding it in the source code itself. Passing command-line arguments might be important for specifying information such as which servers to connect to, which files to work with, or other types of customization.

To show you how you might use this array, here is a new version of the `HelloWorld` class that uses the first argument that you pass on the command line as part of the output:

```
1 /*
2  * The HelloWorld2 Example
3  */
4 public class HelloWorld2
5 {
6     public static void main(String[] args)
7     {
8         System.out.println("Hello, " + args[0]);
9     }
10 }
```

Go ahead and type this code into your editor, save it, and compile it just as you did earlier. Note that this time you should save the code as `HelloWorld2.java`.

Once you have compiled the code, execute it with the following line. Substitute your name where mine is specified, if you like.

```
java HelloWorld2 Todd
```

This time, the string "Todd" (or whatever you put there) is shoved into an array of strings, and that array is passed to the main() method. Because you passed something on the command line, you can now access it from within your code as shown on line 8 of the HelloWorld2 example. Instead of just "Hello World!" being printed to your window, you should now see "Hello, Todd".

The argument you passed on the command line is accessed via the array index. Arrays contain any number of items, but there is only one item per index. Therefore, the string "Todd" is in the first position of this string array. In Java, the first index of all arrays is position zero, not one. To retrieve the argument stored in the array, you use the syntax args[0]. The args is the name of the array, and the [0] portion indicates the first index in that array.

NOTE

You will be learning a lot more about arrays in Chapter 5, "Arrays," including what their syntax consists of, how to create them yourself, how to figure out how many items are inside them, and how to add and remove items from them.

Working with Multiple Arguments

So far, you have passed just one string to the main() method. What if you want to pass 2, 3, or 50 strings? Because the parameter to the main() method is an array of strings automatically created and populated by the interpreter, it always contains all the arguments that you pass. All you need to do is learn how to pass them correctly and how to access them.

Passing them is easy. All arguments to your class are separated by spaces. If you type the following line to execute the new HelloWorld2 class, the subsequent array parameter will contain all three strings:

```
java HelloWorld2 Fred Wilma Dino
```

Of course, without any changes to the source code, the output is simply as follows:

```
Hello, Fred
```

To access all three parameters, you simply need to refer to each new index. Remember that Java arrays always start with index zero. To access these three arrays, you need to access index one and two as well.

Here is the third version of the code, called HelloWorld3, that processes all three parameters:

```
1 /*
2  * The HelloWorld3 Example
3  */
```

```
4 public class HelloWorld3
5 {
6     public static void main(String[] args)
7     {
8         System.out.print("Hello ");
9         System.out.print(args[0] + ",");
10         System.out.print(args[1] + ",");
11         System.out.println(args[2] + "!");
12     }
13 }
```

Compile this code and execute it like this:

```
Java HelloWorld3 Fred Wilma Dino
```

You should see output similar to the following on the command line:

```
Hello Fred, Wilma, Dino!
```

You have seen the use of the addition operator (+) in the past two examples to "add" two strings together. This is a convenience provided by the Java language to simplify appending one string to another. In Chapter 3, you learn more about the use of the addition operator.

NOTE

In lines 8–10, notice that there is a call to System.out.print instead of to System.out.println. The difference is that System.out.print does not append the newline to the output. This is why you see all the output on one line in this example. Just keep in mind that the println method adds the newline but the print method does not.

The Basic Java Data Types

Java has two forms of data types: primitive and reference. A primitive type holds only a single value in memory, such as 9, 4573, or 4.67. A reference type has an object as its value. Objects can contain several primitive types, so a reference type appears to represent multiple values. All objects are represented in your system with a memory address, so a reference type "points" to that memory address.

The Java language has nine basic data types. The first eight are primitive types, and the ninth is a reference type. Of all the items you use from the Java API, you will surely use these nine data types much more than anything else.

Let's start with the eight primitive types. The following table lists each type by name, gives the size of that type, and finally gives example values of each type.

Name	Size	Examples
byte	8 bits	–30, 1, 127
short	16 bits	–30, 567, 15000
int	32 bits	–30, 567, 987654
long	64 bits	–30L, 567L, 987654L
float	32 bits	–3.45F, 1.0F, 567.9876F
double	64 bits	–3.45, 1.0, 567,9876
char	16 bits (unsigned)	'a', 'B', '4'
boolean	–	true, false

If you have used other languages that have primitive types, you may be familiar with having to determine the size of integers and floating-point numbers on a system-by-system basis. Java removes that complexity altogether by mandating the size of all types. When you program in the Java language, you *know* that an integer is 32 bits in size on any system, anytime, anywhere. This is part of Java's promise to run on any system with a compliant JVM.

Earlier, I hypothesized the creation of a bank account as a class and said that a balance could be defined in the source code. To do that, you could use the float type to hold your balance. You could define the methods of the class so that they read this float value when you require amount verification and write a new value for the float when the balance changes.

These primitive types can be thought of as the building blocks of all Java applications. If you take a complex application that might be composed of hundreds or even thousands of objects and can unwrap it, you end up with a whole bunch of primitive types with values that are assigned during the application's processing.

Literal Values

literal value

Any value that can be assigned directly to a variable. Essentially, a literal value is a "real" value and is not represented by a variable, as in 123 or "Hello".

Before you learn about each of the types mentioned in this section, you should know about *literal values*. A literal value is a "real" value that is assigned to one of the primitive data types. In other words, it is not a variable such as abc; it is an actual value such as 100, 45.8 or 'a'.

All the eight primitive data types can be assigned a literal value in your source code whenever you see fit. In the following descriptions of each type, you will see this term used quite a bit to explain some of the rules involved with these primitives.

The ninth basic type, the `String`, can also have a literal value assigned to it. If this is the case, the literal value is a string of characters. In the three classes that you have already created in this chapter, you have been using this type of literal value without even knowing it!

There is technically another literal value in Java called `null`. This is meaningful only in relation to objects, though, so I will bypass it for now and introduce it later in the book.

NOTE

The Integer Types

The first four types—`byte`, `short`, `int`, and `long`—are all considered integer types. In other words, they must be whole numbers with no decimal places at all. The most common of these integer types is the `int`, the true Java integer type. A `byte` is one quarter the size of an integer in memory, but it can also hold values only from –128 to 127. A `short` is half the size of an `int` and can hold values from –32,768 to 32,767. The `int` can hold any value from –2,147,483,648 to 2,147,483,647. The fourth integer type is the `long`, which is twice the size of an `int`, coming in at 64 bits and able to represent values from –9,223,372,036,854,775,808 to 9,223,372,036,854,775,807. That is big!

Notice that in the examples for the `long` type, the letter "L" is appended to each number. This is so that Java can differentiate between a number such as 25,000 stored in a 32-bit `int` and the same value of 25,000 stored in a 64-bit `long`. The literal value 25,000 could be either a 32-bit `int` or a 64-bit `long` because 25,000 falls within the legal range of both numbers. However, if the "L" is appended to the value, the compiler and the Java runtime know 64 bits should be assigned in memory. Truthfully, because all `int` values are within the range of the legal `long` values, you do not need to append the "L" unless you are performing some arithmetic function (something you will be learning more about in Chapter 3).

Using the Integer Types

In the following code, each of the four integer types is assigned a value, and then they are printed to the console window. No arithmetic is being done at this point.

```
1  /**
2   * The integer data types
3   */
4  public class UsingIntegers
5  {
6      public static void main(String[] args)
7      {
8          byte b = 56;
9          short s = 5678;
```

```
10        int i = 123456;
11        long g = 123456789L;
12
13        System.out.println(b);
14        System.out.println(s);
15        System.out.println(i);
16        System.out.println(g);
17    }
18 }
```

After you compile and execute the resulting class file, `UsingIntegers.class`, you should see the following output:

```
56
5678
123456
123456789
```

You may be wondering why you have to specify only the special "L" character for the `long` type but not for `byte` or `short`. Java handles the situation for you in the latter two cases. Go ahead and change the value of the `byte` on line 8 to 567, and try to recompile the code. What happens?

You should get a message from the compiler that looks a lot like this:

```
UsingIntegers.java:8: possible loss of precision
found :    int
required:  byte
byte b = 567;
         ^
```

These lines means that on line 8 of the compiled code, an error was found that forced the compiler to give up trying to create the class file. The error is with the assignment of the value 567 to `byte` b. This should not shock you because you have already seen that the maximum value of a `byte` is 127.

The error message continues by telling you the reason for the failure. The "possible loss of precision" message indicates that the number you assigned to this value is too big and that the Java compiler simply will not alter that value for you. You must change it yourself in the source code. If you think about it, this is a smart way to do things. Some languages allow programmers to make mistakes like this one, and such mistakes often lead to strange results and, even worse, an often tedious process of chasing down and correcting bugs. The Java compiler is a real stickler when it comes to following the rules of the language, but that only serves to reduce the bizarre runtime errors that you might otherwise discover.

The same compile-time error appears if you try to assign a value that is too large to any of the integer types, so it is not just the `byte` that is getting picked on here!

The Floating Point Types

The `float` and the `double` primitive types are numerical types that can contain fractional parts, represented with a decimal point and decimal places. A `float` holds a 32-bit value from $-3.40292347E+38$ to $3.40292347E+28$, and a `double` holds a 64-bit value from $-1.79769313486231570E+308$ to $1.79769313486231570E+308$.

Whenever you specify a floating-point number in Java, it is automatically considered a `double`, *not* a `float`. It is always important to add the "F" to the end of any floating-point number that is being assigned to a `float`. If you forget this rule, you get a compile-time error that tells you once again that there is a possible loss of precision. In these next two lines, the first line would cause a compile-time error, and the second would not.

```
float wrong = 123.45; // compiling fails!
float right = 123.45F; // works like a charm!
```

The Character Type

The `char` is the only Java primitive type that is *unsigned*. When a type is unsigned, it cannot contain any negative numbers; everything is zero or higher. Because the `char` type represents characters, it would make no sense for it to be able to contain negative numbers.

The `char` holds a 16-bit character. If you have used the popular character set, ASCII, you may know that those characters are 8 bits in size. So why is the Java `char` twice as big?

Because the `char` type is based on *Unicode* characters, not solely on ASCII characters. Unicode characters are designed to hold any of the world's languages. The extra size allows characters such as those found in the Chinese, Hebrew, or Cherokee languages to be encoded in a single `char` type. This is important because many of today's applications require the ability to handle a dynamic, global user base.

Of course, you can still use the normal ASCII codes in a Java `char`. Therefore, unless you are using different characters directly in your application, the `char` being a Unicode-based type does not really affect you. Just keep in mind that the Java `char` type is twice the size of a normal ASCII character.

Even though the char is twice the size of a normal ASCII character, you are not necessarily using twice the memory. Many virtual machines can optimize how char is stored if the second eight bits are not used.

unsigned
An unsigned data type can only contain values that are zero or higher. In other words, no negative numbers are allowed as values to an unsigned data type. Java has only one unsigned type, the `char`.

Unicode
A character-encoding scheme that defines a unique number for every character regardless of language or platform.

NOTE

The Boolean Type

The `boolean` type holds either a `true` or `false` value. Unlike some other languages, Java considers these values of `true` and `false` reserved words. You do not (and cannot) use "1" to indicate `true` and "0" to indicate `false` as you can with a language such as C. Also, no size is defined for the `boolean` type, though it is most likely only a bit in size on most virtual machine implementations.

One of the most common tasks in programming logic is to determine whether a condition is `true` or `false` and then take some appropriate action. The `boolean` type is useful for making decisions in Java programs, something you learn more about in Chapter 4, "Flow Control."

Using the Primitive Types

The following is another piece of code that does not do a lot yet, but it does contain all the primitive types and shows correct assignment of each one. Once you learn about things such as operators and flow control, you can use these primitive types in much more interesting ways.

```
/*
 * This code shows the Java primitive types
 * being declared and assigned legal values.
 */

public class PrimitivesInAction
{
  public static void main(String[] args)
  {
      byte aByte = 25;
      short aShort = 50;
      int anInteger = 100;
      long aLong = 1000L;
      float aFloat = 1.34F; // remember the 'F'!
      double aDouble = 1.34;
      boolean aBoolean = true;
      System.out.println("Byte: " + aByte):
      System.out.println("Short: " + aShort);
      System.out.println("Integer: " + anInteger);
      System.out.println("Long: " + aLong);
      System.out.println("Float: " + aFloat);
      System.out.println("Double: " + aDouble):
      System.out.println("Boolean: " + aBoolean):
  }
}
```

Go ahead and compile this code and execute it. Each of the assigned values should print to your window.

These primitive types are definitely going to be important to almost every single piece of Java code you write—especially the int, float, and boolean types. However, you have been using another important basic Java type since the beginning of this chapter that you definitely need to learn about. That type is String.

The *String* Class

Unlike the eight primitive types, the String type is an object defined in a class file. That is, individual String objects are used in your programs. These objects hold strings of characters that can be used for anything you want. Common uses include messages to the user, data pulled from a database, or perhaps a complete web page stored in memory. A String can literally hold any series of characters you want.

You can use String objects in the same simple fashion as you use primitives. You can assign values to them, pass those values around in an application, and eventually display them to a user or store them in a file. However, although using the String type feels a lot like using a primitive type, it is *not* a primitive type. It is a reference type. A reference type is more commonly called an object.

Consider this line of code:

```
String title = "Java";
```

Although this line of code appears simple, in reality, a lot is happening here. First, the variable title is being declared to be of type String. Then the equal sign (=) is used to assign the value "Java" to the title variable. The string of characters, "Java", is a *string literal*. Whenever you use a string literal like this, you are actually referring to an object in memory! The title variable references that object.

string literal
A special form of the literal that contains a string of characters enclosed in double quotes. Note that every string literal is represented as an object in memory.

Primitive Values versus Reference Values

Okay, by now, you are probably a little confused about what the difference really is between a primitive value and a reference value. This is your first lesson on the subject of objects and object-oriented programming, so what you learn here will be discussed further later in this book.

To show you the difference between primitive and reference types, let's look at that char type, which holds a single character value, and the String type, which holds an array of characters.

The char is a primitive type, which means it holds a single value in memory. So the line

```
char theCharacter = 'J';
```

might look something like this in memory:

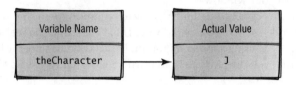

In other words, the variable `theCharacter` directly holds the value, "J".

Now, a `String` is an object that holds an array of characters in memory somewhere. Each element of that array is a primitive `char` type. Another way of looking at the `String` is that it allows you to access a bunch of primitive characters in a simple fashion.

Consider this line of code again:

```
String title = "Java";
```

The variable `title` refers to the string of characters, "J", "a", "v", and "a". However, the way the `title` variable appears in memory is much different from the way the primitive `char` looked.

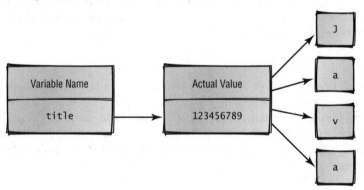

references

Java does not use direct pointers for a variety of good reasons. A reference is really a "pointer to a pointer." This system allows the JVM to manage the memory for you while still allowing you safe access to the objects residing in that memory.

Notice that this time, the `title` variable does not hold the string of characters directly. Instead it holds a pointer to a memory address that knows where the four characters are that form the string "Java". In Java, these pointers are called *references*.

To see a final demonstration of the beauty of using objects, compare the following two sections of code. Both achieve the same thing, but the second is much cleaner and more logical.

First, here is one way you can print "Java" to the command line using only the `char` type:

```
char one = 'J';
char two = 'a';
char three = 'v';
```

```
System.out.print(one);
System.out.print(two);
System.out.print(three);
System.out.println(two);
```

Notice that the variable `two` is used twice in the print statements, once for the second letter and once for the final letter. Because it is the same letter, there is no reason to create a new variable.

Although the previous code works fine, the following code is an improvement:

```
String title = "Java";
System.out.println(title);
```

Remember, the results are identical. The major difference is that `title` refers to an object while each of the `char` variables holds the actual 16-bit value.

Working with String Literals

Any sequence of characters enclosed in double quotes is a string literal. In the previous section, the string "Java" was the string literal. Whenever you are using a string literal, you are actually referring to an object, though. You need to understand a couple of important concepts about the `String` type in Java, however, before continuing to the next chapter.

Java Optimizes String Usage

Because every string literal refers to a `String` object in memory, you may be wondering when these objects are actually created. Essentially, the first time a string literal is encountered in the compiled code, it is created in memory for you. It is not created until you need it, however. This is good because you may have 100 string literals throughout an application that could be holding error details, labels for buttons, or whatever. However, it is possible that you will not need all 100 of these string objects during a particular execution of the program. It would be a waste of memory to have them created and just sitting there going unused, wouldn't it? Java's system of *lazy instantiation* helps minimize memory usage until it is needed.

The other way Java optimizes string literals is by sharing the references. Look at the following three lines of code:

```
String one = "Hello";
String two = "Hello";
String three = "Hello";
```

How many `String` objects can possibly be created here?

If you said three, that is not a surprise. The answer, however, is one. Java notices that the string literal "Hello" was created when the first statement

lazy instantiation
There are two basic choices when it comes to instantiation. The interpreter could create all the objects that you might use before the program even begins executing, or it could delay object creation until it is needed. This latter approach is called lazy instantiation and is the process used by the JVM.

executes, so the following two statements can just refer to the same object. The following diagram shows you how this might look in memory:

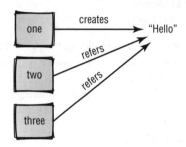

As the picture shows, when the first statement is reached, the string literal "Hello" is created, and the reference is stored in one. When the second and third lines execute, they have the exact same reference stored in them because they hold the same sequence of characters.

WARNING

Don't forget that Java is a case-sensitive language. The string literal "Hello" is *not* the same object as the string literal "HELLO".

Java optimizes String usage like this whenever possible. The end result is much less memory usage for your programs.

String Objects Are Immutable

immutable

When a data type is immutable, it cannot be changed at runtime. By default, both String objects and arrays are immutable, but in different ways. A String cannot have its contents changed, and an array cannot have its length changed.

This may seem quite a shock to you. If String objects are *immutable*, they can *never* be changed! Before you begin to think that the creators of Java were out of their minds, let me explain this immutability.

You *can* say in your code something like this:

```
String title = "Java";
title = "Java Foundations";
```

This appears as if you changed the string itself, but you did not. Remember, whenever Java "sees" a new string literal, it creates a new object. What is really happening in the previous two lines of code is as follows:

1. The variable title is declared a String.

2. The new String object "Java" is created in memory.

3. This new String object's reference is stored in the title variable.

4. The new String object "Java Foundations" is created in memory.

5. The reference to this new String object is stored in the title variable.

After these two lines of code execute, only *one* `String` object is accessible. For all intents and purposes, the first object ("Java") is erased from memory completely because there is no more use for it. Hanging on to `String` objects that nobody is using is not a good idea, so Java just throws them away.

If you are a C or C++ programmer, you may be wondering why you did not have to delete the first `String` object from memory yourself. In Java, the garbage collector handles memory cleanup like this for you. So, no, these two lines of code did not create a memory leak!

NOTE

You cannot change the value of a `String` object. However, you can change the *reference* that your `String` variable holds. This amounts to the same thing, but there is a subtle—and important—difference. Every single time you introduce a new string literal into your code, you are potentially increasing memory usage.

You learn more about `String` objects in Chapter 3 and much more about objects and how they work later in this book.

Terms to Know

access modifier	member
class	method signature
class body	objects
comments	references
compile	source code
compiler	statement
dot notation	string literal
immutable	terminating character
instantiated	Unicode
interpreter	unsigned
lazy instantiation	variables
literal values	

Review Questions

1. Which three types of comments are available when you are writing Java source code?

2. What is the fundamental component of all Java applications?

3. How many primitive types are there in the Java language?

4. What is the significance of a semicolon in Java source code?

5. Name the two major places where the brace characters must be used in Java source code.

6. What is the difference between a primitive type and a reference type?

7. How do you tell the difference between a `char` and a `String` in source code?

8. Why does Java use lazy instantiation of `String` objects?

9. What are the two primitive types in Java that do *not* hold numeric values?

10. What type is the literal value 3.45?

Chapter 3

Keywords and Operators

In This Chapter

- How to create valid names in Java
- All the Java reserved keywords
- The major Java operators
- How to use the operators in practice

Learning the keywords of a programming language is like learning the words of a spoken language, except that there are far fewer keywords to master. Java is a fairly small language—it has only 50 keywords, and two of those are not actually used! So the real total is just 48.

Beyond the keywords, you learn about several operators in this chapter. You use these operators to deal with basic mathematics, assign values, concatenate strings, and work with binary numbers. You will be using operators constantly in Java, so learning them early is important.

Creating Valid Names in Java

In the previous chapter, you were introduced to a few Java classes, but all you learned about were naming conventions. You should follow those conventions if you want to be a top-notch Java developer, but they are indeed conventions, not rules. You can break convention any time you want, and the compiler will not care.

However, there are some rules for naming classes, methods, and variables in Java. For example, all names in Java can contain *only* a combination of letters, numbers, underscores (_), or dollar signs ($). You can never create a class, method, or variable with a name that does not follow this rule. Also, the first character in a variable must never be a number; it can be only a letter, an underscore, or a dollar sign.

As an example, here are some valid variable names that you can use in your Java programs:

```
accountBalance

$firstName

_televisionSchedule

_$_yes_this_will_work_too
```

I am not suggesting that all these are *good* variable names, just that they are valid. I would not like to have to read the source code with variables such as the last one!

In contrast, here are some invalid variable names. Put these in your code, and you will get a compiler error every time:

```
8ball

hello!

never,never,land
```

Java names can be of any length. To decide on a length, keep this in mind: names should be long enough to make clear what they are, but not so long that you are typing a novel every time you try to change a value. Try to limit yourself to 30 characters or fewer as a general rule. Anything longer should be for special situations only.

TIP

Well-defined names are a great alternative or addition to comments. You comment your code to explain portions that may not be abundantly clear, but you can often get away without using them if you choose well-defined names. For example, if you are modeling a bank account and choose balance **as a variable name, no one will have any doubt about what that variable is for. If, however, you named that same variable** xyz_$, **its meaning is unclear.**

The last rule is that you cannot give any of your classes, methods, or variables the same name as any of the reserved words in the Java language. The next section shows you the list of these restricted words.

The Keyword List

The Java language has 52 defined keywords. All these keywords are *reserved words*, which means that you cannot use them as names of variables, methods, or classes in any of your programs. Here are all the Java keywords.

abstract	assert	boolean	break
byte	case	catch	char
class	const	continue	default
do	double	else	extends
false	final	finally	float
for	goto	if	implements
import	instanceof	int	interface
long	native	new	null
package	private	protected	public
return	short	static	strictfp
super	switch	synchronized	this
throw	throws	transient	true
try	void	volatile	while

reserved words
Keywords that form part of the dictionary of a programming language. Java defines 52 reserved keywords that can never be used as names in your source code.

The two reserved words const **and** goto **have no function in the Java language. These words exist only to prevent C and C++ developers from making the mistake of using them. Just remember that you can never use them in your code as names and that they do nothing otherwise.**

WARNING

This book will not discuss all these keywords. For more information about each of these keywords, consult the online version of the Java Language Specification at http://java.sun.com/docs/books/jls/.

The Primitive Type Keywords

In the previous chapter, you learned about the Java primitive types. The basic primitive types account for 11 of the keywords: 9 are the actual types, and 2 are values for the `boolean` type.

- ◆ `boolean`
- ◆ `char`
- ◆ `byte`
- ◆ `short`
- ◆ `int`
- ◆ `long`
- ◆ `float`
- ◆ `double`
- ◆ `false`
- ◆ `true`
- ◆ `void`

Remember that `byte`, `short`, `int`, and `long` are all integer types and decimal places are never attached to them. The `float` and `double` types are for floating-point numbers, and the `char` type is for 16-bit Unicode characters.

The `boolean` type holds either a `true` or `false` value. The list of keywords includes both `true` and `false`.

The `void` keyword is in this list because it is similar to a primitive type. No, you cannot create a variable of type `void`, but in the last chapter you learned that you can return `void` from a method. Returning `void` means you are returning an "empty" type.

NOTE   If you have not yet read Chapter 2, "Java Fundamentals," do so now to learn the basics of using these primitive types. In the discussion of operators coming shortly in this chapter, you will learn how to use these primitive types effectively in your code.

The Flow Control Keywords

flow control
Special constructs in a language that allow simple or complex algorithms to be defined. Essentially, these form the intelligence of your code.

Eleven keywords relate to *flow control*. All the flow control keywords are discussed in detail in the next chapter. Alphabetically, the flow-control keywords are as follows:

- ◆ `break`
- ◆ `case`
- ◆ `continue`
- ◆ `default`

- do
- else
- for
- if
- return
- switch
- while

You use the `if`, `else`, `switch`, and `case` keywords for decision making, and you use the `do`, `while`, and `for` keywords to loop or iterate over a set of values. You use the remaining four keywords in this list—`break`, `continue`, `default`, and `return`—for branching control.

These 11 flow-control keywords form the basis for your programs' intelligence. Because I presume you will be writing code that does a lot more than say "Hello," these keywords are going to be important. Basic code is composed of a series of statements that the interpreter processes sequentially. When you use flow-control constructs, you can alter this simple, statement-by-statement processing by adding conditional testing, iterations, looping, and other enhanced logic. These constructs allow your code to make decisions and perform processing based on dynamic runtime conditions.

Modification Keywords

Six keywords modify classes, methods, and/or variables:

- abstract
- final
- private
- protected
- public
- static

In the last chapter, you learned about the `public` keyword, which allows anyone to access a particular code element (a class, method, or variable). I will now describe the other five.

The *private* Modifier

The `private` keyword is the opposite of `public`. If a method or variable is marked `private`, it can be accessed only by the class that contains it. No external access whatsoever is allowed. You will find that `private` is an important access modifier and that you will use it frequently in your Java programs. As you

encapsulation
An object-oriented concept that protects data from uncontrolled access and modification. The mantra, *private data, public methods*, is concerned with encapsulation.

will learn later in this book, using `private` adds to the *encapsulation* of your classes, an important object-oriented concept.

The *protected* Modifier

subclass

Sometimes called a *child class* or a *derived class*. If you use the `extends` keyword, you are defining a subclass. A subclass essentially inherits the nonprivate members from the extended class.

The `protected` keyword allows less access than does `public`, but more access than using `private`. Don't be confused by the name, `protected`, though it does sound restrictive. When a variable or method is marked `protected`, access from code in the same package is allowed to access via a *subclass*. You learn a lot more about subclasses later, so don't worry too much about them now. When you learn about subclasses, method overloading, and method overriding, we will revisit the `protected` keyword.

_____ **NOTE** _____

One last note about the six access modifiers for now. Although the `public` modifier can be used with classes, methods, and variables, `private` and `protected` cannot be used with classes. Only variables and methods can be modified to be `private` or `protected`.

The *abstract* Modifier

abstract method

A method that has its signature defined, but leaves the implementation for subclasses. The method signature must include the `abstract` keyword. Abstract classes are meant to be implemented in one or more subclasses.

The use of `abstract` is something you learn more about in the advanced discussions of object-oriented programming in Chapter 6, "Introduction to Object-Oriented Programming," and Chapter 7, "Advanced Object-Oriented Programming." An *abstract method* is defined with no body and ends in a semicolon; its body is defined in some other Java class. The idea is that you can define a method that needs to be available, such as *transferFunds()*, without hardcoding the method logic. If you make the *transferFunds()* method `abstract`, you or someone else is forced to provide that method logic in some other class.

Here is an example of this `abstract` method definition:

```
public abstract void transferFunds(float amount);
```

You can use the `abstract` keyword at the class level as well. In fact, if you define even just one `abstract` method in your class, the entire class *must be* abstract.

The use of `abstract` is tied in with the discussion later in this book on object-oriented programming. I know it may be a bit hazy right now, but just keep in mind that an `abstract` method means that the body is defined in some other section of Java code.

The *static* Modifier

In the previous chapter, you saw this modifier as part of the `main()` method, like so:

```
public static void main(String[] args)
```

You learned that it must be marked `static` because the interpreter needs to access the method directly from the class instead of through an object. Both methods and variables can be marked `static`.

Marking a variable `static` is a little different. You can also access the variable directly via the class, and you do not need an object instance to do so; but if you want to do this, you will have only one variable in existence at any one time. For example, consider the following class:

```
public class Counter
{
    public static int theCount;
}
```

The variable `theCount` can be accessed by anything in the current JVM. Perhaps every time a new object is created, this variable is incremented by one, thus allowing you to find out how many objects are in memory at a given moment. As objects are removed, they can decrement this variable. Remember that a class defines a *kind* of object and that an object is an actual instance of that type.

The point here is that the static variable is the same for everyone who accesses it. This is in contrast to the other kind of variable defined in a class—the *instance variable*. An instance variable exists once for each particular object instance, hence its name. A static variable is sometimes referred to as a class variable because it is bound to the class itself.

instance variable
A variable that can be accessed only when an object exists. Instance variables are initialized upon instantiation, and each object instance holds its own copies of each variable, independent of any other objects of the same type.

Basically, a `static` method or variable is the same for all objects of the class type; an `instance` method or variable is particular to each individual object. In a way, you can think of an ISBN number for a book as being static; all copies of the same book have the same ISBN number. However, my copy of that book could have a torn cover while the cover on your copy is in great shape. The condition of each book cover is particular to each instance of the book.

The *final* Modifier

You can use the `final` modifier with classes, methods, or variables, and it means semantically the same thing in all cases—no changes are allowed.

When you use `final` with a variable, the value is fixed and can *never* be changed. You will find this useful if you want to define a *constant* in your code. For example, you might want to hardcode a minimum starting balance for all new bank accounts of $5.00. You could define a variable for this value like this:

constant
A variable that has a fixed value that cannot be changed at runtime. Typically, constants are shared by many pieces of code because they are read only.

```
public final float minBalance = 5.00F;
```

By making this a `final` variable, you assure that nobody can change the value to something other than 5.00 at runtime. Such a change is now possible only if someone makes a physical change in the code itself and then recompiles the code.

════════════════ *TIP* ════════════════

If you are a C or C++ developer, you are familiar with the const keyword. Essentially, Java's final keyword is the same as const. Remember that Java *does* define const as a reserved word, but it does not do anything. If you want to define a constant in Java, use final.

Class-Related Keywords

Six significant keywords are related to defining classes:

- ◆ class
- ◆ extends
- ◆ interface
- ◆ implements
- ◆ package
- ◆ import

These are described in detail in the following pages.

The *class* Keyword

The first (and most obvious) keyword in this list is the class keyword itself. A class is an object template that defines an object's variables and functionality. In Chapter 2, you wrote your first class; you will write many more as you progress through this book.

The *extends* Keyword

inheritance
An object-oriented concept that involves a child class deriving structure and data from a parent class. Inheritance is used to create object hierarchies and form complex relationships.

The extends keyword is used for a special situation called *inheritance*. Inheritance allows you to create one class as a "child" of another class. When you define a class to be a child class (or a subclass, as it is commonly referred to), you use the extends keyword right in your class declaration. When you extend a class, you have full access to all its public methods and variables.

You can extend only a single class in the Java language. You cannot inherit from multiple classes, and if you try, the compiler gives you an error message.

For a quick example, consider this class definition that defines a generic appliance:

```
public class Appliance
{
    public void powerOn()
    {
        System.out.println("On");
    }

    public void powerOff()
```

```
    {
        System.out.println("Off");
    }
}
```

All appliances are powered somehow, so this class defines two methods: powerOn() and powerOff(). This is the first time you have seen user-defined methods in a class file, and as you can see, they follow the rules spelled out in Chapter 2. Though this discussion concentrates only on the structure of a class, you will learn how to create objects and call these methods shortly.

Okay, so we have created this Appliance. Think about it for a moment, though. Do you have anything in your kitchen that is called an appliance? Do you say, "Please get me some water from the *refrigerator*," or do you say, "Please get me some water from the *appliance*"? I would hope you chose the former! An appliance is an abstract type. In other words, it is not a "real" thing, but only a concept. The refrigerator is much more real.

So, if you want, you can create the refrigerator type in a class file. You can also create a stove, a microwave, a dishwasher, a coffee maker, and a toaster. All these are types of appliances, and they can all either be "powered on" or "powered off." In other words, they all share some common traits. It is this set of traits that makes them appliances as opposed to, say, shoes!

Take a look at another class, this one called Refrigerator. You could define the class to have its own methods for power control, but it makes more sense for this class to inherit from the original Appliance class. This is achieved using the extends keyword:

```
public class Refrigerator extends Appliance
{
    /*
     * No method definitions are needed
     * because they are defined in our "parent"
     * class, Appliance
     */
}
```

Normally you refer to the Appliance class as the "superclass" or "parent" class and the Refrigerator as the "subclass" or "child" class.

TIP

At first, it seems as if the Refrigerator class is empty, but in reality, it already has two methods. Because Refrigerator extends the Appliance class, and both of the two methods defined in Appliance are public, this subclass automatically has both methods available. It is just as if you defined them right inside this class!

This brief description of inheritance and using extends is not meant to be complete. The concepts are the important part right now. You learn more about the details and the reasons for extending classes in Chapters 6 and 7.

The *interface* Keyword

concrete class
A class that has all its method bodies defined and could be a standalone class, requiring no further extension.

There are really two types of classes in Java. A *concrete class* has all method bodies provided and is a complete, functional unit of code. An *abstract class* has one or more undefined method bodies, thus making the class incomplete. For example, in the previous example of the Appliance, two methods are defined for power control that will be, presumably, shared by all specific appliance types (refrigerators, stoves, toasters, and so on). It is agreed that all appliances require some concept of power control, but how they provide that power control is specific to each appliance. The toaster is on only when you press the button; the refrigerator is on as long as it is plugged in.

abstract class
A class that must be extended by a subclass. Typically, an abstract class contains one or more abstract methods. An abstract class must include the abstract keyword in the class declaration.

It might make more sense for the powerOn() and powerOff() methods in the Appliance class to be abstract methods. Essentially, this means that the methods signatures are defined, but the implementation of those methods is the responsibility of any subclasses. In this case, the subclass is Refrigerator.

So what does all this have to do with interfaces? A lot, really. An interface is a purely abstract class because *all the methods defined in it* must be abstract. No method bodies whatsoever are allowed. When you define an interface, you are simply defining a new type and declaring what methods need to be implemented in the subclasses.

Here is another look at defining an appliance, this time using an interface to define the appliance instead of a class:

```
public interface Appliance
{
    public void powerOn();
    public void powerOff();
}
```

Notice that the method signatures are defined the same way, but no bodies are provided. Creating an interface such as this is like creating a contract. If any subclass of this interface does not define those two methods, the code will not even compile.

However, the way a class "extends" an interface is *not* with the extends keyword. Instead, another interface-specific keyword is used—implements. In the next section, you learn about implements and see how the Refrigerator class changes to fulfill the "contract" created with the Appliance interface.

If you compile an interface, it still ends up with an extension of "class" in your file system. This is because an interface *is* a class; it is just a special *form* of class.

The *implements* Keyword

When a class "extends" an interface, the `interface` keyword must be used instead of `extends`. Remember that each class can extend only *one* concrete class in Java; you can implement any number of interfaces. The ability to implement one or more interfaces is how Java provides *multiple inheritance*.

The previous section defined an interface named `Appliance`. You can now create a new `Refrigerator` class, but with two major differences. First, you will not use `extends`; you will use `implements` instead. Second, you now have to define your own versions of the two methods, `powerOn()` and `powerOff()`.

Here is the rewritten `Refrigerator` class that now implements the `Appliance` interface:

```
public class Refrigerator implements Appliance
{
    /*
     * Must define both methods now since they
     * are undefined in our "parent" interface.
     */
    public void powerOn()
    {
        System.out.println("Refrigerator is on.");
    }

    public void powerOff()
    {
        System.out.println("Refrigerator is off.");
    }
}
```

You can be sure we will revisit this concept in the object-oriented discussions (Chapters 6 and 7), but the concept should at least be clear right now. Basically, an interface is completely abstract and defines only type and method signatures. You *must* define the interface methods of any class that implements an interface before you can compile and use it.

The *package* Keyword

A *package* lets you control the naming of your classes. For example, you have already worked a little with one standard Java class, `String`. This class is actually located in a package named `java.lang`. So the full name of this class is actually `java.lang.String`.

This is important because it provides an order of uniqueness to your class files. For instance, if I wanted to model a guitar as a class, I might want a related

multiple inheritance
The ability to inherit from more than one parent. Java does not allow inheritance of more than one class, but you can implement more than one interface.

package
A mechanism for grouping related classes in the same namespace. Packages provide both class organization and inherent protection.

class that models the guitar strings. Though I can choose any name I prefer, the simple name String makes a lot of sense. But how can I create a class that already exists?

This is where packages come into play. If you keep in mind that the *fully qualified name* of the standard Java String class is actually java.lang.String, you can begin to see the solution. In the case of *guitar*, all I have to do is create my String class in a package of its own.

The following code snippet shows you how I might do this:

```
package music.guitar;

public class String
{
    /*
     * Variables and methods would be defined here.
     */
}
```

Even though I appear to have created a new class with the same name as an existing Java class, in reality they are different names altogether. The Java class is java.lang.String, and my class is music.guitar.String. They are completely separate from each other.

Notice that the package statement is the first line in this code. This is required; only comments can come before the package statement. Also, because a class can belong to only one package, only one package statement can exist in each source-code file.

NOTE   Every class in Java is in a package, even if you give no package statement. When you do not specifically assign a class to a package with such a statement, it is in the "default package," which essentially means that it is in the directory where the class file resides in your file system.

You have already learned that classes contain methods and variables. Packages are conceptually like containers that contain only classes. The statement we have been using to print a message to the console window is System.out.println(). You may recall that the dot notation in that line signifies ownership. The println() method is part of the out object that is part of the System class.

The System class lives in the same package as String does—the java.lang package. Therefore, the following is also a completely valid line of code:

```
java.lang.System.out.println("Hello World!");
```

fully qualified name
When you include the package name with the class name, it is fully qualified. So java.lang.String is a fully qualified name while just String is not.

Here, the System class is "owned" by the lang subpackage of the ultimate java package.

Compiling Classes Defined in Packages

The compilation process is a bit different when you define a class to be in a package. This is because the package structure is physically modeled in your file system. So for the package music.instrument, eventually you will encounter a directory somewhere named music that contains a subdirectory named instrument. The instrument subdirectory holds the actual compiled class file.

To demonstrate this concept, let's take our original HelloWorld class from Chapter 2 and add a package statement. I have left out the comments in this example for brevity:

```
package test;

public class HelloWorld
{
    public static void main(String[] args)
    {
        System.out.println("Packaged Hello World!");
    }
}
```

The standard Java compiler has a flag you can pass to ensure that the package structure is correctly modeled on your file system. When you have a class with a package statement, you should compile your code like this:

```
java -d /code TestClass.class
```

This line includes the -d flag to the compiler. This flag means "destination" and is used to tell the compiler that the resulting compiled class file should be sent to a location other than the current directory. You specify the destination that you want right after the -d flag. In the preceding line, the destination is a directory named code. Consequently, the compiled class file actually ends up in that directory.

If you try to do this process right now, be sure that the destination directory you pass to the compiler (/code, in this example) actually exists. The compiler will *not* create that directory for you, so if it does not exist, you will receive a compiler error.

WARNING

Using the -d flag also does one other task that relates to packages. If your source code includes a package statement, the compiler is sure that the package structure is mimicked in your file system when you use -d. Because the

HelloWorld class is now defined to be in the package test, the resulting class file is stored in /code/test/.

TIP

If you work on a Windows-based system, you usually use a backslash (\) as your path separator. If you work on a UNIX-based system, you use a forward slash (/) as your path separator. You can, however, use the system-specific separator on your command line because the compiler is smart enough to convert the slash for you. Thus, even on a Windows system, you can type the command exactly as given.

Remember, if you use the package specified in the earlier code, the name of the class is really test.HelloWorld now. In other words, to run this new version of the HelloWorld class, you need to give the fully qualified name to the interpreter, and you also need to include the code directory in your classpath, like so:

```
java -classpath /code test.HelloWorld
```

In this command, the -classpath flag is passed to the interpreter; this allows you to append other directories where the interpreter should look for class files. By default, the interpreter looks only in the Java API classes and the local directory. If you need to add other directories, you can do so on an application-by-application basis with the -classpath interpreter flag as shown in the previous line.

TIP

You can also set the CLASSPATH environment variable if you want. If you do this, all Java applications on that system will use the same CLASSPATH settings. See http://developer.java.sun.com/developer/onlineTraining/new2java/programming/learn/ for details on setting the CLASSPATH environment variable on your specific operating system.

Import One or All: Which Is Better?

A common question among developers is, does importing everything hurt performance? There is a lot of confusion about the answer, but the answer is, quite simply, no. There is no runtime performance hit whatsoever.

The truth is that import statements are a compile-time feature only. When you import from a package, you just tell the compiler that it can attempt to find the classes in that package. The compiler actually prefixes all your short class names with the correct package. So in the class files, it is as if you typed fully qualified names for everything yourself.

If you import everything (as in import java.lang.*) instead of importing only what you need (as in import java.lang.String), the compiler may have to work a bit harder, but the interpreter will not know the difference.

If you created this code with the message "Packaged Hello World!" as I did, you can verify that this new version of the class is executing. If you see the standard "Hello World!" message, you are not accessing the correct class. This is probably because you either did not compile it into a package or are not specifying the fully qualified name on the command line.

The last thing to say about packages involves another Java coding convention. The standard way to create a package name is to take your domain name, reverse it, and append your specific package names. For example, I might create a package called com.sybex.test. The idea here is that if everyone follows this rule, packages will be uniquely named.

The *import* Keyword

The import keyword is related to using packages. You can use one or more import statements to "link" to a particular class or even to an entire package. To be able to reference classes by their short name (such as String) instead of their fully qualified name (such as java.lang.String) all the time, you must use import statements.

You must place such import statements after any package statements and before the class declaration. You can either specify a specific class or import an entire package. If you want to import the java.lang.String class, you can use either of the following import statements:

```
import java.lang.*;
import java.lang.String;
```

Both statements allow you to reference the java.lang.String class as simply String. The difference is that the first statement allows you to use the short name for *all* the classes in the java.lang package (for example, the System class as well), and the second statement allows you to do so only for the String class itself.

The Special Package: *java.lang*

You might already be thinking that something is amiss here. You just read that the only way to reference a class by its short name is if you have an import statement in your source file. Yet the HelloWorld class includes references to both System and String, but no import statement. How can you use those classes like that without actually importing the java.lang package?

Well, the truth is the java.lang package has so many commonly used classes that it is always imported automatically. Every piece of Java source code that you write can reference any class in the java.lang package directly because the compiler adds the following line to your source file when it compiles it:

```
import java.lang.*;
```

The compiler does not actually change your source code, mind you. This is just a conceptual addition made by the compiler. The bottom line is that you never need to import anything from the java.lang package explicitly because it is always part of your import statements anyway.

Dealing with Subpackages

The import statement can import only public classes from a package. If a class does not have the public modifier attached to its declaration, it is considered *package private*. This means that only other classes in the same package can access non-public classes. No cross-package referencing to a non-public class is possible.

Some developers have been confused by how to deal with subpackages. You may already see the similarity between the way import statements reference classes and the way you reference files in your file system. Something like music.instrument.Guitar, which says "the Guitar class in the instrument package in the music package," looks much like what you would use to access a file in a file system. Conceptually, this is as if the music package is the top-level directory, instrument is a subdirectory within music, and Guitar is a file of some kind.

Of course, this subpackage structure is a lot more than just a conceptual relationship. Packages, if you recall, are mapped to your file system when you compile those classes (and use the -d flag). So for the package music.instrument, there will indeed be a music directory that contains a subdirectory named instrument in an appropriate location on your system.

Along with the rule that import statements can only import public classes, there is a second point to remember. You can only import class files, and any subpackages are not automatically accessible. For example, a package in the standard Java classes named java.awt contains classes for creating user interfaces. A subpackage is also defined named java.awt.event, and it contains classes you need to handle mouse clicks and keyboard commands. If you are creating a user interface for an application, you probably need classes from both these packages.

However, just saying

```
import java.awt.*;
```

is not enough. Though this line allows you to access the classes you need to create buttons and windows, it will *not* link to the java.awt.event subpackage. You have to give both lines explicitly to access all the required classes:

```
import java.awt.*;
import java.awt.event.*;
```

Object-Related Keywords

Five keywords relate to object-oriented programming, and we'll look at these in Chapters 6 and 7. All these keywords are meaningful only to an instantiated object. Because all of them are discussed in greater detail in the object-oriented chapters, only brief descriptions are given now.

- new
- instanceof
- null
- super
- this

The *new* Keyword

Classes are templates for creating objects, as you have learned already. However, you have yet to actually create any objects. You create objects using the **new** keyword. This is something you will do more and more throughout the remainder of this book, so here is a quick introduction to how to use the **new** keyword.

The following class defines a robot:

```
public class Robot
{
    public String name;
}
```

This class defines just one variable called *name*. The relationship between the Robot class and the Robot objects that we will create in a moment is the same as in real life. A factory would have a schematic for creating a robot. In this sense, all the robots created based on this schematic are alike, but each constructed robot is a separate unit with separate characteristics, such as its name. The schematic is like a class, and each robot is like an object.

Now you can make individual instances of this Robot class. To do this, use the **new** keyword, which tells the interpreter to set aside the appropriate memory for this particular object and return a reference. A reference is the "pointer" to the memory address where the object is stored. The reference is stored in a variable, just like primitive types are.

To demonstrate the basics of this process, here is a Java class that creates two robots, gives them each a unique name, and then prints each name:

```
1  public class RobotUser
2  {
3      public static void main(String[] args)
4      {
```

```
5        /*
6         * Create the two robots
7         */
8        Robot firstRobot = new Robot();
9        Robot secondRobot = new Robot();
10
11        /*
12         * Give each robot a unique name
13         */
14        firstRobot.name = "Harold";
15        secondRobot.name = "Maude";
16
17        /*
18         * Print out the robot names to prove there are
19         * two separate instances here
20         */
21
22        System.out.println("There are two robots here.");
23        System.out.println("The first is named " +
             firstRobot.name);
24        System.out.println("The second is named " +
             secondRobot.name);
25    }
26  }
```

In the main() method on lines 8 and 9, the two Robot objects are created. Notice that the new keyword is being used, and note the syntax of the command. The new keyword is followed by the name of the class and a pair of parentheses. You can always tell that an object is being created when you see this new keyword syntax.

NOTE

What is really happening here is that a special portion of code, a constructor, is being called. You will learn how to work with constructors later in Chapter 6. For now, just know that whenever you create an object, a special method called a constructor is always called first.

Jump down to lines 14 and 15. Here we are once again using dot notation. In this case, the only member of the Robot class is the variable, name, which is a String. On these two lines, we assign the value "Harold" to the first Robot object and the value "Maude" to the second. At this point, there are two individual objects based on the Robot class. This essentially means both of them have a *name* variable. If we created 1,000 Robot objects, they would all have their own copy of the *name* variable. However, each of them could have a completely different value for that name, just as the two objects in this code do. This is one of the important keys to understanding objects: they are separate entities based on the same class.

Lines 23 and 24 also use the objects and dot notation, this time to access the stored values. These lines print the names of each Robot instance to the command line.

Compiling and Executing the Code

As always, you must first compile the code and correct any errors that you find. Once the compilation is successful, you are ready to run the code and watch those robots appear.

1. Compile both files with the following command:

```
javac Robot.java RobotUser.java
```

2. Run the RobotUser code with this command:

```
java RobotUser
```

You should see the following printed to your command line:

```
There are two robots here.
The first is named Harold
The second is named Maude
```

The *instanceof* Keyword

The instanceof keyword is for conditional testing between objects. With this keyword, you can test an object to be sure that it is a specific type, like a String or Robot. This is more like an operator than a keyword. The next section of this chapter is all about the operators in Java; the instanceof keyword is addressed further momentarily.

The *null* Keyword

The null keyword is used only with object references. When you assign null as the value of an object reference, there is *no* reference. All object references start with null as their default value. Until you assign a value to a reference, it is always null.

Let's borrow the Robot class from the previous section for a moment. In the following section of code, a variable named testRobot is created that is of type Robot. Next, a new Robot object is instantiated and the reference is stored in testRobot in the first line. Finally, the object is explicitly set to null, wiping out the reference altogether.

```
Robot testRobot; // the value is null here
testRobot = new Robot(); // live reference created here
testRobot = null; // the reference is nullified here
```

Effectively, setting an object reference to null ends the usefulness of that object entirely and makes it eligible for garbage collection. Once an object is set to null, it is gone forever. There is no resurrection from null! Note that the variable itself can be used again, but only if a new object is assigned to it; the original object that was set to null is no longer "alive."

NOTE

The previous example shows only a single variable referencing an object. If you have multiple variables referencing the same object, setting one variable to null does not nullify the object for the other variables.

In the next chapter, you learn how to test to see if an object is null before using it. This is one of the most important tests that you will make in your Java classes because it is illegal in Java to do anything with a null reference except assign it a new object reference.

WARNING

In C and C++, there is a constant called NULL that is equal to zero. Do not confuse that NULL with the null found in Java.

The *super* Keyword

super class

Sometimes called a *parent class* or a *base class*. The class listed to the right of an extends clause is the super class. The class to the left is the subclass.

Earlier in this chapter, you learned a little bit about the extends keyword and how it relates to inheritance. When you have a child class, it is sometimes important to be able to "talk" directly to the parent class. For example, you might want to call a method of your parent class at some point in your own functionality. To do so, you must have a reference to your parent class. This reference is always available to you and is always called super because your parent class is also known as your *super class*.

The syntax for referencing a method named parentMethod from a child class would simply be

```
super.parentMethod();
```

WARNING

You can go up only one level to your direct super class. If your parent class also extends another class, there is no way to directly access the "grandparent" class. A call such as super.super.method() is not allowed.

The *this* Keyword

Much like super, the this keyword is a standard name for a reference that you will need from time to time. In this case, the reference is not to any parent class, but to yourself. In other words, when you use this, you are referring to *this instance*.

You use the this keyword inside your method bodies in two different cases. First, you can use it to clarify that the variables and methods being called belong to one particular instance. Second, you can pass it as a parameter to or a return type from a method.

As a quick example of how `this` works, here is a modified version of the Robot class. Notice that the *name* variable is now `private` and that there are two new methods, one for setting the value of *name* and one for getting the value of *name*.

```
1   public class Robot2
2   {
3       private String name;
4
5       public void setName(String name)
6       {
7           this.name = name; // cannot say name = name;
8       }
9
10      public String getName()
11      {
12          return name;
13      }
14  }
```

The Robot2 class works quite a bit differently from the original Robot class, but the results are the same. Make a note of how this class looks because this is well constructed. In the previous example, the *name* variable was declared as `public`, which is perfectly legal but not good practice. Generally, all the variables defined in the class should be `private` so that no external users can modify their value directly. Instead, you should provide one or more `public` methods that handle access and modification of the variable. In Robot2, the `setName()` method takes a `String` as a parameter that is then assigned to *name*, and the `getName()` method returns this value to the caller.

Line 7 is an example of why `this` is needed. In this case, it is a question of *scope*. The parameter to the `setName()` method is called `name` and the variable defined on line 3 is also called *name*. It would make no sense to provide the following method definition:

```
5   public void setName(String name)
6   {
7       name = name;
8   }
```

The reason that this makes no sense is that you are essentially assigning the value of the `name` parameter to the `name` parameter. If the previous sentence confuses you, that kind of proves the point, doesn't it?

scope
Scope refers to the accessibility of a variable within a class. Everything in Java has some form of scope. At the class level, you can identify a scope by a matched pair of braces. Whatever is between the braces is in the same scope and cannot be "seen" outside those braces. Each new pair of nested braces is yet another level of scope.

This is an example of one of the fundamental rules of the Java language. It is another rule you should memorize, because if you can rattle this off the top of your head, you will find it much easier to understand what is going on in a particular piece of source code: *Java always starts in the local scope and then looks outward.*

This rule relates directly to the braces surrounding method and class bodies. Those braces define scope and, within the same scope, all variable names (and method signatures when you talk about classes) must be unique. In the `Robot2` code, the goal is to assign the value of the `name` parameter to the *name* variable defined on line 3. The *name* variable is defined in the class scope, so all the methods defined in this class can access this variable. The `name` parameter on line 5 is only "alive" for the duration of the method body. Once the statement on line 7 completes and the closing brace on line 8 is reached, the `name` parameter vanishes into thin air. We call this vanishing act *going out of scope.*

Okay, so let's wrap `this` up for now. When you put `this` in front of a variable, you are saying that you want to access the instance variable, the variable defined in the class scope. If you leave off the `this` keyword in this example and just say `name`, Java thinks that you mean the name parameter because that is the most local scope. That is obviously not a useful thing to do!

In Chapter 6, I'll discuss some other uses for `this`. What you have learned so far concerning `this` is a good start, though.

Wrapping Up the Keywords

Obviously, this lengthy discussion of keywords is a lot to handle all at once. However, you should not feel you have to master all of them right now. As these keywords come up in the rest of the book, you can always refer to this chapter for a quick, friendly refresher on the basics. Also, as each keyword is used throughout the book, especially if they are used differently from the simple examples shown here, a full explanation will be given.

Once you feel comfortable with the immersion that you just received in the Java keywords, move on to the final section of this chapter, which covers the major operators in the Java language. Trust me, it is a much gentler topic to handle!

The Java Operators

You have already seen the Java primitive types and some classes, including `String`. Up to this point, you have not really done much with them, though. In this section, you learn how to use the major operators found in the Java language. These operators can be used with both primitive types and objects themselves.

You will learn about four major categories of operators:

◆ Arithmetic

◆ Assignment

◆ Relational

◆ Conditional

The Arithmetic Operators

One of the primary functions of code is to do math. After all, we do call it a *computer*, don't we? There are seven arithmetic operators, and most of them are basic indeed.

The Binary Operators: +, –, *, and /

These are the four standard arithmetic operators that you would find in any programming language. There is little to say about them because they do exactly what you would expect, but next is a small class that demonstrates them in use. You can use these operators with any integer or floating-point primitive.

```
public class MathDemo
{
    public static void main(String[] args)
    {
        int x = 6;
        int y = 3;

        System.out.println(x + y); // 9
        System.out.println(x - y); // 3
        System.out.println(x * y); // 18
        System.out.println(x/y); // 2
    }
}
```

One More Binary Operator: %

The *modulus operator* is a lesser known, but still fairly common operator. This operator divides the first number by the second and returns the remainder. This can be used with integers and floating-point primitives.

To see how the modulus operator is used, you can change the existing MathDemo class slightly:

```
public class MathDemo
{
```

modulus operator

A special arithmetic operator that returns the value of the remainder of division between two numbers. If it returns 0, one number is a power of the other.

```
    public static void main(String[] args)
    {
        int x = 6;
        int y = 3;

        System.out.println(x + y); // 9
        System.out.println(x - y); // 3
        System.out.println(x * y); // 18
        System.out.println(x/y); // 2

        System.out.println(x % y); // 0
        x = x + 1;
        System.out.println(x % y); // 1
    }
}
```

Because 6/3 is 2 without any remainder, the first of these new statements prints 0. In the next line, the x variable has 1 added to it, and then this new value of 7 is used in the subsequent modulus operation, which prints 1. This is because 3 fits into 7 2 times, with 1 left over.

The Unary Arithmetic Operators

Some operators in Java do not require two operands, making them unary in nature. Some of them have to do with arithmetic while others have to do with logical operations. Here are the main unary operators:

◆ ++

◆ --

◆ -

The Increment Operator: ++

The unary operator is an increment operator and can be used before or after a variable. When used before, it is called a preincrement operator; when used after, it is called a postincrement operator.

Here is a code snippet that shows both the preincrement version and postincrement version of this operator in action:

```
int f = 10;
System.out.println(f++ + 2); // 12
System.out.println(++f + 2); // 14
```

The difference between these two forms of the increment operator is seen in this example. The call to (f++ + 2) uses the postincrement operator. What happens here is that 2 is added to the current value of f (which is 10, as specified on the previous line), and that is what is printed. However, the ++ operator means to increase the value by one. Because this is a postincrement, the increase is not actually carried out until the operation completes. In other words, the *next* time the f variable is used, it will be 11, not 10.

This is further proven in the final line of the example. This time, the preincrement operator is being used. In this case, the f variable should be incremented by one *before* it is added to 2. So it is really saying ((11 + 1) + 2).

The Decrement Operator: --

The decrement operator works exactly the same as the increment operator, including having both a postdecrement and predecrement version.

Here is an example of using this operator, though the process is just the opposite of the increment operator previously discussed.

```
int f = 10;
System.out.println(f-- + 2); // 12
System.out.println(--f + 2); // 10
```

Remember that the postdecrement occurs *after* the operation completes and the predecrement occurs *before* the operation completes. In this example, f starts with a value of 10. On the next line, 2 is added to this value, so the printout is 12. However, the postdecrement operator executes, so f is 9 when the final statement begins. The predecrement operator immediately drops the value to 8 and then 2 is added to it, making the last printout 10.

The Unary - Operator

This is a simple one. All the unary form of the - operator does is negate a numeric value. It is just like using a negative sign in algebraic equations.

```
int s = 100;
System.out.println(-s); // prints out -100
```

Here, this operator just negates the current value of a primitive, numeric type. So after the printout, what is the value of s? The negation affects only the output, not the variable itself. If you want to actually negate the value of the variable, you need to add a line like this one:

```
s = -s;
```

The Parentheses Operator

This operator does not really fit into any single category, but it has two main uses: grouping arithmetic operations and casting.

precedence

The predefined order in which operators execute, enforced by the rules of Java. Understanding precedence helps you ensure that your operations function exactly as you intend. Often, parentheses are used to group expressions to better control the precedence.

casting

Whenever you convert a variable of one type to another type, you are casting. For example, you might convert a `float` value to an `int` value. You can cast primitive number types between each other, and you can cast objects back and forth. *Upcasting* is converting one type to a bigger type, for example, casting a `byte` to an `int`. *Downcasting* is converting one type to a smaller type, for example, casting an `int` to a `byte`. The only time you must explicitly cast is if you are downcasting.

Parentheses as a Grouping Operator

You can use parentheses to group an operation. This is important to avoid precedence issues. *Precedence* is the order in which operations execute. In Java, precedence is clearly defined for every operator so that there should be no doubt about which operations come first. It is not as simple as reading a statement from left to right; certain operators take precedence over others. The parentheses operator is number one in precedence order. In other words, anything inside parentheses is calculated before everything not in parentheses.

For example, these two lines look similar, but the use of parentheses forces a different result:

```
int a = 1 + 2 * 3; // this is 7
int b = (1 + 2) * 3; // this is 9
```

These are different because the * operator takes precedence over the + operator. So in the first line, the 2 * 3 happens first, then the 1 is added to give the result of 7. In the second line, because parentheses surround the 1 + 2, the addition will occur first, followed by the multiplication. The resulting statement is actually 3 * 3, which is, of course, 9.

You can also nest parentheses. In the following situation, the inner parentheses take precedence over the outer parentheses:

```
int a = ((1 + 2) * 3) + 4; // 13
int b = (1 + 2 * 3) + 4; // 11
```

In the previous lines, the first line has nested parentheses, so the 1 + 2 operation happens first. This result is multiplied by 3, and finally the resulting 9 is added to 4. The second line contains only the single parenthetical pair, so normal precedence takes over: the 2 is multiplied by 3, the result is added to the 1, and then this result of 7 is added to 4.

> **NOTE** Precedence is an important facet of the language to become accustomed to, because not understanding it can lead to strange results in your code. You'll find a precedence chart at http://java.sun.com/docs/books/tutorial/java/nutsandbolts/expressions.html.

Parentheses as a Casting Operator

Casting is the process of converting from one type to another. Though you can cast objects as well, for now you will only learn about casting primitive types.

Upcasting Is Always Safe

You may have an *int* variable that you wish to convert to a *long*. This is called upcasting and is always allowed in Java without any special routines on your part. The concept is that there is no danger and no possible loss of information if you are casting from a 32-bit int to a 64-bit long.

In other words, the following code would work just fine:

```
int small = 145;
long big = small;
```

The following list has the primitive numeric types in upcasting order. Everything under a specific type can be cast to that type automatically.

- double
- float
- long
- int
- short
- byte

As you can see, the floating-point types are the highest on this list. Everything can be upcast to a double, for example.

Downcasting Is Not Safe

The trouble arises when you want to take a 64-bit long value and shove it into a 32-bit int value or when you want to put a floating-point number into a normal integer type. Neither of these actions is safe because you could lose data as a result. For example, if you convert the number 4.567 to an integer, the .567 portion is lost. That is something the Java compiler does not allow unless you specifically cast the value yourself.

To perform this casting, you simply wrap the target type in parentheses and place it before the variable in question. In the following code, a float is being converted to an int, something that would not be allowed without the explicit cast:

```
float f = 1.567f;
int i = (int)f; // value is 1
```

Note that casting just chops off the decimal places; there is no automatic rounding up as you might expect. You can cast any numeric type to another numeric type in this fashion. However, you can *never* cast a number to a boolean value; the compiler does not accept such a cast. When you are working with primitives, casting works only on numbers.

Technically, the char type is a number, so it can be cast just like other numeric types. This is rare, however.   *TIP*

promotion
The upcasting of one primitive type to another as the result of a mathematical operation. Essentially, the biggest type in an expression is how big the result of that expression will be. All the variables in the expression are promoted to the result type before the operation completes.

Automatic Casting

Automatic casting is usually referred to as *promotion*. In the following lines of code, the result of adding this `int` and this `float` is a `float`:

```
int x = 10;
float y = 5.5f;
float result = x + y; // 15.5
```

Essentially, this promotion system always makes the type of a result of an operation the same as the largest type in the operation. Because a `float` is technically bigger than an `int`, the promotion now makes sense.

You can use the casting operator to downcast if you need to, even the result of an entire operation:

```
int x = 10;
float y = 5.5f;
int result = (int)(x + y); // 15
```

Remember that whenever you downcast like this, you are willingly losing precision. Instead of the actual result of 15.5, this second example is only 15. Because the cast needs to be performed on the result of the addition, the parentheses wrap the `x + y`.

The Assignment Operators

Six major assignment operators are defined. All do the same thing, of course: assign a value. The difference is that five of them involve an extra step before assignment occurs.

- `=`
- `+=`
- `-=`
- `*=`
- `/=`
- `%=`

The Basic Operator: =

You have been using this assignment operator since Chapter 2. The equal sign (=) assigns a value to a variable. It is used for primitives and objects alike.

```
int x = 50;
Robot robot = new Robot();
```

The single equal sign is used only to assign values and is never used for equality checking. Equality checking is a conditional operation that will be discussed in the next section.

The Combination Operators

The final five operators in the list of assignment operators all perform their action (add/subtract/multiply/divide/modulus) on the value to the right of the equal sign to the variable on the left. They are just shorthand; the same thing could be said in a more verbose fashion. You are never required to use these five combination operators, but you may find that they make your code more legible.

For example, both of the following two lines add 10 to the current value of x. The first statement uses the combination assignment operator, which performs the addition, and then the assignment. The second statement does exactly the same thing, but in a more verbose fashion. Which form you use is your choice; the JVM will execute both statements exactly the same way.

```
int x += 10;
int x = x + 10;
```

The remaining four combination assignment operators work exactly the same way except that the actual operation changes.

The Relational Operators

Six operators determine the relationship between two operands. Each of these operators returns either `true` or `false`. You will use conditional operators quite a bit when you work with flow control in Chapter 4, "Flow Control."

- ◆ ==
- ◆ >
- ◆ <
- ◆ >=
- ◆ <=
- ◆ !=

The Equality Test Operator: ==

When you want to test a variable to see if it is equal to a specific value, this is the operator to use. This is sometimes called the "double equal" operator to differentiate it from the "equal" operator (=) that you use for assignment only. You can use this operator with both primitive types and reference types.

Testing the Equality of Primitive Types

When you use this operator with primitive types, it just compares the value on the right with the value on the left. If they are equivalent, true is returned. Otherwise, false is returned.

```
int x = 100;
System.out.println(x == 100); // prints out "true"
System.out.println(x == 10); // prints out "false"
```

Testing the Equality of Reference Types

When you test reference types such as objects with this operator, it compares the actual value of the memory addresses. If they match, the result is true. For the memory addresses to exactly match, the two objects being tested must be the same object.

Here is an example of this referential testing in action:

```
Robot one = new Robot(); // new object
Robot two = new Robot(); // new object
Robot three = one; // reference to the first Robot object
System.out.println(one == two); // prints out "false"
System.out.println(two == three); // prints out "false"
System.out.println(one == three); // prints out "true"
```

In this code, only two objects are created. Remember that whenever you see the new keyword, a new object is being created. Because the third Robot object is not using the new keyword to assign a reference, you know that it must point to the same object as was defined on the first line.

The <, >, <=, and >= Operators

These operators test how two values relate. The < operator tests to see if the value on the left is less than the value on the right. The > operator tests to see if the value on the left is greater than the value on the right. The other two operators, <= and >=, work the same way, but tests involving them return true if the values are equivalent as well. Note that you can use these operators only with primitive numbers.

Here is a short example of these simple operators:

```
int a = 10;
int b = 10;

System.out.println(a < b); // prints out "false"
System.out.println(a > b); // prints out "false"
```

```
System.out.println(a <= b); // prints out "true"
System.out.println(a >= b); // prints out "true"
```

As with the == operator, you use these operators extensively when working with the flow-control constructs in the next chapter.

The Non-Equality Operator: !=

The "not equal" operator, !=, is simple to use; it tests to ensure that two values are *not* equal. In this sense, it is the opposite of ==. If the two values involved are not equal, the operation returns true. If they are equal, the operation returns false. You can use this operator with both primitive types and reference types.

```
int a = 10;
int b = 10;

System.out.println(a != b) // prints out "false"
System.out.println(++a != b) // prints out "true"
```

The first operation returns false because the two values are equal. The second operation returns true because the preincrement operator makes the value of a equal to 11.

The Conditional Operators

You use the conditional operators to test for logical truth. Conditional operators work by testing for truth in two operands. These operands are commonly the result of relational operations that are used to form more complex algorithms. There are six conditional operators: five are binary in nature, and one (!) is unary.

- &&
- ||
- &
- |
- ^
- !

The && Operator

This operator tests the results of two operands and ensures that both are true. This is sometimes called the Boolean AND operator and is often referred to as a "short-circuit" operator, because it automatically returns false if the first test returns false. In other words, if the first test fails, this operator does not even test the second operand.

Take a look at this operator being used in the following code:

```
int x = 9;
int y = 55;
boolean b = x < 10 && y > 20; // true
boolean c = x == 9 && y == 100; // false
boolean d = x == 10 && y == 55; // false
```

In the final line, the y == 55 operation is never executed because the x == 10 operation returned false.

The || Operator

This operator works a lot like the && operator, except that instead of performing a Boolean AND test, it performs a Boolean OR test. If either of the operations returns true, the || operator returns true. This is also a short-circuit operator because if the first test passes, the second test is not even executed.

Take a look at this operator being used in the following code:

```
int x = 9;
int y = 55;
boolean b = x < 10 || y > 20; // true
boolean c = x == 9 || y == 100; // true
boolean d = x == 10 || y == 55; // true
```

Notice that all three tests pass in this case even though both relational operations return true only in the first case.

The & Operator

The & operator is different from the && operator because it has no short-circuit functionality. Both relational tests must pass for this conditional operation to return true. Both relational operations are *always* executed with this operator. This is commonly called the binary AND operator.

Here is an example of how this operator works:

```
int x = 9;
int y = 55;
boolean b = x < 10 & y > 20; // true
boolean c = x == 9 & y == 100; // false
boolean d = x == 10 & y == 55; // false
```

In the final line, the y = 55 operation is executed even though the x == 10 operation already returned `false`. This is the difference between the & operator and the && operator.

The | Operator

The | operator differs from the || operator because it has no short-circuit functionality either. When you use this operator, you will find that one of the tests must pass, but that both relational operations are *always* carried out. This is commonly called the binary OR operator.

Here is the example code for the | operator:

```
int x = 9;
int y = 55;
boolean b = x < 10 | y > 20; // true
boolean c = x == 9 | y == 100; // true
boolean d = x == 10 | y == 55; // true
```

Though the results are the same as using the || operator in this case, keep in mind that the big difference between | and || is that both relational operations are executed regardless of the result of the first operation.

The ^ Operator

The ^ operator is used to ensure that one of the relational tests returns `true` while the other does not. Another way of putting this is that the ^ operator makes sure the results are never equal—neither both `true` nor both `false`. This is usually called the exclusive OR operator.

Take a look at this operator being used in the following code:

```
int x = 9;
int y = 55;
boolean b = x < 10 ^ y > 20; // false
boolean c = x == 9 ^ y == 100; // true
boolean d = x == 10 ^ y == 55; // true
```

This operator always evaluates both operands, of course, because it has to ensure that they never match.

The Unary Operator, !

This conditional operator does not use two operands. Instead, it is used to negate a logical value. Earlier you learned about the arithmetic operator, -, that negated the value of a number. The ! operator is similar, except that it is used only with `boolean` values. The result is the opposite of the current `boolean` state. If it was `true`, it becomes `false`. If it was `false`, it becomes `true`.

Here are some examples of using this unary conditional operator:

```
int x = 9;
int y = 55;
boolean b = !(x == y); // true
boolean c = !(x < 10 && y == 100); // true
boolean d = !(y == 55); // false
boolean e = !b; // false
```

TIP

The operators covered in this chapter are just the most common. This is not an all-inclusive list. Consult the Java Language Specification for a complete discussion of all the Java operators. You can find the language specification discussion of expressions and operators at `http://java.sun.com/docs/books/jls/second_edition/html/expressions.doc.html#44393`.

Terms to Know

abstract class	modulus operator
abstract method	multiple inheritance
casting	package
concrete class	package private
constant	precedence
encapsulation	promotion
flow control	reserved words
fully qualified name	scope
inheritance	subclass
instance variable	super class

Review Questions

1. Which of the following is not a Java keyword: `sizeof` or `const`?

2. What does the `new` keyword do?

3. Which of the following is not a valid name for a variable in Java: `licenseNumber`, `34jump`, `$inTheMoney`, or `_$____`?

4. What does making a variable `final` mean?

5. What are the characteristics of a `static` method?

6. How many interfaces can a class implement?

7. How many classes can a class extend?

8. Which operator tests equality of primitive types?

9. Name the two functions of the parentheses operator, `()`.

10. If x equals 6, what is the result of `!((x < 7) ^ (x == 0))`?

Chapter 4

Flow Control

So far, all the programs you have created have been composed of simple, linear code. Most code requires some form of intelligence built into it so that processing decisions can be made at runtime. This intelligence is created with flow control.

Flow control allows you to conditionally execute statements, skip statements, jump between statements, and perform looping. Most of your code logic will be composed of combinations of flow-control statements and regular statements.

Application Scope

As you will see, the flow-control constructs involve the use of braces just as classes and methods do. Before you begin "getting into the flow," we need to look at scope a little more. Scope refers to the "accessibility" of a class member, whether a variable or a method. Essentially, anything defined within a pair of braces is accessible only from within that same pair of braces. Another way to say this is that a variable defined inside a pair of braces is *not* accessible outside those braces.

There are various levels of scope. The primary level is class scope, which refers to everything defined between the class braces themselves. This, of course, refers to everything defined in the class. Anything defined in the class scope is accessible from anywhere within that class.

A narrower form of scope is method scope. This refers to all the declarations inside a particular method body, enclosed by the pair of braces. Variables defined within a method are accessible only from within that method body and are not visible anywhere else in the class. A variable defined within a method scope is often called a *local variable*.

local variable

A variable whose scope is the body of a method. Local variables are only "active" while their containing method is being invoked.

NOTE

The basic rule of scope is the same everywhere. A pair of braces defines the scope. Variables and methods defined within those braces are visible only in that scope. Variables and methods defined outside those braces are accessible as well.

In essence, a class file is just a series of nested scopes. The ultimate scope is the class itself, and each method defines its own scope. You need to understand scope and visibility so that you can be sure to define your class members appropriately.

Along with classes and methods, there are other areas of scope. Any time you see a pair of braces, you know that you are defining a new scope. When you use flow-control statements, you use a pair of braces again, so you know that you have created yet another scope. You will come across some examples of the implications of this scope in this chapter as you learn about each of the flow-control statements available in the Java language.

The *if* Statement

The if statement is the basic flow-control statement. Using the if statement, you can selectively execute other statements. In this sense, you use the if statement to make decisions in your code based on some criteria. You decide whether to execute a section of code based on a test condition that will be either true or false.

The if statement works much like real, human logic. For example, you might think something like this if you are deciding what to have for dinner:

If I am really hungry, I will make a large salad.

Inherent in that statement, of course, is the contrary statement:

If I am not really hungry, I will not make a large salad.

The logic is clear and concise, and that is exactly how an if statement works in your code. Here is the *pseudocode* for an if statement:

```
if(expression is true)
{
    execute this block of code
}
```

Okay, let's see the if statement in action. Before you look at the following code, let me introduce you to a new class from the standard Java API: java.lang.Integer. This is a *wrapper class*, which means it matches a primitive type. So for the primitive int, we have the class Integer; for the primitive float, we have the class Float, and so on.

These wrapper classes exist because primitive types are *not* objects. No methods are associated with them. The only thing you can functionally do with a primitive is combine it with some of the operators you learned about in Chapter 3, "Keywords and Operators." However, when we "wrap" a primitive int inside an actual Integer object, some methods are now available to use.

I'm introducing the Integer class now so that I can present you with some more interesting, useful code. After all, there are only so many times you need to print out "Hello World"! In the following code, I am using the Integer class to convert the String passed in on the command line into a primitive int. This is accomplished by calling a static method named parseInt(). This method takes a String as a parameter and, assuming String actually contains a valid integer value, returns the primitive int.

The following code expects you to pass in an integer, and when you do, it tells you if that number is even. Notice how the if statement works by evaluating the expression passed to it for a true or false value. This expression uses the modulus operator that you learned about in Chapter 3.

```
1   public class EvenTest
2   {
3       public static void main(String[] args)
4       {
5           int number = Integer.parseInt(args[0]);
6           int mod = number % 2;
7           if(mod == 0)
8           {
9               System.out.println("The number is even.");
10          }
11      }
12  }
```

pseudocode

Code written in a logical, natural language style to express process or flow. Pseudocode cannot be compiled; it is used only to explain the steps required for actual code to work.

wrapper class

Java provides classes that "wrap" around primitive types. For example, the Integer class contains a primitive int, but provides methods to process or retrieve the "wrapped" primitive. All primitive types have an associated wrapper class.

When you run this code, you have to pass an integer as a command-line argument. Remember that these arguments you pass in are stored in the `String` array, `args`. The first argument is parsed into a primitive `int` on line 5. Line 7 shows the `if` statement that checks to see the results of the modulus operation on line 6. If the number you pass in is divisible by 2, this expression evaluates to `true`, and line 9 executes, printing a message. Otherwise, there is no output, which means that the number you passed in was simply not even.

WARNING

If you forget to pass in something on the command line, you get a message from the interpreter saying that you had an `ArrayIndexOutOfBoundsException`. This is because nothing is there when line 5 attempts to access the value of `args[0]`! Also, if you pass something that is not a valid integer (perhaps a `String` or `float`), you receive this message: `NumberFormatException`. This happens if the `String` passed to `Integer.parseInt` does not contain a valid integer value. You learn how to handle these problems gracefully in Chapter 5, "Arrays."

Adding the *else* Statement

So far, the `EvenTest` code responds to you only if the number you provide is divisible by 2. If you pass an odd number, you get no output. A complete version of this code would have both options presented. In other words, you are told if the number is even or if it is odd.

We can accomplish this by adding an `else` statement to the code. If we incorporate `else` into our original human logic about salad making, we could add some more useful logic:

If I am really hungry, I will make a large salad

else

I will make a small salad

In other words, using `else` is like saying "otherwise." This way, you get to eat either way, but you can adjust the amount you eat to your hunger level. Hey, learning Java is cool, but you still have to eat! The pseudocode looks like the following when you add the `else` statement to the mix:

```
if(expression is true)
{
    execute this block of code
}
else
{
    execute this other block of code
}
```

Let's change the EvenTest code to include an else statement that guarantees output:

```
1   public class EvenTest2
2   {
3       public static void main(String[] args)
4       {
5           int number = Integer.parseInt(args[0]);
6
7           int mod = number % 2;
8           if(mod == 0)
9           {
10              System.out.println("The number is even.");
11          }
12          else
13          {
14              System.out.println("The number is odd.");
15          }
16      }
17  }
```

Now when you run the code, it outputs a message to you either way, indicating whether the supplied number was even or odd. Notice that the code is actually making a decision here based on the if statement on line 8. This is much more realistic code than the simple statements you have been working with up to this point.

Working with Multiple *else* Statements

We are not done yet, however. This code is still not as smart as it should be. For instance, if you pass in the number zero (0) on the command line, this code tells you that the number is even. Zero is, of course, a special case that is neither even nor odd, so this needs to be corrected. To do this, we need to add yet another else statement.

You can "stack" else statements if you want to provide decision making beyond the simple binary method shown here. To do this, you actually combine else with another if. Every if and else statement must be based on unique criteria. For example, in the EvenTest2 code, the if statement tests the truth of the modulus operation, and the else statement assumes truth for everything else. You can effectively read line 12 of the EvenTest2 code as "Otherwise, no matter what the criteria, execute the following statement."

This is perfectly fine, but if a second else statement is added, it must have criteria of its own. The only way to test criteria here is with another if statement.

What we need to do is test to see if the number is zero. If it is, we print a new message. This adds a third decision point to the code and makes the code smarter and able to handle any integer you pass on the command line.

```
1   public class EvenTest3
2   {
3       public static void main(String[] args)
4       {
5           int number = Integer.parseInt(args[0]);
6           int mod = number % 2;
7           if(number == 0)
8           {
9               System.out.println("The number is zero.");
10          }
11          else if(mod == 0)
12          {
13              System.out.println("The number is even.");
14          }
15          else
16          {
17              System.out.println("The number is odd.");
18          }
19      }
20  }
```

You should immediately notice that this code not only has a new else statement, but it also has been reorganized. Now the initial test is whether the number is zero, not the modulus operation. Why?

Because, when you work with flow-control statements, the *first* test that returns true is where the logic stops. The original version of this code printed that the number was even when the number was actually zero. If the modulus test were still first, the test for the zero value would never even happen!

Another rule about using else statements is that if two or more of the statements would return true for a given input, you must order your statements appropriately. If you think of each else statement as a distinct option, you will understand that only one such statement can ever execute in an if/else construct.

Testing the Array of Arguments

To make this code as robust as possible, let's add one more example of using if statements. In Chapter 5, you will learn a lot about arrays, but right now you will learn how to determine if any arguments were passed in and, if so, how many.

Another Style for *else-if* Statements

Though the EvenTest3 code example documents how most production code will look, it can lead to some confusion. When you combine an else statement with an if statement, you may occasionally find it difficult to keep those braces aligned. You might be more comfortable writing code like the following instead.

```java
if(number == 0)
{
    System.out.println("The number is zero.");
}
else
{
    if(mod == 0)
    {
        System.out.println("The number is even.");
    }
}
else
{
    System.out.println("The number is odd.");
}
```

This code executes exactly the same, but some people find that including all the braces like this makes their code more legible. In all my years of Java development, I have seen both styles used, so it really helps to be able to make sense of each of them. Which style you prefer in your code is completely up to you; just use the style that you find most comfortable.

All arrays have a length, and you can query by finding the value of the property named length. This is not a method call; you use it just like you would if it were a variable defined in all arrays. Assuming the array has been created (which the argument to the main() method is guaranteed to have been), you can always determine how many items are in the array. The value will be zero or more.

The EvenTest code and all its variations assume that you are passing a command-line argument. If you do not pass one, you receive a runtime error message, the ArrayIndexOutOfBoundsException. This is because you are trying to access an index in the array (in this case, the first index, 0) that does not contain anything.

To handle this possible user error gracefully, just add yet another if statement to test the value of length. If it is zero, you know that the user forgot to
pass in any arguments, and you can handle this right in the code.

```
1  public class EvenTest4
2  {
3      public static void main(String[] args)
4      {
5          if(args.length == 0)
6          {
7              System.out.println("Usage: java EvenTest4
                   <num>");
8              System.exit(1);
9          }
10         int number = Integer.parseInt(args[0]);
11         int mod = number % 2;
12         if(number == 0)
13         {
14             System.out.println("The number is zero.");
15         }
16         else if(mod == 0)
17         {
18             System.out.println("The number is even.");
19         }
20         else
21         {
22             System.out.println("The number is odd.");
23         }
24     }
25 }
```

Line 5 makes the initial test to be sure that you did not call this code without
any command-line arguments. If you did, and the args.length is 0, a usage
message prints to remind you to pass an argument. On line 8, a new method call
allows you to exit the virtual machine altogether. This call to System.exit(1)
shuts down the application immediately. The parameter to this method is an
arbitrary error code. If you make a call to this method and it is a normal shut-
down not instigated by user error, it is conventional to pass 0. Otherwise, you
can assign a number of your choosing as the parameter.

The number passed to System.exit() is not meant to be used for error handling. There is no way to recover from this method call. If you exit the virtual machine, no more processing is possible. Later in this chapter, you learn how to handle logic errors in your code.

The *switch* and *case* Statements

Another way to perform decision-oriented flow control is with the switch statement. While if/else statements are used to process true and false results, the switch statement is used to process integer results. This statement is used in conjunction with a series of case statements. The switch statement has a conditional expression associated with it, and each case statement is bound to one of the possible values for that expression. Each case statement is followed by one or more statements that are executed in order.

The switch statement can process only four primitive types: byte, short, char, and int. No other types are allowed for evaluation in a switch statement. Although char may not seem to be an integer, it is. The value it actually holds is the Unicode value, which is a 16-bit integer value. It is represented in code normally as an actual character, of course.

Some languages (notably Visual Basic) allow you to associate strings with switch statements. However, Java does not allow anything other than integer types.

This is a good time to explore a more complex piece of code. The SwitchDemo class that follows is the most elaborate class you have seen so far in this book. The concept of this code is that you select one of four arithmetic operations (addition, subtraction, multiplication, or division) and provide two operands to work with. When you execute this code, you must pass three command-line arguments. The first argument is the code for the arithmetic operation that you want to perform. You pass 1 to select addition, 2 to select subtraction, 3 to select multiplication, and 4 to select division. The remaining two arguments are the numbers that you want to use in the calculation. If you fail to pass all three arguments, a usage message prints to the console window to remind you how to use the code correctly. Nothing like a friendly reminder from time to time!

Take a look at the SwitchCommand class to familiarize yourself with the code. As usual, a discussion of the class follows.

```
1  public class SwitchCommand
2  {
3      public static void main(String[] args)
4      {
5          if(args.length != 3)
6          {
```

```
 7            System.out.print("Usage: java SwitchDemo
                 (1)-add,");
 8            System.out.print("(2)subtract,(3)multiply,");
 9            System.out.print("(4)divide <num_one>
                 <num_two>");
10            System.out.println();
11            System.exit(1);
12        }
13        byte command = Byte.parseByte(args[0]);
14        float numOne = Float.parseFloat(args[1]);
15        float numTwo = Float.parseFloat(args[2]);
16        String output = "The result is ";
17
18        switch(command)
19        {
20            case 1:
21                // add operation
22                System.out.println(output + (numOne +
                     numTwo));
23                break;
24            case 2:
25                // subtract operation
26                System.out.println(output + (numOne -
                     numTwo));
27                break;
28            case 3:
29                // multiply operation
30                System.out.println(output + (numOne *
                     numTwo));
31                break;
32            case 4:
33                // divide operation
34                System.out.println(output + (numOne/
                     numTwo));
35                break;
36            default:
37                // unknown command
38                System.out.println("Unknown command");
39        }
40    }
41 }
```

A number of things are going on in this code. It starts on line 5 with an `if` statement that tests the length of the parameter array. This is followed on lines 13–15 with statements that parse the input values into primitive types. The first parameter is parsed into a `byte`, which represents the selected command. The second and third parameters are both parsed into primitive `float` types.

Why use a `byte` for the first parameter? Because the value expected is between 1 and 4, numbers small enough to fit in the size of a byte. Using the smallest type possible takes less memory at runtime— always a good idea.

Earlier you learned how to use the `Integer` class to parse a `String` into a primitive `int`. Much like the `Integer` class, the `Byte` and `Float` classes have corresponding methods for parsing strings into the corresponding primitive types. Both of the operand arguments are parsed into primitive `floats`, by the way, because the division works much better if they are. If they were just primitive `int` operands, the division would not have the correct precision. For example, if you tried to divide the integer 9 by the integer 2, the result would print as 4 without any decimal places. Therefore, using the `float` type for the operands is a better choice.

The Java API provides classes that match each of the primitive types. These classes are commonly called wrapper classes. Besides just `Integer`, `Float`, and `Byte`, there are the `Character`, `Short`, `Long`, `Double`, and `Boolean` classes. You will learn more about these classes in Chapter 9, "Common Java API Classes."

The code continues with a new `String` being created on line 16. This is the prefix of all the output messages that show the arithmetic results.

Finally, the `switch` statement appears on line 18. Following the `switch` keyword is the integer value that will be evaluated. Remember that this value *must* be an `int`, a `short`, a `char`, or a `byte`. In this case, it is a `byte` because the menu command is only a value in the range 1 through 4.

Lines 20–35 are the corresponding `case` statements. Each `case` statement represents a possible value for the `byte` evaluated in the `switch` statement. For example, if the first argument is a 1, the `case` statement on line 20 executes. Line 22 prints the result of the addition of the two operands.

Line 23 is an important part of every `case` statement; it houses the `break` keyword. You will learn more about this a bit later in this section, but let me sum it up for you now. The `break` statement ends all processing in the `switch` statement at the point it is executed. If you do not follow each `case` statement with a `break` statement, the processing continues into the next `case` statement and does not end until either a `break` statement is finally found or you reach the end of the `switch` statement. This is called "falling through" the `case` statement and is usually not desirable. I will show you a situation in which leaving out the `break` statement can be useful later in this section.

If you look at each of the four `case` statements, you will notice that they all print the results of the arithmetic operation and include a `break` statement. Technically, the final `case` statement does not require a `break` statement because it marks the end of the overall `switch` statement anyway. However, you might want to add more `case` statements in the future, so it is not a bad idea to include the `break` statement anyway.

The *default* Statement

Line 36 is a `default` statement. If you remember how an `else` statement works, you get the idea of the `default` statement. It represents what to do in all other cases. If none of the `case` statements match the value evaluated in the `switch` statement, the `default` statement matches everything else.

In the `SwitchCommand` class, the `default` statement is triggered if you enter a command that is not 1, 2, 3, or 4, and a message is output, indicating that the input command is unknown. Including a `default` statement like this is always a good idea because it can account for values that you do not want to handle or are not prepared to handle.

Deciding between *if/else* and *switch/case*

The preceding code could have been written using `if/else` statements instead of `switch/case` statements with the same results. The following is the same code rewritten to work with `if/else` statements. Remember, the results are *exactly* the same. The code is just stylistically different.

```
1   public class SwitchDemo
2   {
3       public static void main(String[] args)
4       {
5           if(args.length != 3)
6           {
7               System.out.print("Usage: java SwitchDemo (1)-
                    add,");
8               System.out.print("(2)subtract,(3)multiply,");
9               System.out.print("(4)divide <num_one> <num_
                    two>");
10              System.out.println();
11              System.exit(1);
12          }
13          byte command = Byte.parseByte(args[0]);
14          float numOne = Float.parseFloat(args[1]);
15          float numTwo = Float.parseFloat(args[2]);
```

```
16          String output = "The result is ";
17
18          if(command == 1)
19          {
20              // add operation
21              System.out.println(output + (numOne +
                    numTwo));
22          }
23          else if(command == 2)
24          {
25              // subtract operation
26              System.out.println(output + (numOne -
                    numTwo));
27          }
28          else if(command == 3)
29          {
30              // multiply operation
31              System.out.println(output + (numOne * numTwo))
32          }
33          else if(command == 4)
34          {
35              // divide operation
36              System.out.println(output + (numOne/numTwo));
37          }
38          else
39          {
40              // unknown command
41              System.out.println("Unknown command.");
42          }
43      }
44 }
```

Because you can write code that works exactly the same way using either if/else or switch/case statements, how do you decide between the two? Essentially the decision is arbitrary. Often the choice comes down to readability of the code and the overall "elegance" of the processing. One difference between the two types of statements is that if statements can process only conditional tests that result in either true or false values and switch statements evaluate only integers.

Personally, in my own coding, if I am processing a range of integer values, I tend to use the switch/case statements. I find the code easier to maintain over time. If my code is making decisions based on truth conditions, I rely on if/else statements. You will learn which statements you prefer in various situations as you write more of your own code.

Processing a Range of Values

In the last section, I mentioned that if you leave out the break statement follow-ing your case statement processing, a condition called "falling through" occurs. For example, the following code prints both "Yes" and "No."

```
int x = 1;
switch(x)
{
    case 1:
        System.out.println("Yes");
    case 2:
        System.out.println("No");
}
```

This happens because without a break statement to terminate the enclosing switch statement, the Java interpreter has no way to know that it should stop. This is an easy mistake to make and can lead to bugs that are difficult to track down; so be sure to use your break statements correctly.

However, on some occasions you can leverage this "falling through" behavior to your advantage. For example, you want to determine whether a character argument is a vowel. The following code expects a single character to be passed as an argument. Note that this is still input to the array as a String, so the char-acter needs to be extracted from it.

```
1   public class VowelCheck
2   {
3       public static void main(String[] args)
4       {
5           if(args.length == 0)
6           {
7               System.out.println("Usage: java VowelCheck
                    <char>");
8               System.exit(1);
9           }
10          char c = args[0].charAt(0);
11          switch(c)
12          {
13              case 'a':
14              case 'A':
```

```
15              case 'e':
16              case 'E':
17              case 'i':
18              case 'I':
19              case 'o':
20              case 'O':
21              case 'u':
22              case 'U':
23                  System.out.println(c + " is a vowel.");
24                  break;
25              case 'y':
26              case 'Y':
27              case 'w':
28              case 'W':
29                  System.out.println(c + " is sometimes a
                        vowel.");
30                  break;
31              default:
32                  System.out.println(c + " is not a
                        vowel.");
33          }
34      }
35  }
```

Line 10 bears some explanation. The purpose of this line is to convert the input String into a primitive char, so the method charAt() is called. This method is defined in the String class. The parameter is the index of the character to return. For example, if you have the String "Hello", the character at index 0 is 'H', the character at index 1 is 'e', the character at index 2 is 'l', and so on. Unlike the other wrapper classes, the Character class has no method for parsing a String into a primitive. Thus, this method is used to do the conversion for us.

NOTE

Because the charAt() method returns the primitive char at the specified index, technically, you could pass more than one character on the command line, and this code would still work. It would simply always use the first character in the provided String argument.

The real key to this code is that lines 13–22 are all case statements, but only the one on line 22 has a break statement. If any of the characters on lines 13–22 are input, they will result in the same output. Namely, this output indicates that the character is definitely a vowel. A similar situation exists on lines 25–28 when 'y', 'Y', 'w', or 'W' is tested. The switch statement includes a default statement to handle everything else.

The Ternary Operator

You learned a lot about operators in the previous chapter, but there is one more that you may find useful in your programming. I'm introducing it in this chapter because it is a special operator that works like an if/else statement, but in a single line. This operator is called the ternary operator because it takes three operands. The first is a conditional test, the second is the result if the conditional test evaluates to true, and the third is the result if the conditional result evaluates to false.

The syntax for the ternary operator is as follows:

```
test ? trueResult : falseResult
```

As an example, here is the EvenTest2 class rewritten using the ternary operator instead of if/else.

```
1   public class EvenTestTertiary
2   {
3       public static void main(String[] args)
4       {
5           int number = Integer.parseInt(args[0]);
6           int mod = number % 2;
7           String result = (mod == 0) ? "even." : "odd.";
8           System.out.println("The number is " + result);
9       }
10  }
```

Line 7 reads, "If the remainder is zero, set the value of result to 'even.' If the remainder is not zero, set the value of result to 'odd.'" The output from this is exactly the same as that of the original EvenTest2 class, but processing the conditional test requires only a single line.

The ternary operator can be used only for binary decisions. It cannot simulate the action contained in EvenTest3, for example, which has multiple else statements.

You might look at this operator and think that it is the ugliest thing you have ever seen; many developers would readily agree with you. It is another matter of stylistic choice. There is no reason you should use this operator instead of a standard if/else pair, but some developers feel this is a more elegant solution. Consider it an option and use it at your whim.

The *for* Loop

Another kind of flow-control statement is the for loop. While the if/else state-ments are used for decision processing, the for statement is used for looping. This statement allows iteration over a range of values at runtime. The pseudocode of a for loop is shown next.

```
for(initialization_exp; termination_exp; iteration_exp)
{
    //code
}
```

The initialization expression is executed only once before the loop begins. This expression allows you to set up the starting conditions of a loop, which is typically an integer value.

The termination expression must be a boolean expression. The code within the for loop executes until the termination expression returns false. Note that if this condition is false before the first iteration of the loop, the body of the for loop never executes.

The iteration expression is executed after the last statement in the body of the for loop executes. Immediately following this expression, the termination expression executes again, and if that expression is still true, the body of the loop executes again. The iteration expression alters the value of the initialization expression, and then this new value is used by the termination expression.

Here is an example of using the for statement:

```
class ForDemo
{
    public static void main(String[] args)
    {
        for(int i = 0; i < 10; i++)
        {
            System.out.println("The number is " + i);
        }
    }
}
```

The output from this code is as follows:

```
The number is 0
The number is 1
The number is 2
The number is 3
The number is 4
```

```
The number is 5
The number is 6
The number is 7
The number is 8
The number is 9
```

initialization expression

The portion of a for loop that is executed only once when the loop starts. It allows the setup of the starting conditions of the loop.

In order, the portion in parentheses contains the initialization, the termination, and the iteration expressions. The *initialization expression* is used to declare a variable called i with a starting value of 0. The *termination expression* indicates the end point of the range and is separated from the initialization statement by a semicolon. In this example, the termination expression is i < 10, which means "as long as the variable i holds a value less than 10, execute the statements in the body of the loop." The *iteration expression* modifies the value i that was defined in the initialization expression. This is done using the ++ operator; so every time this expression executes, i is increased by one.

termination expression

The portion of a for loop that tests the value of the for loop for true or false. If this expression returns false, the for loop ends at that point.

This example prints the String ten times, stopping only when the variable i finally equals 10. You can always determine the number of iterations that will be performed if you subtract the value in the initialization expression (in this case, 0) from the value in the termination expression (in this case, 10). You can also get ten iterations of a for loop with this code:

```java
for(int i = 50; i < 60; i++)
{
    System.out.println("The number is " + i);
}
```

iteration expression

The portion of a for loop that is executed after the last statement in the loop executes. The value resulting from the iteration is then checked by the corresponding termination expression to determine if the for loop should continue.

The for loop is useful for iterations of known values. That is really what it is designed for. The termination expression can be anything you like, perhaps the length of an array. In fact, for loops are useful for processing arrays. I will show you more about this in Chapter 5, but we already have an array we have been using—the array passed to the main() method.

The following code shows you how to use a for loop to print all the command-line arguments passed to a program.

```java
public class ArrayLoop
{
    public static void main(String[] args)
    {
        for(int i = 0; i < args.length; i++)
        {
            System.out.println(args[i]);
        }
    }
}
```

If you compile and execute this code, you can pass any number of command-line arguments, and they will all print. Not exactly mind-blowing, but it does demonstrate how a for loop can be used to iterate through an array. If you pass no arguments, you will not see any output because the termination expression will return false immediately because the length of the array would be zero. Code can be strange sometimes, but zero is still not less than zero!

Multiple Increment Steps

The iteration expression commonly adds or subtracts one from the variable defined in the initialization expression. This is because you usually use for loops to iterate through a series of values. However, you do have the flexibility to increment or decrement by more than one. Imagine you have the dates of an annual calendar that you want to process. You might want to add a note for a meeting scheduled for every Wednesday of every week. You could accomplish this by starting on the first Wednesday of the year and then use the iteration expression to increment by seven days each time it executes. This would allow you to skip the other six days each week and deal only with the specific day in which you are interested.

Instead of actually trying to create a working calendar processor, the class below simply decrements the i variable by 2 each time the loop executes. The end result is that all the even numbers are printed in descending order, from 20 to 2.

```
public class MultiStepFor
{
    public static void main(String[] args)
    {
        for(int i = 20; i > 0; i -= 2)
        {
            System.out.println("The number is "+ i);
        }
    }
}
```

The output from executing this code is as follows:

```
The number is 20
The number is 18
The number is 16
The number is 14
The number is 12
The number is 10
```

```
The number is 8
The number is 6
The number is 4
The number is 2
```

The point is that you can add or subtract any value that you want from the variable to control the steps in your iteration.

But wait, there is more! You are not limited to addition and subtraction; you can do any type of arithmetic operation that you want. For example, the following code actually uses the multiplication operator to double the variable i each time the loop executes.

```java
public class MultiplyFor
{
    public static void main(String[] args)
    {
        for(int i = 20; i < 100; i *= 2)
        {
            System.out.println("The number is " + i);
        }
    }
}
```

Here is the output of this code:

```
The number is 20
The number is 40
The number is 80
```

You can also do various operations in the termination expression. Normally, the less-than (<) operator is used for the test, but you can perform any test that returns true or false.

You can create countless examples of termination expressions, but I will show you just one such possibility. In the following code, instead of checking to be sure that the value of i<100, the code performs a division and checks to be sure that the result is not 80. It returns false until the fourth iteration of the loop when i*2 is 160.

```java
public class ForTerminationDemo
{
    public static void main(String[] args)
    {
```

```
for(int i = 20; i/2 != 80; i *= 2)
{
    System.out.println("The number is " + i);
}
}
}
```

Also notice that the output is exactly the same as the last class, `MultiplyFor`. In other words, the termination expressions can be different in function, but they both terminate the loop at the same exact point (the fourth iteration).

```
The number is 20
The number is 40
The number is 80
```

Don't be creative in your `for` loops needlessly. An old adage is perfect to have burned into your memory as you write code: *keep it simple*. Good code is efficient, logical, and maintainable and works as it is supposed to. Adding unneeded complexity is never a good approach. Having said that, you should also keep in mind that you are not "locked in" to one way of doing things. Whether it is `for` loops or some other code construct, you have the power to be creative to solve unique or unusual problems!

Beware the Infinite Loop

Have you ever seen the movie *Groundhog Day*? In that film, the main character keeps reliving the same day over and over again. This is the same thing that happens if you create an *infinite loop*. However, in the movie our hero eventually breaks out of the loop; an inadvertent infinite loop just keeps right on going. As mentioned previously, the infinite loop is usually considered a problem. It is an especially nasty bug if you are not careful when you define your `for` loops. For example, consider the following example:

infinite loop
A looping construct that has a test condition that always evaluates to `true`. Infinite loops can be useful, but are often dangerous bugs.

```
for(int i = 10; i > 0; i++)
{
    System.out.println("Infinity!");
}
```

If you execute this code, you see the word "Infinity!" printed to the command line, well, infinitely. The termination expression will *never evaluate to* `false`. The variable `i` is *always* going to be greater than zero in this example.

If you do execute this code, press Control-C in your terminal window to stop execution of the program.

The *while* Loop

A for loop is excellent when you need to execute a series of statements a fixed number of times. However, what if you do not have a fixed limit before the loop begins? Let's compare two real-world examples. If you deposit some change into a pay telephone and make a call, you know that you have a limited amount of time available before the call is cut off. If you never add more change and do not manually hang up the phone, the call terminates at some fixed time. A for loop is best suited for situations like this when there is a predetermined number of iterations.

Now consider making a call on your home telephone. Assuming that all your bills are up-to-date, you can make that call and "iterate through a conversation" until you or the other party hangs up. Notice that in both examples there is a point at which the call ends. The difference is that on your home phone, no fixed time limit is imposed; you continue the conversation as long as you want. A while loop is better suited for situations like this in which the termination condition can vary.

Just like the for loop, a while loop continually processes a series of statements as long as a condition remains true. A for loop is usually used to loop over a known range of values. A while loop is usually used to loop for an unknown number of iterations. In the previous phone call example, the pay phone had a fixed number of iterations before the call was even made (the imposed length based on the amount of change you deposited). When you use your home phone, there are an unknown number of iterations.

All right, enough about telephones. Let's look at some real code that uses a while loop. The following code takes an argument and loops until it finds the '!' character. It prints everything that it finds up to that point. This provides a rudimentary form of command processing in which every command ends with an '!'.

```
1   public class WhileDemo
2   {
3       public static void main(String[] args)
4       {
5           if(args.length == 0)
6           {
7               System.out.println("Usage: java WhileDemo <str>");
8               System.exit(1);
9           }
10          char [] chars = args[0].toCharArray();
11          int index = 0;
12          while (index < chars.length && chars[index] != '!')
13          {
14              System.out.print(chars[index]);
```

```
15              index++;
16          }
17      }
18 }
```

After the argument is processed, line 10 shows the expression that converts a String into a char array. The method toCharArray() is another method defined in the String class. This method converts the entire String into a correctly sized char array.

So far in this chapter, you have seen some interesting methods defined in the String class. There are a lot more useful methods in this class, and you will continue to encounter them throughout this book.

NOTE

Once the char array is derived from the argument, the processing can begin. You need to "walk" through this array until you encounter either a '!' character or the end of the array itself. An int is defined on line 11 that represents the index and is initialized to zero.

Finally, the while loop is defined. The conditional test is enclosed in the associated parentheses. In this case, that conditional test is complex because it actually is designed to be sure that two facts are true. First, it makes sure that the end of the array has not been reached. If the end has not been reached, the second part of this conditional test executes. That second half of the test checks to see whether the current char in the array is a '!'. If both tests return true, the currently indexed char is printed on line 14. Line 15 increments the index, and the while loop begins the next iteration. This process continues until the conditional test returns false.

The order of the two tests in the conditional expression is important. If you reverse them, you'll see an error message at runtime once the end of the array is reached. Be careful when you define complex conditional expressions like this, and be sure the order of each test is logical.

WARNING

If you compile and run this code with the following command, the word "Apple" prints to the console window:

```
java WhileDemo Apple!Tart
```

Comparing *for* and *while* Loops

In reality, anything you can do with a while loop, you can do with a for loop. The choice between the two comes down to the type of processing. As mentioned, if you have a known, fixed range of iterations to perform, a for loop is usually more convenient. If you have an unknown or varying range of values (as you do in the WhileDemo class), a while loop makes a lot of sense.

Here is code that works the same as the ForDemo code but uses a while loop.

```
public class WhileForComparison
{
    public static void main(String[] args)
    {
        int i = 0;
        while(i < 10)
        {
            System.out.println("The number is " + i);
            i++;
        }
    }
}
```

The output is exactly the same as before. Ten messages are printed, indicating that the value of the number is 0–9. Because you can accomplish the same results using either a for loop or a while loop, how do you decide which one is best in a given situation?

One large difference between a for loop and a while loop is that the while loop is associated with *only* a conditional test. Any variables used to control the iterations must be defined outside the while loop and incremented or decremented manually. Because the variable i is not ever used anywhere but inside the body of the loop itself, a for loop probably makes more sense in the previous code. Again, there is no rule necessarily; it is simply a matter of how the loop is being used.

Both types of loops have something in common—the danger of creating an infinite loop. It is easy to mistakenly turn a while loop into an infinite loop because no automatic increment expression is provided. It is even easier to make this mistake in a while loop than in a for loop. A while loop just keeps right on processing as long as the conditional test remains true.

Take a look at the following code and notice that there is no way for this while loop to ever stop.

```
int x = 0;
while(x < 10)
{
    System.out.println("The number is " + x);
}
x++;
```

This code prints "The number is 0" infinitely. Although the variable x is incremented in the code, it is not done until *after* the while loop completes processing. Because x is not ever incremented within the scope of the while loop, the conditional test always returns true.

Let me stress again: be careful not to create infinite loops!

The *do* Statement

You can add the do statement to a while loop to alter the normal iterative processing slightly. There is a big difference between a normal while loop and a do/while loop. With a normal, standalone while loop, the statements defined within the braces do not execute if the conditional test fails the first time. For example, the following code does not output anything because the conditional test returns false right away:

```
int x = 10;
while (x < 10)
{
    System.out.println("Hello!");
}
```

Now, if you use a do-while statement, things change because you are guaranteed that the statements between the braces execute at least once.

```
int x = 10;
do
{
    System.out.println("Hello!");
}
while(x < 10)
```

The reason for this difference is that with a do/while loop, the conditional test comes *after* the block of code, not before, as it does with a normal while loop. Even though the condition in the previous code fails the first time it is tested, the message "Hello!" is printed once.

The choice of whether to use a while or do/while loop really comes down to the type of processing. If you want to execute a series of statements one or more times, use the do/while statement. If you want to execute a series of statements zero or more times, use a standalone while statement.

branching statements
Allow a change in the normal flow of a flow-control statement. You can use branching statements to escape from a flow-control statement if the need arises.

The Branching Statements

The Java language provides three *branching statements*. A branching statement allows you to interrupt the normal processing of flow-control statements. The three branching statements are as follows:

◆ break

◆ continue

◆ return

Let's take a look at each of these statements in detail.

The *break* Statement

You have already seen the basic break statement several times in this chapter—first with the switch/case statements, specifically to prevent case statements from "falling through." You also saw the break statement in the discussion of alternative switch for loops. In both cases, break was used to stop processing and move on to the next statement after the flow-control block. In other words, the statement following the closing brace of the flow-control block is the next statement to execute.

You can actually use break statements in two ways, however. The first is by themselves, as you have seen already. This use of break terminates processing in a for, while, or do/while loop at the point that the statement is found and continues with the first statement following the closing brace. In the following code, when i==5, the for loop is exited completely. This results in only the numbers 0–4 being printed.

```
for(int i = 0; i < 10; i++)
{
  if(i == 5)
  {
    break;
  }
  System.out.println(i);
}
```

Using *break* with a Label

label
A special identifier followed by a colon that allows a continue or break statement to escape to a specific location in the code.

You can also use a break statement when it is associated with a *label*. A label is an arbitrary word placed in your code that marks the location to which you want to "break." Using a label like this is useful if you have nested loops, for example.

Here is an example of using a label with a **break** statement to terminate processing in the inner **for** loop and return processing to the outer **for** loop:

```
1   public class NestedLoopsWithBreak
2   {
3       public static void main(String[] args)
4       {
5
6           test:
7           for(int i = 0; i < 3; i++)
8           {
9               int j = 0;
10              System.out.println("Outer loop: " + i);
11              while(true)
12              {
13                  System.out.println("Inner loop: " + j);
14                  if(j++ > 2)
15                  {
16                      break test;
17                  }
18              }
19          }
20          System.out.println("Out of both loops");
21      }
22  }
```

The output from executing this class is the following:

```
Outer loop: 0
Inner loop: 0
Inner loop: 1
Inner loop: 2
Inner loop: 3
Out of both loops
```

Do you see why this is the output? Before you read the following explanation, see if you can figure it out just by reading the code itself. I have reinforced my understanding of several programming languages—including Java, of course—by reading lots of source code and ensuring that I can understand exactly what is happening.

For the answer, let's walk through what actually happens in this code. First, the label on line 6 marks the first **for** loop. This indicates which loop we want to escape to when the break statement is eventually reached on line 16. It appears as if the outer for loop defined on line 7 iterates three times. The first iteration results in the variable j being created and initialized to zero. Line 10 prints the first of the messages, "Outer loop: 0".

On line 11, the code hits a new loop, this time a while loop that has true in the parentheses. This would be an infinite loop if it were not for the test condition and break contained in the body of the loop itself. First, a message is printed to indicate that the code is in the inner while loop and the current value of j. As you can see from the output, this message prints four times. It stops only when the if statement on line 14 returns true. This happens, of course, when j==3 and line 16 finally executes.

The break test statement means "break out of all the loops until you get to the one labeled test." When you find that particular loop, continue the processing at the statement following that loop." That statement is line 20, which prints the message "Out of both loops".

As a comparison, here is the same code without a label:

```
1   public class NestedLoopsWithBreak2
2   {
3       public static void main(String[] args)
4       {
5
6           for(int i = 0; i < 3; i++)
7           {
8               int j = 0;
9               System.out.println("Outer loop: " + i);
10              while(true)
11              {
12                  System.out.println("Inner loop: " + j);
13                  if(j++ > 2)
14                  {
15                      break;
16                  }
17              }
18          }
19          System.out.println("Out of both loops");
20      }
21  }
```

This time, the output looks like this:

```
Outer loop: 0
Inner loop: 0
```

```
Inner loop: 1
Inner loop: 2
Inner loop: 3
Outer loop: 1
Inner loop: 0
Inner loop: 1
Inner loop: 2
Inner loop: 3
Outer loop: 2
Inner loop: 0
Inner loop: 1
Inner loop: 2
Inner loop: 3
Out of both loops
```

Notice that the outer loop completes all three of the iterations specified by the termination expression. This is because the standalone break statement only ends the processing of the inner loop. When line 15 is reached, processing returns to where the outer for loop left off.

The *continue* Statement

Like break, the continue statement allows you to end the processing in a loop. However, continue does not escape the loop. Instead, it returns processing to the beginning of the loop and continues with the next iteration. In effect, then, when a continue statement is found, it "skips" the rest of the processing for the current iteration and jumps to the next one. You can use continue in while, do/while, or for loops.

To demonstrate the use of continue, here is a class that counts the number of vowels in the argument you pass on the command line. This is a more complex piece of code, but a full explanation follows as usual.

```
1   public class Vowels
2   {
3       public static void main(String[] args)
4       {
5           if(args.length == 0)
6           {
7               System.out.println("Usage: java Vowels <str>");
8               System.exit(1);
9           }
10          String str = args[0].toLowerCase();
```

```
11              char [] chars = str.toCharArray();
12              int count = 0;
13              for(int i = 0; i < chars.length; i++)
14              {
15                  switch(chars[i])
16                  {
17                      case 'a':
18                      case 'e':
19                      case 'i':
20                      case 'o':
21                      case 'u':
22                          count++;
23                          break;
24                      default:
25                          continue;
26                  }
27              }
28              System.out.print(args[0] + " has ");
29              System.out.println(count + " vowels.");
30          }
31 }
```

On line 10, the input String stored in args[0] is converted to all lowercase
letters. This is accomplished by calling yet another method in the String class,
toLowerCase(). This step simplifies working with the case statements. Instead
of checking for both uppercase and lowercase forms of each of the five main
vowels (as was done in the VowelCheck class shown in the switch/case section), only the five lowercase vowels need to be checked for. This new String
variable, str, is then converted into a char array so that each letter can be
inspected.

Line 12 defines a new int named count that stores the number of vowels
found in the input string.

Line 13 defines a for loop that iterates through the array until it reaches
the end.

The real work gets done in the switch statement (see line 15). Every character
in the array is evaluated, and if it is one of the five main vowels, the *count* variable is post-incremented on line 22. This is followed by a break statement that
ends the switch statement processing and allows the for loop to process the
next iteration.

Line 24 is the default statement that triggers when anything other than a
vowel is found. Because you are not interested in anything except vowels, this is
where the continue statement comes into play. When line 25 is executed, the next

iteration of the for loop begins, and the next character (assuming that you have not already reached the end of the array) is evaluated in the switch statement.

Once the entire array has been processed, lines 28 and 29 execute, outputting a message that indicates how many vowels were found in the argument you passed in. Notice that the original String stored in args[0] is used here, not the converted version stored in str. This is because the printout should include the actual, case-sensitive String originally passed in to the code.

If you run this code and pass the String "Apple", you receive the following output.

```
Apple has 2 vowels.
```

Go ahead and pass other arguments to this code to prove to yourself that it works and, even more important, to ensure that you understand *why* it works.

How Do I Pass Arguments That Contain Spaces?

When you pass command-line arguments, the interpreter considers each space character as the separator. If you pass the String "Apple Pie" to this class, the results are still "Apple has 2 vowels". As far as the interpreter is concerned, you passed *two* arguments on the command line, yet reference only the first one in your code.

You can wrap your arguments in quotes if you want to pass full String arguments that contains spaces, as in:

```
java Vowels "Apple Pie"
```

The output from the Vowels class in this case is "Apple Pie has 4 vowels".

Using *continue* with a Label

As with the break statement, you can associate a label with a continue statement to allow control to pass to a specific outer loop. When the continue statement executes, it returns control to the loop that has the label preceding it and continues the next iteration of that loop.

Here is similar code shown in the section on break statements and labels, though it has been modified a bit. It uses continue instead, and the inner loop is now a for loop instead of a while loop.

```
1  public class NestedLoopsWithContinue
2  {
3      public static void main(String[] args)
4      {
5
```

```
6              test:
7              for(int i = 0; i < 3; i++)
8              {
9                  System.out.println("Outer loop: " + i);
10                 for(int j = 0; j < 10; j++)
11                 {
12                     System.out.println("Inner loop: " + j);
13                     if(j == (i * 2))
14                     {
15                         continue test;
16                     }
17                 }
18             }
19             System.out.println("Out of both loops");
20         }
21 }
```

The output of this code is a bit different from when the break statement was used on line 15 instead of continue. Here is the output; see if you can figure out why this is the output before you read the explanation that follows.

```
Outer loop: 0
Inner loop: 0
Outer loop: 1
Inner loop: 0
Inner loop: 1
Inner loop: 2
Outer loop: 2
Inner loop: 0
Inner loop: 1
Inner loop: 2
Inner loop: 3
Inner loop: 4
Out of both loops.
```

The processing begins on line 7 with the first iteration of the outer for loop that is associated with the test label. When the inner for loop is reached, i==0. When line 13 is reached for the first time, the test condition in the if statement is actually 0 == 0 * 2, which evaluates to true. Therefore, the body of the if statement executes, and line 15 returns the processing to the outer for loop because it specifies the label, test. On the next iteration of the outer loop, i==1 and the inner loop begins processing all over again, starting at 0. The if statement on line 13 returns `false` the first time because 0 `!=` 2 and also returns `false` on the second iteration of the inner loop because 1 `!=` 2. On the third iteration of the inner loop, however, the `if` statement returns `true` because 2==2.

This process continues until the termination expression in the outer `for` loop returns `false` and ends the processing, printing the final message "Out of both loops."

NOTE You might have to examine this code a few times to really be able to follow what is happening, but stick with it. Nested loops and the ability to define complex processing like this within them is a powerful technique that you can use in your own code.

The *return* Statement

The `return` statement is a little different from the other two because it does not just exit a loop; it exits an entire method. The truth is that *all* methods defined in Java classes must have a `return` statement. This is even true for the `main()` method you have been using in all the code examples thus far. But wait! There are no `return` statements in any of them! Is the `main()` method somehow special?

The answer is no. What is happening is a compiler trick. When a method is defined to return `void`, which essentially means that it returns nothing to the caller of the method, the `return` statement can be left out for convenience. When you compile your code, the Java compiler sticks in the `return` statement as the last line of your method. This does not alter your source code, of course. The `return` statement is simply added to the class file that the compiler creates.

This means that your `main()` methods could look like this:

```
public static void main(String[] args)
{
    // do your processing
    return;
}
```

Remember, you do not now have to start adding `return` statements to your methods that return `void` (like the `main()` method does). The lesson right now is that all methods have such a statement, whether you define it explicitly or not.

NOTE Typically, the last line is where you want your `return` statement because you do not want to end method processing until the entire method body has been executed. However, you can actually place `return` statements anywhere in a method body. Just be sure you understand that when a `return` statement is reached, no code that comes after the `return` actually executes. Also, if the compiler notices that code following a `return` statement can *never* be reached, you receive a compiler error forcing you to fix your code.

Returning Values from a Method

The only time that you do not have to explicitly define a return statement is if the method is declared to return void. As you will learn in Chapter 6, "Introduction to Object-Oriented Programming," and Chapter 7, "Advanced Object-Oriented Programming," you can define methods to return any type. If the return type is not void, the compiler issues an error message, stating that you have to return the type defined in the method signature itself.

You have not yet learned how to create your own methods, but the following code shows a quick working example of returning something other than void. In this case, we return to our old friend, HelloWorld, but this time two methods are defined in the class. The first is the main() method that we require to kick off the processing. The second is named getMessage() and actually returns the String that is printed in the main() method's body. The output of the code is the same as the original HelloWorld class.

```
1   public class HelloWorldRevisited
2   {
3       public static void main(String[] args)
4       {
5           String message = getMessage();
6           System.out.println(message);
7       }
8
9       public static String getMessage()
10      {
11          return "Hello World!";
12      }
13  }
```

In this code, line 5 actually calls the getMessage() method defined on line 9. There is only one statement in the method body, and that is the return statement. Notice that this time a String is given right after the return keyword itself. This is how you return a specific type. This method must return a String, because the method signature on line 9 says that it does. If you leave out the return statement on line 11, the compiler will tell you that it is missing.

The important point here is that every return statement you define must return the same type that is defined in the enclosing method's signature. If you create a method that returns an int, the statement return "Hello World!" will not compile. You have to return either an int variable or literal to fulfill the "contract" specified by the method signature.

NOTE   **You will learn a lot more about defining methods and returning values from them in Chapters 6 and 7, when I begin discussing classes and objects in more detail.**

Terms to Know

branching statements

infinite loop

initialization expression

iteration expression

label

local variable

pseudocode

termination expression

wrapper class

Review Questions

1. How do you define scope within a class, method, or flow-control statement?

2. What are the decision-making flow-control statements?

3. What is the rule that you must follow when using `else` statements with an `if` statement?

4. What is the difference between a `while` and a `do/while` loop?

5. What statement is used to handle all other results not already associated with `case` statements?

6. What does the `break` statement do?

7. What does the `continue` statement do?

8. If a method is defined as the following, is `return 1987;` a valid `return` statement?

   ```
   public static int getValue()
   ```

9. What is wrong with the following code?

   ```
   for(int i = 0; i < 10; i++)
   {
     if(i = 5)
     {
       System.out.println("Found a 5!");
     }
   }
   ```

10. Typically, why should a `break` statement be the last line of all `case` statements?

Chapter 5

Arrays

So far, you have learned about some of the simple data types in the Java language and various flow-control constructs that you can use to build logic into your programs. There is a lot more to this language than just adding numbers together! You are getting closer and closer to leaping into the world of objects.

Before you get immersed in this new topic, though, you will spend some time in this chapter learning about a predefined object type called an array. Arrays are useful for holding collections of similar items. Instead of defining a variable to hold a single number, now you will be able to define a variable that holds as many numbers as you like!

Understanding Arrays

array

An ordered collection of primitives or objects. When you declare an array, you specify the element type, and the resulting array can contain only elements of that type.

If you have not used arrays before, this section is for you. An *array* is a data structure that contains zero or more elements, and each element's location is denoted by an index. Once you have mastered how to use arrays, you have a powerful addition to your growing number of skills with the Java language.

Simply put, an array is an object that contains multiple items. However, an array can only hold items of the *same type*. In other words, you can put a bunch of int primitives in an array or a lot of String objects, but you cannot mix the two. That is your first lesson in this chapter: arrays can contain multiple items of the same type.

Imagine a car dealership that has rows and rows of new and used cars on display. If you saw this while traveling somewhere, you would not think it strange at all, right? This is because you *expect* a car dealership to have those rows of cars. If you think about this as an array of cars, you can begin to see the point of the same-type-only rule. After all, if you saw this same car dealership, and circus animals were mixed in with all the cars, you would surely look twice. That does not fit with the collection you expect to find.

This somewhat silly analogy serves to demonstrate why each array that you create must always contain the same type of values. Don't go trying to stick giraffes in with the convertibles!

NOTE Java does provide other collection types that can hold a variety of types, unlike arrays. You will learn about some of these in Chapter 9, "Common Java API Classes."

Conceptually, an array looks like the following diagram.

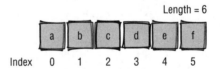

The array in this diagram holds six char primitives. Therefore, the length of the array is six. At the bottom of the diagram are the indices of each element in the array. Notice that the first index is 0, not 1. This is another important point about arrays in the Java language—all arrays begin with index 0.

The number one error that new (and even veteran!) developers make is that they forget that the first index of an array is 0 and that the last index is always one less than the array length. In the previous diagram, you can see that the length of the array is 6, but the last index in the array is 5. If you can find a place to burn these rules into your head right now, you will be way ahead of the game when you write your own code.

Each item in an array is called an *array element*. Therefore, you might refer to the character *b* in the diagram as "array element one" or "element one." Don't forget, each of these elements is always the same type in a particular array.

Once an array is created and stored in memory, its length can never change. In other words, all arrays are immutable. If you have an array with six elements in it and you want it to hold seven, you must create a new array. An array is not meant to be a dynamically sized collection type, so don't try to use it that way. Java provides other collection types that you can dynamically resize, and you will be able to check these out in Chapter 9.

Think about the main method that you have been working with so far:

```
public static void main(String[] args)
```

Earlier, you learned that the parameter to this method is in fact an array of `String` objects. Each element in this array is one argument passed on the command line to the class that holds this main method. What is the length of that array? You have no way to answer that right now, do you? Until you actually pass the command-line arguments, there is no way of telling. If you pass two arguments, the length of `args` will be two. If you pass zero arguments, the length will be zero. This demonstrates an array's length being determined at runtime. Once the array length is determined, however, it cannot change.

A critical step is being left out of this discussion right now. Before an array can actually have contents or a length, it must be created. What really happens when you pass command-line arguments is that the JVM creates a new array and populates it with each of the arguments that you passed (if any). Make sure you read on a bit to find out how to create arrays before you try to use them in your code.

Although you cannot change the array itself, you can change its contents. You can replace the value of any element in the array whenever you want. Just like the car dealer who makes a sale and replaces the sold car with new one, you can change array contents as you need to in your code. Thus, an array is a useful container for multiple elements that you can pass back and forth throughout your code.

Regardless of the element type, all arrays are objects. This means that you create them differently from the way you created the primitive types you already learned about. If you review the brief introduction to objects at the beginning of this book, you may be able to see why arrays are objects. Primitive types can hold only a single value. Objects, on the other hand, can hold multiple values. Because an array is meant to contain a collection of elements, it simply has to be an object.

array element
Each item stored in an array is considered an element of the array. Each array element must be the same type as the array itself. For example, an `int` array contains some number of `int` array elements.

WARNING

TIP
This chapter focuses on arrays, of course, but you also get a basic introduction to creating and working with objects along the way. In Chapter 6, "Introduction to Object-Oriented Programming," and Chapter 7, "Advanced Object-Oriented Programming," you finally learn how to create your own classes and objects, but the techniques that you learn in this chapter give you a little head start.

Let's wrap up the important points in this section before we move on and actually create and work with arrays.

♦ Arrays contain multiple items.

♦ Each item in an array is called an element.

♦ All the elements in an array must be the same type.

♦ The length of an array is determined at runtime.

♦ The length of an array can never change.

♦ The contents of an array can be changed dynamically.

♦ All arrays are objects, regardless of their content type.

♦ Array indexes start at zero and go to (length − 1).

Declaring Arrays

Just like all the other data types that you have learned about, arrays are always bound to a variable you define. You use this variable to access the array as needed throughout your code. All array declarations indicate the type of the elements, a pair of brackets ([]), and the variable name for the array.

The following are valid array declarations:

int [] ages;   An array of primitive `int` values

String[] names;   An array of `String` object references

float [] salaries;   An array of primitive `float` values

The key difference between a normal variable declaration and an array variable declaration is those brackets, of course. In source code, you can always identify an array by those brackets. If you do not include the brackets, you are simply defining an individual variable; so be sure to remember using them. If you do not and then later try to create an array for that variable, you get a compiler error.

Some people prefer to declare their array variable a little differently. The truth is that the brackets can come before or after the variable name itself. In other words, the three arrays declared previously could optionally be declared like this:

```
int ages [];
String names [];
float salaries [];
```

Although this format is completely legal, I suggest using the earlier style, with the brackets coming before the variable name. The reason is a purely logical one. When you declare a variable, you always precede the name with the type, right? So what is the type of the *ages* variable in the first example? Is it an `int`? No, it is an `int` array. Because the type of the variable *ages* is `int []`, that type should precede the variable name. Which way you declare the arrays is entirely up to you, but keeping the type-name for your variables consistent can make your code much easier to read and maintain.

As I climb down off my soapbox, let me explain something else. So far, all you have done is *declare* arrays; you have not yet created any. Therefore, none of these arrays have a length or any content whatsoever. As mentioned earlier, all arrays are objects. When you declare an object as a class variable, it automatically has a value of `null`. In Java, it is illegal to access a `null` object or array, and attempting to do so results in a runtime exception.

You have already read a bit about exceptions in this book, and you will read even more in this chapter. At this point, you will learn only how to avoid exceptions, but later, you learn how to handle them elegantly at runtime and how to keep your code from crashing when exceptions are discovered.

NOTE

When you declare a simple, single value variable as a class member, it automatically defaults to a valid value. For example, if you define the variable `int age;` at the class level, it has a value of zero. All the numeric primitive types default to a zero value when they are declared. However, when you declare an array variable such as `int [] ages;`, there are no contents to initialize yet. Remember, declaring an array (or any object) and creating it are two different tasks.

Up to this point, you have only been declaring variables inside a method. In this chapter, you continue working only inside methods. The "automatic initialization" rule applies only to those variables defined at the class level. No initialization is performed on variables defined inside a method unless you do it explicitly. I touch on this subject again in the next chapter, in which you begin creating your own classes and objects.

WARNING

Creating Arrays

All right, you have learned how to declare arrays, and now it is time to actually create them. As with all variables, you give a variable a value to hold when you create it. With primitive types, you accomplish this with just the assignment operator (=) and a literal value. This does not work for objects such as arrays, however. Instead, you need to use the new keyword.

Way back in Chapter 3, "Keywords and Operators," you were introduced to the new keyword, and you saw a short example of how it worked. To refresh your memory, when you use new, the interpreter sets aside the appropriate memory for an object and returns a reference. Recall that this reference is the pointer to the memory address where the object is stored. When you use the new keyword with an array, you "turn on the power" so to speak; you make it ready to use in your code.

The new keyword works the same way with arrays; this should not be at all surprising because arrays are in fact objects. The JVM performs a secondary step in this process, however; it initializes all the array elements to their default value. Using new to create an object is called *instantiation*. When you instantiate an array, it becomes a valid, live object, and you can access and change the elements to new values at your whim.

instantiation
The process of creating an object. This usually involves using the new keyword. Instantiation results in the JVM setting aside memory for the created object's contents. An object's members cannot legally be accessed until it has been instantiated.

You *must* specify the size of the array as part of the array-creating process; you cannot create an array with an unknown size in Java code. The size must be a valid, nonnegative int value. Remember, this number defines the length of the created array for its entire life cycle—arrays' lengths cannot be changed at runtime. You put this int inside the brackets on the right side of the expression.

To see how this is done, let's take the three arrays introduced in the last section and add the appropriate code to instantiate them.

```
int [] ages = new int [5];
String[] names = new String[10];
float [] salaries = new float[100];
```

Now we are talking! Once these three lines of code execute, you have three references to arrays in memory. All of them initialize their elements to their default values. Therefore, the ages array currently holds 5 int elements, all with a value of zero. The salaries array holds 100 float elements with a value of zero. The names array holds String elements (which are objects, remember), so each of these String elements currently has a value of null.

Note that you have to specify a size when you create an array. There is no way around this rule. Code such as the following is illegal:

```
int [] ages = new int[];
```

In some languages, you can use code like this without a problem if you create a dynamically sized array, but not in Java. The compiler will not even let code like this pass.

Getting the Length of an Array

After you create an array, you can access its length. In essence, all arrays have a member variable named *length* that you can query to find out how many elements a particular array holds.

You learned earlier that all objects have a class file that contains all the variables and methods that can be called using that object. Arrays are a strange case because they do not have a class that we can actually look at. Although the *length* variable is always part of any array you create, this is the only member available to you. Just think of all arrays as having a class that is controlled and hidden by the JVM itself, and keep this *length* variable in mind, because it will be immensely useful to you when you write your own code.

NOTE

If you have jumped ahead, you may have realized that all arrays also have access to all the methods defined in the ultimate `java.lang.Object` **class. Although this is absolutely true, it is not overly relevant right now, so I do not discuss it at this time. You will learn more about the** `Object` **class in Chapter 7.**

Not surprisingly, the value of the *length* variable is the actual length of the array in question. You might wonder why you would ever need this in the first place. After all, you have to pass a size to the array when you create it, so surely you know how big it is, right?

That is not necessarily true in most code. Sure, if you are hardcoding the size when you create the array, you know the length, but you often create arrays using an *int* variable as the length, not a hardcoded literal. If you do this in code, the *length* variable becomes important because using it is the only way that you can determine how many elements are in the array.

A common example of this occurs when you are processing command-line arguments. So far, all our code has assumed that you pass the correct arguments when arguments are required. If you do not, you receive an exception, and your program crashes. Wouldn't it be much nicer if you could handle this problem dynamically and give the user a helpful message?

The following code is simply a variation of HelloWorld, but this time it makes sure that you pass an argument on the command line. If you do not, a message prints, explaining how the code should be executed.

```
public class EnforcedArg
{
    public static void main(String[] args)
    {
        if(args.length == 0)
        {
            System.err.println("Usage: java EnforcedArg
<arg>");
            System.exit(1);
        }

        System.out.println("Hello " + args[0]);
    }
}
```

Go ahead and compile and execute this code, but do *not* pass any arguments. You will receive the message that tells you how to run the code. The `<arg>` simply represents an argument that should be passed, and it holds no special significance to the JVM itself; it is only for human viewing.

TIP

So far you have been using `System.out.println()` to output messages to the command line. When you output error messages, you should normally use `System.err.println()` instead. This outputs the message to the standard error of your system. This is normally just the command line, but using `System.err` ensures that all error messages go to the right place.

The key to making this code work is that the `if` statement checks to see if the length of the array is zero. If it is, you know right away that no arguments were passed. This works because the array argument to the main method is *always* instantiated, even if you do not pass any arguments at all. If no arguments are passed, the JVM creates the array like this:

```
String[] args = new String[0];
```

Although it may seem strange to create an array with no size that can therefore never hold any elements, it is perfectly legal. You will probably never do it yourself, but it is a good thing that you and the JVM can because it allows elegant argument processing code as shown in the `EnforcedArg` class to be created!

Be sure you understand the big difference between an array created with a length of zero and an array that is not created at all. If the JVM only created the array if you passed arguments, code like that shown in the `EnforcedArg` example would not work. Why? Because the `args` array would be `null`. Remember that it is illegal to try to access the members of a `null` object reference, so you would not be able to access `args.length` without causing an exception that would crash your code...and that is what you were trying to avoid in the first place!

Just like the array itself, the *length* variable is immutable. It is illegal to write a statement such as the following:

```
int [] stuff = new int[10];
stuff.length = 20; // illegal!
```

If you try to do this in your code, you get a compiler error because the *length* variable is defined as `final`. You will use the *length* variable later in this chapter when you begin iterating through arrays.

Populating an Array

Typically, after creating an array, the next step is to populate it with more useful values than the defaults of zero or `null`. To help demonstrate this, let's take one of the arrays that we have seen so far—the `names` array.

You might want to maintain a list of names in an address book and be able to access and modify them at your convenience. Typically, the names are read from some file stored on a computer system somewhere, but we will cheat a bit and put the values right in our code. We will create an array that holds six names.

The syntax for accessing an array element is `arrayName[x]`, in which *x* is the index of the element you are after. Don't forget that the first element in an array is always at index zero, and the last is always at (`arrayName.length - 1`). So for the following six-element array, the last index is 5.

Take a look at the code that populates the `names` array:

```
public class AddressBook
{
    public static void main(String[] args)
    {
        String[] names = new String[6];
        names[0] = "Kelby";
        names[1] = "Suzanne";
        names[2] = "Georgianna";
        names[3] = "Kathy";
        names[4] = "Lee";
        names[5] = "Sean";
        System.out.println("There are " + names.length +
    " names in the address book.");
    }
}
```

Granted, this code does not do much right now, but we will add to it as we move though the remainder of this chapter. Right now, let's concentrate on the population of the array itself. The output tells you there are six elements in the array.

The first element in the array is now `"Kelby"` (located in `names[0]`), and the last element is `"Sean"` (located in `names[5]`). Any index value given to this array other than those shown in this code would cause an exception at runtime. The compiler, however, would not care even a little if you tried to access `names[900]`, so you cannot rely on it to warn you of mistakes like that.

Using Array Initializers

Although you can manually add the elements of an array with a known size, you may often find it more convenient to use a special syntax called an *array initializer*. This time, you do not have to explicitly use the `new` keyword and give a length because those things are automatically provided in a list of elements. The number of elements you provide becomes the array length, and the elements are contained in the array in the same order in which you give them.

array initializer

A special variation to creating an array that does not require you to explicitly set the length. Instead, the contents of the array are put right inside a pair of braces ({}), and a comma separates each element. The resulting array's length equals the number of elements listed between the braces.

Here is an example of adding names using this syntax:

```
public class AddressBook
{
    public static void main(String[] args)
    {
        String[] names = {"Kelby", "Suzanne",
        "Georgianna", "Kathy", "Lee", "Sean"};

        System.out.println("There are " + names.length +
        " names in the address book.");
    }
}
```

The braces identify the list of elements that you want to add to the array. The results of this code are equivalent to those of the previous example, but as you can see, this method requires less coding on your part.

Array initializers are only useful if you know the exact number and the values of the elements in an array at compile time, of course. This is a useful technique when you want to hold a known range of values because you can add and remove them from the list in your source code and recompile them to have a different array length and new contents at runtime.

There is one caveat to this, however. You can only do this type of array initialization on the *same line of code*. Don't be thrown off by the fact that the source code actually spans two lines; Java ignores white space, and it is written this way only for readability. As far as Java is concerned, the entire array initialization statement is on one line.

As usual, though, there is another option...

An Array Initializer Variation

You can actually combine the two forms of initialization that you have seen so far. The syntax is somewhat strange, but if you read it closely, you will see exactly what is happening. Take a look at this variation, and then I will explain what is going on:

```
public class AddressBook
{
    public static void main(String[] args)
    {
        String[] names;
        // do some other work perhaps
```

```
        names = new String[]{"Kelby",
                             "Suzanne",
                             "Georgianna",
                             "Kathy",
                             "Lee",
                             "Sean"};

        System.out.println("There are " + names.length +
    " names in the address book.");
    }
  }
```

Once again, you are using the new keyword, but this time you are not explicitly giving a length inside the brackets. Instead, the same list of values in the braces that you used before follow the brackets. This results, once again, in all six elements being put into the array. This is useful if you need to declare an array in one location but populate it in another while still taking advantage of the array initializer. You probably will not use it often, but it is there when you need it. In my own development, I have found this to be a useful syntax indeed on more than a few occasions.

Accessing Array Elements

Of course, an array is really useful only if you can access the contents. You do so with something called a *subscript*. The subscript syntax consists of a pair of brackets that follow the array name with a valid array index inside them. So, to access the first element of the names array, you would say names[0]. By using the subscript, you can retrieve the value of the element in an array if it is a primitive, or you can retrieve a reference to the element in the array if it is an object.

subscript
The syntax for specifying the element of an array that you want to access. A subscript is shown as a pair of brackets containing an int that represents an index. For example, the statement names[2] refers to the third element in the array called names.

You have already used this form of array access every time you worked with the array passed to the main method of your classes.

NOTE

There is an important difference between an array of primitive types and an array of objects, however. Remember that when you create an array of primitives, all the elements are initialized to the default value of zero (or '\0' in the case of a char array) or null if the element is an object. Immediately after you create the array, you can access the value of the elements, and they will all be zero. When you create an array of objects such as a String[], the elements are not initialized; all the elements of the array default to null. Sure, you can access those values if you really want to, but they will not typically do you a lot of good! Be sure your arrays are fully initialized with correct, meaningful values before you access the elements.

Here is the AddressBook class once again, this time with code added to print the contents of the array itself. Notice the use of subscripts to access each element.

```
public class AddressBook
{
    public static void main(String[] args)
    {
      String[] names;
      // do some other work perhaps

      names = new String[]{"Kelby",
                           "Suzanne",
                           "Georgianna",
                           "Kathy",
                           "Lee",
                           "Sean"};

      System.out.println("There are " + names.length +
        " names in the address book.");

      System.out.println(names[0]);
      System.out.println(names[1]);
      System.out.println(names[2]);
      System.out.println(names[3]);
      System.out.println(names[4]);
      System.out.println(names[5]);
    }
}
```

When you execute this code, all the names in the array are printed. Don't forget that the last element of an array is always one less than the length of the array. That is why the final printout is of names[5].

The previous example explicitly accesses the exact subscripts of the array. This is fine if you know the exact length of the array before runtime, but that is often not the case. Here, our old friend, the for loop, comes into play. Using for loops with arrays is extremely common because they provide the perfect iteration mechanism with which to access each element of the array.

The following code uses a for loop for array access. The class AddingMachine allows you to pass two or more numbers as arguments, and then it adds them up for you. When the addition is complete, the final sum is printed. Notice in this code that because there is no way to know the length of the array until runtime, the for loop handles the iteration for you.

```java
public class AddingMachine
{
    public static void main(String[] args)
    {
        if(args.length < 2)
        {
            System.out.println("Pass at least two numbers");
            System.exit(1);
        }

        int sum = 0;
        for(int i = 0; i < args.length; i++)
        {
            sum += Integer.parseInt(args[i]);
        }

        System.out.println("The sum is " + sum);
    }
}
```

Every time the for loop executes, the array index increases by one. The only line in the body of the loop adds the number you passed in to sum. The entire array processing takes just three lines. As you work more with arrays in the Java language, you will find that for loops are a great help when you need to access elements such as this.

Multidimensional Arrays

So far, you have worked with simple arrays that contain a range of elements, and you have accessed each element with a single subscript. However, you have already learned two facts that allow you to create more complex arrays. First, arrays can contain objects. Second, all arrays are objects. It is therefore completely logical for an array to contain other arrays, which creates a *multi-dimensional array.*

multidimensional array
An array that contains other arrays as its elements. The most common type of multidimensional array is the two-dimensional array. In Java, all multidimensional arrays are just arrays of arrays.

Java does not truly have multidimensional arrays such as those found in some other languages. In Java, a multidimensional array is simply an array of arrays. There is no rule that says each of the subarrays must have the same length.

WARNING

Think of the data stored in a table. The table has rows and columns, and at any specific coordinate, there is a piece of data. When working with tabular data like this, you can refer to the location of each piece of data by its row number and column number. For instance, in the following diagram, a set of letters is stored in a table. The numbers running down the left side of the table signify the row number, and the numbers running across the top of the table signify the column number. Oh, and just for consistency with our array discussions, I have chosen to begin the first row and column index with zero.

When you look at data in table form like this, you can say things like, "The letter B is at column 1, row 0" or "The letters A, B, C, D are in row 0, columns 0 through 3." You can map any row and column index to a specific piece of data, which is the whole beauty of tabular data.

Now imagine that each row of data is a single char []; in this case, you end up with four such arrays. Those four arrays could then be added to another array to give you the tabular form of the data. This final array would be a two-dimensional array.

You define a two-dimensional array by simply adding another set of brackets to the declaration. To declare the two-dimensional array in this case, we must first determine the arrays type. Because it will be holding the four simple char arrays as its elements, the two-dimensional array will be "an array of character arrays." Such an array would be declared as char [] [] table;.

NOTE

You can create arrays with as many dimensions as you like, but it is unusual to have anything beyond two or three dimensions. Anything beyond that is most likely needlessly complex and should be avoided.

Okay, we have the array declaration. Now we need to populate it. If you keep in mind that each element of the table array is in fact a char array, this should not be as complex as you might think. All you have to do is create each of the four simple arrays and add them one by one to the table array.

The best way to see how this works is to jump right into the code, so let's do it. The following class creates the two-dimensional array and models the table of data that you looked at before. When you run the code, you specify a coordinate (row and column in that order), and the letter found at that location prints. You can use the previous graphic as a point of reference to be sure that the code is working correctly.

```java
public class TwoDimArray
{
    public static void main(String[] args)
    {
        if(args.length < 2)
        {
            System.out.println("Enter the coordinates!");
            System.exit(1);
        }

        char [] row0 = {'A', 'B', 'C', 'D'};
        char [] row1 = {'E', 'F', 'G', 'H'};
        char [] row2 = {'I', 'J', 'K', 'L'};
        char [] row3 = {'M', 'N', 'O', 'P'};
        char [] [] table = new char[4][4];
        table[0] = row0;
        table[1] = row1;
        table[2] = row2;
        table[3] = row3;

        int row = Integer.parseInt(args[0]);
        int column = Integer.parseInt(args[1]);
        if(row >= table.length || column >= table.length)
        {
            System.out.println("Invalid coordinates: " + row +
", " + column);
            System.exit(1);
        }
        System.out.println("The data at " + row +
            "," + column + " is " + table[row][column]);
    }
}
```

The TwoDimArray class first ensures that you have entered two coordinates. The simple, one-dimensional char arrays are created next. These four arrays represent each row in the table. Of course, they also implicitly define the columns as well. Just like the previous diagram, there are four rows and four columns. All four of these char arrays are then added in order to the two-dimensional array named table.

Do you see what is happening here? Just as before, we specify the index in question by using a subscript. The result is that each of the `table` array's elements is actually a one-dimensional `char []`. The result is a two-dimensional array that holds four one-dimensional arrays and exactly models the diagram of the table this section started with.

A quick check is made by the initial `if` statement to be sure that you entered valid coordinates to avoid any exceptions. It is easy to enter the wrong coordinates because you will be inclined to say that the character 'P' is located at row 4, column 4. Remember that the final row and column in this array is 3, not 4.

When you execute this code and enter a pair of coordinates, it prints the letter found there. For example, if you start the program with `java TwoDimArray 2 2`, the following message prints:

```
The data at 2,2 is K
```

As with simple arrays, you access the contents of a two-dimensional array with subscripts. If you give just a single subscript, you are accessing the entire array element itself. If you pass the two arguments just mentioned in the printed message, you are accessing `table[2][2]`. This translates to "give me the `char []` at index 2 of the `table` array, and then give me the primitive `char` contained in that `char` array at index 2."

Two-Dimensional Array Initializers

In the `TwoDimArray` code, the four one-dimensional arrays are created using the array initializer syntax that you learned earlier. You can do the same thing with multidimensional arrays. Instead of using the four lines required to add each individual `char` array to the two-dimensional array, you can alter the code to look like the following.

```
char [] row1 = {'A', 'B', 'C', 'D'};
char [] row2 = {'E', 'F', 'G', 'H'};
char [] row3 = {'I', 'J', 'K', 'L'};
char [] row4 = {'M', 'N', 'O', 'P'};
char [] [] table = {row1, row2, row3, row4};
```

The results are exactly the same as before, but there are fewer lines of code. At the least, this code is easier to read.

Let's take a look at yet another way to do this initialization. There is no reason you cannot just use array initializers for everything to produce the same two-dimensional array. This may seem a bit complex at first, but give it a look.

```
char [] [] table = { {'A', 'B', 'C', 'D'},
                     {'E', 'F', 'G', 'H'},
                     {'I', 'J', 'K', 'L'},
                     {'M', 'N', 'O', 'P'} };
```

If you remember how you did this array initialization with a simple array, this should make sense. The first pair of braces denotes the boundaries of the `table` array itself. The contents of the `table` array are declared to be four simple `char` arrays, right? So all you do is define these arrays with their own braces, separated by commas. This is exactly the same syntax as you would use to initialize any simple array. The only thing that makes it seem complicated is that the comma-separated elements are themselves arrays!

Whichever style you choose to use to initialize your arrays, whether simple or multi-dimensional, you will not see any great performance gains in the JVM. The choice is purely a stylistic one for the most part, so choose whichever style you prefer and run with it!

TIP

Nonrectangular Arrays

A *nonrectangular array* is a multidimensional array that does not contain equally sized array elements. You might have a two-dimensional array that contains three other arrays, but those three arrays can all be of different lengths. Although it is far more common to have a completely even two-dimensional array that is logically like a table, you are not forced to follow this rule.

When you define a two-dimensional array, you are only required to specify the length in the *first* subscript. The second subscript can remain empty until you initialize each of the subarray elements. As an example, imagine a company that owns three soft drink vending machines around town. At any given time, each machine has a specific set of soft drinks contained in it, but each probably has a different selection. This situation can be modeled with a nonrectangular, two-dimensional array as follows.

nonrectangular array
A multidimensional array whose sub-arrays are not all the same length. This type of array requires some special care because you will usually have to determine the length of each subarray before you can process its elements.

```
String[] [] machines = new String[3][];
machines[0] = new String[] {"Root Beer", "Orange", "Cola"};
machines[1] = new String[] {"Cola", "Lemon-Lime"};
machines[2] = new String[] {"Root Beer", "Orange", "Grape",
    "Cola"};
```

The resulting two-dimensional array, `machines`, contains three array elements. The first has a length of three, the second a length of two, and the third a length of four. You access the elements just as before with the subscript pair, but now the range of the index for each simple `String[]` representing each soft drink machine is different.

Note that the first subscript in the `machines` array can *never* be empty; you absolutely have to define a length for the `machines` array. The second subscript can be empty until later because each of the subarrays can be of a different length.

The *java.util.Arrays* Class

Let me introduce you to a helpful class, `java.util.Arrays`. Remember that the `java.util` portion of the name refers to the package in which the `Arrays` class resides. You learn more about a lot of useful classes in the `java.util` package later in Chapter 9. When you are working with arrays, though, the `Arrays` class can be useful indeed.

I want to discuss three main method types in this class. These three methods let you search an array for a value, sort an array, and automatically fill an array. If you look at the `Arrays` class documentation, you will find several versions of each method. These multiple versions allow you to work with all the different types of arrays possible (the primitive types and arrays of objects). I am not going to go through each and every method here, but I will show you how all three methods work and how to use them with a specific array type.

NOTE

All the methods in the `Arrays` class are declared as `static`, so you can just call the methods using the class itself. The syntax is always `Arrays.`*methodname*.

Filling an Array

When you create an array, you already know that the contents are initialized to their default values. If you want to change these values, you must assign the new value to each element of the array. If the elements can each hold a different initial value, you still have to do that processing yourself. However, sometimes you just want to create an array that contains all the same values initially. This is where the `Arrays.fill()` method comes in handy.

The following code creates an `int []` and then uses the `Arrays.fill()` method to set all the contained elements to 100. Notice the required `import` statement so that you can use the `Arrays` class in the code.

```java
import java.util.Arrays;
public class FillArray
{
    public static void main(String[] args)
    {
        int [] numbers = new int[10];
        Arrays.fill(numbers, 100);

        for(int i = 0; i < numbers.length; i++)
        {
            System.out.println("Index " + i + "=" + numbers[i]);
        }
    }
}
```

The `Arrays.fill` method takes two parameters. The first is the array that you want to fill, and the second is the value to which you want all the elements set. Of course, the type of the second parameter must match the element type of the array in the first parameter. As mentioned, various versions of this method work with all the array types that you might have, including arrays of objects.

When you run this code, you will see that every element of the `numbers` array is set to 100. Of course, you can still change the value of each element as you need to in your code. All the `Arrays.fill()` method does is provide you with an initial value that is different from the default of zero.

Sorting an Array

At one time, sorting arrays was often a challenge for new developers. Hey, it was also often a pain in the neck for us experienced developers! Well, not anymore. You now have another method available to you: the `Arrays.sort` method. This method sorts the contents of an array according to its *natural ordering*, which is essentially the common ordering that you would expect. Numbers are sorted in increasing order, and `String` objects are sorted alphabetically. You will find this method helpful when you have a `String` array that you want to ensure is in alphabetic order.

All you have to pass to the `Arrays.sort()` method is the array you want to sort. Once again, you can pass any type of array. The following code creates a `String[]` and then sorts it alphabetically.

natural ordering
A process used in sorting algorithms to determine how a specific set of data should be ordered. This is normally an ascending order for numbers and alphabetic order for characters and strings.

```
import java.util.Arrays;
public class SortArray
{
    public static void main(String[] args)
    {
        String[] names = {"Kelby", "Suzanne", "Kathy",~CR
        "Georgianna", "Lee", "Sean"};
        Arrays.sort(names);

        for(int i = 0; i < names.length; i++)
        {
            System.out.println(names[i]);
        }
    }
}
```

When you run this code, you will see the names printed in alphabetic order like this:

```
Georgianna
Kathy
Kelby
Lee
Sean
Suzanne
```

With this method, it is that easy to sort arrays, and the performance is quite acceptable as well. Of course, the larger the array, the more time it is going to take to sort it; so don't expect an array of 1,000 elements to sort as fast as an array of 6. Using this method sure beats writing your own sort algorithms for simple sorting like this!

Searching an Array

The Arrays class also gives you the ability to search an array. This allows you to find out if a particular array contains a specified element value or reference. You can search any type of array using the Arrays.binarySearch() method.

You have to be careful, though. This method is guaranteed to work correctly only if the array being searched has already been sorted. So you have to be sure to use the Arrays.sort() method before you try your search. If you do not sort the array, the results may not be what you expect, so don't forget: sort before you search!

The Arrays.binarySearch() method takes two parameters: the array it should search and the element for which it should search. The method returns an int that will be either the index of the element if it was found or a negative number if no matching element was found. You simply need to retrieve this int and find out the value to determine if the search was successful and, if it was, where in the array the element was found.

Let's take the code from the sorting example and add searching to it. Now you can specify a name on the command line, and if it is found, you will be told the index where it was discovered in the array.

```java
import java.util.Arrays;
public class SearchArray
{
    public static void main(String[] args)
    {
        if(args.length == 0)
        {
```

```
        System.out.println("Give me a name!");
        System.exit(1);
    }

    String[] names = {"Kelby", "Suzanne", "Kathy",
    "Georgianna",~CR"Lee", "Sean"};
    Arrays.sort(names); // must do this!!!

    int index = Arrays.binarySearch(names, args[0]);
    if(index < 0)
    {
        System.out.println(args[0] + " was not found.");
    }
    else
    {
        System.out.print(args[0] + " was found at ");
        System.out.println("index " + index);
    }
    }
}
```

If you run this code and enter one of the names in the array, you receive a message telling you the index where it was found. Remember, the array is being sorted first, so if you search for "Georgianna", you will be told it is at index 0, not index 3 as it appears in the code.

WARNING

Don't forget that Java is a case-sensitive language. The name "Georgianna" and "GEORGIANNA" are two different things entirely. In this case, the former will be found; the latter will not be found.

Terms to Know

array	multidimensional array
array element	natural ordering
array initializer	nonrectangular array
instantiation	subscript

Review Questions

1. What is the starting index of all created arrays?

2. What is the last index of all created arrays?

3. What is the value at index 2 of the following array?

   ```
   String[] names = new String[10];
   ```

4. Is the following code snippet legal?

   ```
   int [] points;
   points = new int[900];
   ```

5. Is this a legal array declaration?

   ```
   float f [10];
   ```

6. Is the following array created legally?

   ```
   int [][] points = new int[5][];
   ```

7. What kind of arrays can you search using the `Arrays.binarySearch()` method?

8. Which method should you always call before you use the `Arrays.binarySearch()` method?

9. In the following array, what is the length of `points`?

   ```
   int [][] points = new int[10][5];
   ```

Chapter 6

Introduction to Object-Oriented Programming

You have learned a lot about the Java language already, but so far we have paid little attention to objects and object-oriented programming. To unleash the power of the language completely, you need to know about this methodology. Except for the primitive types, everything in the Java language is an object. Obviously then, understanding how objects work and why they are so beneficial is an important stage of learning the language.

I was first introduced to the object-oriented paradigm many years ago. It was downright challenging to learn! You may find yourself in a similar situation, but trust me; you *will* understand objects if you keep plugging away at the concepts introduced in this chapter.

The Object-Oriented Paradigm

Up to this point, all the code you have written has been completely contained in a single method, the main() method. This method is static, which means it does not need an object to be invoked. The main() method is a special method because it is the entry point for the interpreter.

Truthfully, putting all the code for a program inside a single method like this is normally not a good idea. Instead, you usually create programs from one or more objects. Each object can communicate with other objects to provide the complex logic and functionality that today's programs so often require. This form of object-to-object communication is often termed *messaging*. Messaging is actually accomplished by calling the methods of your objects. Each of these methods typically alters the internal state of an object (though that is not a requirement by any means). The state of an object is represented by the variables defined in the class itself.

Objects are created based on the methods and variables defined in an underlying class. A class is like a blueprint for your objects, and all objects that are built from that class share the same basic characteristics. However, each object maintains its own private state; two objects that share the same class type are independent of each other when it comes to state.

This may be a bit confusing, so think back to the primitive types that you have already learned about. If you create two variables, int x and int y, both of them share the same basic characteristics. They can hold both positive or negative numbers (or, of course, zero). Neither can have any decimal places; they can hold whole numbers only. Addition, subtraction, and all the other mathematical operations can be performed on them. In that sense, the two variables are the same.

However, what if we assign a value to each variable? Let's say x=10 and y=20. Although they still share the same basic characteristics, they obviously are not the same anymore. Both of them are still int primitives, but they have different values. Does changing the value of x also change the value of y? Of course not! They are separate variables with their own particular values. The only thing they will always have in common is their basic nature as integer types.

Now, an object is not a primitive, but the concept is exactly the same. All objects are based on a particular type, however, just like primitives. In the case of objects, the type is a class definition. You have already been using one type of object in particular, the String object. All String objects are based on the standard String class. Therefore, all String objects have the same characteristics (they are all immutable sequences of characters) and share the same behavior (such as converting all the characters to lowercase or uppercase, finding specific characters, or retrieving substrings). All this common behavior is defined in the String class, yet there can surely be two String objects in memory with completely different values.

As you progress through this chapter and begin defining your own classes and instantiating your own objects, these concepts become clearer.

messaging
In object-oriented programming, messaging is the way that two objects communicate. This messaging is realized by invoking instance methods on objects within a program.

Real-World Objects

The concept of objects and classes in programming is essentially the same as its corollary in the real world. The world is full of types of things, such as lamps, chairs, and books. These are abstract concepts because they are only a *kind* of thing. Of course, luckily for us, the world is also full of particular instances of those types. It is these particular instances of the abstract types that we interact with daily. After all, it is not the *idea* of a chair you sit in; it is an actual *realization* of a chair!

Take a look around the room you are in right now, and you will find a slew of objects. You are holding a book. You might be sitting in a chair. Probably a lamp of some kind will be either on or off at the moment. The book, the chair, and the lamp...even *you*...can all be considered distinct objects. Each is a unique entity with specific characteristics, and each object can have some set of actions performed on it. You *read* the book, you *sit* in the chair, and you *turn on* the lamp. Those actions are akin to the methods that you create in a Java class definition.

Consider just a lamp for a moment. What is it? How would you describe a lamp to someone who had no idea what it was? You might say it has a lightbulb, a shade, a base, a power cord, and a switch. You might describe what it does; namely, it provides light when the switch is on. This is not the perfect definition perhaps, but it captures the basic construct of a lamp and gives a brief detail of its purpose.

Now consider *your* lamp for a moment. It probably shares most of the same characteristics as the generic lamp, but you can go into much more detail. For example, my lamp has a brown, ceramic base, a tan shade, and a three-way lightbulb, and the switch is on the base itself. Those specific details are the *state* of my lamp, and it is probably different from the state of your lamp. They are different instances of the same abstract type.

In the Java language, the abstract type of the lamp would be a class definition. Your lamp and my lamp, with their own particular state, would be different objects based on that lamp class. It is important to understand this difference between classes and objects. A class is an abstract type; an object is a realization of that type.

Objects are independent of each other once they are created. When I turn off my lamp, your room does not suddenly go dark. You can throw your lamp away and replace it with a new one; mine stays right where it is. Each lamp belongs to one of us, and each individual controls the lifetime of their lamp.

Software objects behave in a similar fashion. Each object is "owned" by a particular reference. An *object reference* is basically the memory address of an object. Altering the state of one object does not alter the state of all objects of that type because each reference is pointing to one object.

object reference
Whenever a variable holds an object, its value is actually a reference to that object. The reference essentially equates to a pointer to the memory address of the object. While you use the reference, the JVM is responsible for both assigning it and maintaining it at runtime.

It is possible to have multiple references to the same object, however. This would be the same situation as if you and a roommate owned one lamp. If one of you turned it on, the other would benefit from the light.

NOTE

We are not quite done with this lamp analogy. Consider your lamp again. How does it work? How does the electricity get passed from the wall outlet to the lamp to the bulb to the filament of the bulb? How does the filament produce light? How does the switch control that electricity flow? These may be interesting questions to investigate some day, but do you need to know all those details to operate the lamp? Certainly not! If you were a guest in my house and I asked you to turn on the lamp in the living room, would you freeze, confused and unable to perform the task? No, you would walk over to the lamp, find the switch, and presto! Light appears. The point I am making is that the internal workings of the lamp are not critical to your use of the lamp. If the lamp is in good working order, you simply turn it on and off and occasionally replace a blown lightbulb. The lamp hides the working details from you and provides a simple, standard interface to allow you to use it.

Software objects also hide details. A software object can often be seen as a "black box" because the details of how the object functions are not usually evident. Instead, you call a method, and the method takes care of the details. A well-designed class provides a standard interface composed of `public` methods that you invoke. Everything that happens after that invocation is up to the object. All you normally care about is the results of the method call, not how it works. This concept is called encapsulation. Encapsulation is also referred to as information hiding, and it is an essential part of well-designed objects.

Defining a Class

Okay, it is time to take that lamp discussion and try to use those concepts in your own code. Because we have been talking about lamps so much, you will create a class to describe a lamp. Eventually, you will use this class to create individual objects that you can control.

Following is a simple class called Lamp. It is not really complete yet, but it is a good starting point. You will add more detail as you get deeper into this chapter.

```
1   public class Lamp
2   {
3       private boolean on;
4
5       public void turnOn()
6       {
7           if(on)
8           {
9               System.out.println("The lamp is already on!");
```

```
10          }
11          else
12          {
13              on = true;
14              System.out.println("The lamp is on.");
15          }
16      }
17
18      public void turnOff()
19      {
20          if(!on)
21          {
22              System.out.println("The lamp is already off!");
23          }
24          else
25          {
26      on = false;
27              System.out.println("The lamp is off.");
27          }
28      }
29 }
```

Line 3 defines a single variable. Because this variable is created at the class level and is not contained in any methods, it is called an instance variable. Instance variables represent the state of particular objects. Notice that this variable is declared `private`. Although this is not required, it is almost always a good idea. If you recall, any class member that is declared `private` cannot be accessed by anything other than instances of that class. In other words, because this variable represents whether the lamp is "on" or "off," it needs to be controlled by the `Lamp` itself so that any details of this process can be taken care of.

Line 5 is the first of the two methods defined. These methods do not have `static` as part of their definition because they can be used only by object instances. A method that is not defined to be `static` is technically called an *instance method*. The set of `public` instance methods that you define compose the interface for your objects.

instance method
A method that can be invoked only via an object reference. This is opposed to a `static` method that can be invoked via the class name alone.

You are not limited to creating only `public` instance methods. You can also use the `private`, `protected`, and default access modifiers on instance methods. Typically, any method that can be invoked from outside the object is defined as `public`, however. Truthfully, the two most common access modifiers are `public` (full access allowed) and `private` (no access allowed outside instances of the class).

NOTE

The turnOn() method first checks to see if the on instance variable is set to true, which would indicate that the lamp is already on. If it is, a message is printed. Otherwise, the *on* variable is set to true, which indicates that the lamp is now on, and then a message is printed.

The turnOff() method does just the opposite. If the *on* variable is already false, an informational message is output. Otherwise, on is set to false, and an appropriate message is printed to your command line.

You learned earlier that a class could be considered a blueprint for objects of that class type. That is what the Lamp class accomplishes. When you want to create individual Lamp objects, you instantiate the objects, and then you can call methods on them. Note that you can never call the instance methods turnOn() and turnOff() without an instance of the Lamp class. They are not accessible via the class alone as static methods are.

TIP You have seen two terms in this section: *object* and *instance*. The two terms are interchangeable. An object is just the normal term for an instance of a class.

Instantiating and Using Objects

Now that you have the Lamp class definition, you can create objects of this type and invoke the instance methods on them. The following code is a simple class that provides only a main() method, just like the classes that you have worked with in previous chapters. Remember, you need the main() method to give the interpreter an entry point into your program. Whereas all the previous programs you have written have been composed of a single class, this program is composed of two classes. The first is the Lamp class that you just created, and the second is the LampTest class shown here:

```
1  public class LampTest
2  {
3      public static void main(String[] args)
4      {
5          Lamp lampOne = new Lamp();
6          Lamp lampTwo = new Lamp();
7
8          lampOne.turnOn();
9          lampTwo.turnOn();
10         lampOne.turnOn();
11         lampTwo.turnOff();
12         lampOne.turnOff();
13     }
14 }
```

The first thing the `LampTest` code does is create two `Lamp` objects on lines 5 and 6. The syntax is the same as when you created primitive types or arrays. On the left of the assignment operator (=), you give the type and variable name. On the right, you provide the value. In the case of objects, the "value" is the reference that the JVM creates automatically for you. You trigger this reference creation by instantiating an object using the new keyword. Notice that after the new keyword, you give the type name again (in this case, `Lamp`), followed by a pair of parentheses. This is the basic syntax for instantiating an object.

The parentheses make this look like a method call, but it is not truly a method call at all. The parentheses actually signify something called a constructor, which you will learn about later in this chapter. Essentially, a constructor works much like a method and allows you to perform some initialization functions before a valid reference is returned and the object can be used.

NOTE

Once lines 5 and 6 complete, there are two `Lamp` objects in memory. They share the same structure provided by the `Lamp` class, but their state can be altered independently. Of course, because no methods have been called on either object yet, their state is exactly the same (the variable *on* holds the default value of `false`). The difference between the two objects is the reference that was returned by the JVM. Each object is located in a distinct area of your system's memory.

Lines 8–12 call methods on each of the objects so that you can see what happens. First, the `turnOn()` method is invoked via the `lampOne` object. This results in the variable *on* changing to `true` and a brief message being printed because that is the logic provided back in the `Lamp` class. The same thing occurs on line 9, but with the `lampTwo` object. On line 10, the `turnOn()` method is called again, but this time the state is not changed because the *on* variable is already set to `true`. Finally, on lines 11 and 12, both lamps have their `turnOff()` method invoked.

The output from running the `LampTest` code looks like this:

```
The lamp is on.
The lamp is on.
The lamp is already on!
The lamp is off.
The lamp is off.
```

A Closer Look at a *Lamp* Object

It might help at this point to have a visual of a `Lamp` object. Traditionally, an object is diagrammed as a circle with compartments for each method around the circumference, and a smaller compartment inside the circle for the variables. A Lamp object would look something like the following diagram.

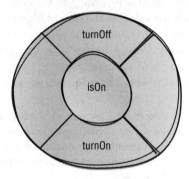

A Lamp Object

What this diagram is showing you is that the turnOn() and turnOff() methods are accessible to outside callers and that the on instance variable is hidden. This should make sense because you defined the two methods to be public and the lone instance variable to be private. You could say that the methods surrounding the instance variables are the interface of your object. The diagram clearly shows the encapsulation inherent in a Lamp object; the only way to alter the state of the *on* variable is by invoking one of the provided methods.

This concept of a clearly defined interface is important. Imagine that your real-world lamp has a warranty. If you turn on the lamp and a short circuit ends up blowing a fuse in your house, you should be able to return the lamp to the store that you bought it from and get a new one. This is because the lamp did not work as it is supposed to. However, if you had previously taken the lamp apart in a fit of insatiable curiosity and messed around with the wiring and *then* the short circuit occurred, the store might refuse your request for a new lamp. In the second case, you voided the warranty by directly accessing the internals of the lamp instead of using the standard interface it provides you.

This warranty concept is the same with your object interfaces. Your object should work "as advertised" when the public instance methods are invoked correctly, and you should make every effort to prevent direct access to your object's state. When you define private variables, you practically guarantee that your variables are protected from illegal access. Probably the only way that someone could alter them directly would be if you provided them with the source code. (And you would not do that, right?)

This brings up one of the mantras of object-oriented programming: "private data, public methods." If you adhere to that advice, you will find yourself creating encapsulated objects without even trying!

Sharing a Reference

Before we move on, you should know that the only way you can create an object is with the new keyword. If you do not use new, no instantiation takes place whatsoever. Take a look at the following class.

```
public class AClass
{
    private int number;

    public void setNumber(int n)
    {
        number = n;
    }

    public int getNumber()
    {
        return number;
    }
}
```

Now imagine that the following lines of code are executed in another class. How many objects exist when these four lines complete? What is the value of number for each reference?

```
AClass one = new AClass();
AClass two = one;
AClass three = two;
AClass four = new AClass();
one.setNumber(10);
System.out.println("one: " + one.getNumber());
System.out.println("two: " + two.getNumber());
System.out.println("three: " + three.getNumber());
System.out.println("four: " + four.getNumber());
```

The answer to the first question is that two objects are created. The first line creates a new AClass object and assigns the reference to one. The second line does *not* create a new object, but simply assigns the reference stored in one to two. The third line does the same thing, assigning the single existing reference to three. The fourth line actually instantiates a new AClass object and assigns the reference to four. Because the new keyword is used only twice, only two objects can be in memory.

The second question essentially asked what the printouts would be. If you ran this code somewhere, you would see the following output:

```
one: 10
two: 10
three: 10
four: 0
```

Do you see why? Because one, two, and three all refer to the same object in memory, the value of number is the same for all three. Because four is a new object but that object never changed the default value of number, the value is zero.

The point is that a single object can have multiple references. The implication is that if any of those references change the state of their object, *all* the references to that object see this new state. This can be both powerful and dangerous, depending on the care you take in designing your code.

Object Messaging: Adding a Lightbulb

Q: How many programmers does it take to change a lightbulb?

A: It depends on how well the class is defined.

The Lamp class is workable, but not really complete. A lamp is not really a self-contained object if you think about it. The lamp itself provides only the structure and electrical system to supply light. To actually get the light, you usually need a lightbulb. When you design software objects, you often model real-world counterparts. So, to really capture a lamp in software, you need a lightbulb.

Another way to look at this is that when you define classes, you essentially model the world of your program as you want it to be. The Lamp class defined earlier says that to be a lamp, you must be able to be turned on and off. Of course, a more realistic lamp might include color, size, and a shade—you get the idea. The point is, a Lamp as defined right now is a simplified, workable version of a real-world lamp. However, lamps are of many types. Some run on electricity, some on gas, and some are really just candleholders. It is up to you to define the details and the flexibility of your class types. For our current purposes, we will stick to the electrical lamp style, but later in this chapter and in the next one, you will learn how to define a more generic "lamp" that could provide any type of light source.

The following LightBulb class provides a simple view of a real-world lightbulb. Eventually, the Lamp class itself will be altered a bit to work with this new LightBulb type. Like the Lamp class, it defines only one instance variable to indicate whether the bulb is lit or unlit. Two methods are defined that allow you to set the state and get the current state of the bulb.

```
1  public class LightBulb
2  {
```

```
3      private boolean lit;
4
5      public void setLit(boolean param)
6      {
7          if(lit && param)
8          {
9              System.out.println("The bulb is already lit!");
10         }
11         else if(!lit && !param)
12         {
13             System.out.println("The bulb is already unlit!");
14         }
15         else
16         {
17             lit = param;
18             String str = lit ? "lit." : "unlit.";
19             System.out.println("The bulb is " + str);
20         }
21     }
22
23     public boolean isLit()
24     {
25         return lit;
26     }
27 }
```

Line 3 defines the lone boolean instance variable, lit. Line 5 houses
the method that is called whenever the bulb's state changes, setLit(). This
method takes a boolean parameter that indicates the desired action to take. If
the parameter is true, the bulb should be lit; if the parameter is false, the bulb
should be unlit. Line 7 performs a boolean AND (&&) on the instance variable
and the parameter to determine if both of them are true. If they are, you are
trying to light an already-lit bulb, and only a message prints. The opposite test is
made on line 11 to ensure that both variables are not false. Finally, on line 15,
the code is provided that executes if the state of the LightBulb object actually
changes. On line 17, the instance variable is given the value of the param
parameter, and on line 18, the ternary operator is used to create a String that
holds the state of the object, either "lit" or "unlit." Line 19 tells a message to
print to the command line to show you the current state of the object. The
setLit() method is often called a *mutator method* because it can potentially
alter the state of the object.

mutator method
A method that sets the value of a
portion of an object's state. This state
is typically stored in a private
instance variable. By convention, a
mutator method begins with set and is
followed by the instance variable name.
So, for an instance variable named
value, the mutator method would be
called setValue(). Mutator methods take a parameter that is the same
type as the instance variable with which
it is associated. This parameter holds the
new value to which the instance variable
should be set.

Line 23 defines the second method, `isLit()`. This method returns a `boolean`, not `void`, as `setLit()` does. This is because the instance variable is defined to be `private`; it cannot be directly accessed from outside the object. However, once you incorporate a `LightBulb` object with a `Lamp` object, the `Lamp` object may need to know the state of the `LightBulb` object. This is why the `isLit()` method exists. It simply returns the value of the instance variable to the caller. The `isLit()` method is often called an *accessor method* because it returns a value pertaining to the object's state.

To use this new class, we must rework the original `Lamp` class. Now, the basic idea is that turning on the lamp calls the `LightBulb` object. For this to work, the `Lamp` class needs to declare a reference to a `LightBulb` that you pass in to the `Lamp` object. You will also find that both the `turnOn()` and `turnOff()` methods have changed. Check out the `LampWithBulb` class that follows.

```
1   public class LampWithBulb
2   {
3        LightBulb bulb;
4
5        public void setLightBulb(LightBulb b)
6        {
7            bulb = b;
8        }
9
10       public void turnOn()
11       {
12           if(bulb == null)
13           {
14               System.out.println("There is no lightbulb!");
15           }
16           else if (bulb.isLit())
17           {
18               System.out.println("The lamp is already on!");
19           }
20           else
21           {
22               bulb.setLit(true);
23               System.out.println("The lamp is on.");
24           }
25       }
26
27       public void turnOff()
28       {
29           if(bulb == null)
```

```
30              {
31                   System.out.println("There is no lightbulb!");
32              }
33              else if(!bulb.isLit())
34              {
35                   System.out.println("The bulb is already off!");
36              }
37              else
38              {
39                   bulb.setLit(false);
40                   System.out.println("The lamp is off.");
41              }
42         }
43 }
```

The LampWithBulb class declares a LightBulb object on line 3. This object is given a valid reference when the setLightBulb() method defined on lines 5–8 is called. You will be instantiating a LightBulb and passing it to a LampWithBulb object in the LampWithBulbTest class that you define next.

Line 10 begins the new version of the turnOn() method. On line 12, the if statement checks to see if a LightBulb object is already created. If no such object exists, the method prints a message to let you know that no further action can be taken. Line 16 contains the first else statement, which checks to see if the LightBulb is already "lit." If it is, the message on line 18 prints. The final else statement on line 20 contains the block of code that calls the setLit() method of the LightBulb object. The turnOff() method is similarly altered to support the addition of the LightBulb object to the logic of the code.

This process of one method invoking another method is called *delegation* because the object is delegating responsibility to another method in another object. Delegation is a common approach in object-oriented programming that provides the logic of your code.

The following code is the final class you will need, the LampWithBulbTest class. This class contains just a main() method to make things go. First, a LightBulb is instantiated, and then a LampWithBulb object is instantiated. The LightBulb object is passed to the LampWithBulb object, and then some calls are made to demonstrate how the two objects work together.

delegation
The process of invoking a method in another object from a method in the current object. This allows complex logic to be handled by separate objects to form the overall logic of your program.

```
1  public class LampWithBulbTest
2  {
3      public static void main(String[] args)
4      {
5          LightBulb bulb = new LightBulb();
6          LampWithBulb lamp = new LampWithBulb();
7          lamp.turnOn();
```

```
8              lamp.setLightBulb(bulb);
9              lamp.turnOn();
10             lamp.turnOn();
11             lamp.turnOff();
12         }
13 }
```

If you compile all three classes and execute the `LampWithBulbTest` class, you should see the following output to your command line:

```
There is no lightbulb!
The bulb is lit.
The lamp is on.
The lamp is already on!
The bulb is unlit.
The lamp is off.
```

This is a simple example, to be sure, but it demonstrates some important concepts that you need to understand when you are working with objects and methods.

Passing by Value

pass by value
The pass-by-value semantics mean that parameters and return types are copied when they are passed to and from methods. All primitive types in Java follow the pass-by-value rule.

You can pass parameters and return types to methods in the Java language in two ways: by value and by reference (which is discussed in the next section). When you pass by value, you pass a primitive type to a method as a parameter or from a method as a return type. The term *pass by value* means that the value of the variable passed is *copied* to or from the method.

Copying the value has an important implication. Take the following code example. First, a simple method is defined and takes an `int` as a parameter. A second method is then defined and is called by the first one. Printouts show you the value of the parameter before it is passed, after it is passed, and after both methods change the value.

```
public class PassByValueTest
{
    public void methodOne()
    {
        int x = 100;
        methodTwo(x);
        System.out.println("methodOne: x == " + x);
        x = 200;
        System.out.println("methodOne: x == " + x);
    }
```

```
    public void methodTwo(int x)
    {
        System.out.println("methodTwo: x == " + x);
        x = 500;
        System.out.println("methodTwo: x == " + x);
    }

    public static void main(String[] args)
    {
        PassByValueTest test = new PassByValueTest();
        test.methodOne();
    }
}
```

Run this code and you will see the following output:

```
methodTwo: x == 100
methodTwo: x == 500
methodOne: x == 100
methodOne: x == 200
```

The point of this class is to show you how a parameter to a method is a copy of the original value: methodTwo() changes the value of the parameter to 500, but this does not affect the original variable defined in methodOne(). The two values are completely distinct from each other.

NOTE

If the body of the main() method confuses you because it is actually instantiating an instance of the class in which it is defined, hold tight. The reason is that static methods cannot call instance methods without an object reference. You will learn why this is the case later in this chapter. For now, just use the code as provided here.

Let me show you another, slightly different example. This time, an instance variable is involved instead of just local variables inside the methods. See if you can predict the two outputs from each method.

```
public class PassByValueTest2
{
    private int x = 50;

    public void methodOne()
    {
        System.out.println("methodOne: x == " + x);
        methodTwo(x);
```

```
            System.out.println("methodOne: x == " + x);
        }

        public void methodTwo(int y)
        {
            System.out.println("methodTwo: y == " + y);
            y = 100;
            System.out.println("methodTwo: y == " + y);
        }

        public static void main(String[] args)
        {
            PassByValueTest2 test = new PassByValueTest2();
            test.methodOne();
        }
    }
```

Can you see what happens here? First, the value of x is 50, the value it is given when it is declared. This value is then passed to methodTwo(). When the first printout happens in methodTwo(), the value is still 50. The next line then changes this value to 100, and the output reflects this change.

When methodTwo() completes, control returns to methodOne(), and a final printout results. The printed value is 50, *not* 100. This is because primitive types are passed by value, so the change made inside methodTwo() is seen only during the scope of methodTwo(). The value of the original instance variable *never* changes in this code.

The output is as follows:

```
    methodOne: x == 50
    methodTwo: y == 50
    methodTwo: y == 100
    methodOne: x == 50
```

Passing by Reference

pass by reference
Instead of copying the values of parameters and return types like you do with primitive types, only the reference of objects is passed. This allows one object to be referred to from many points in an application and ensures that state and behavior are consistent.

The other way that parameters and return types can be passed is by following the rule of *pass by reference*. This happens only if you are passing an object. Objects are always passed by reference; primitives are always passed by value. Passing by reference can lead to some interesting situations, so it is important that you understand what this implies.

Let's take code similar to what you found in the previous section when you learned about passing by value. This time, you pass an object that is based on a simple class called IntHolder, which is defined in the following code. This class holds only one instance variable and a pair of methods to mutate and access the value of that variable.

```java
public class IntHolder
{
    private int x = 100;

    public void setX(int newX)
    {
        x = newX;
    }

    public int getX()
    {
        return x;
    }
}
```

In the following PassByRefTest class, you now create an instance of the IntHolder class and pass it to methodOne().

```java
1   public class PassByRefTest
2   {
3       public void methodOne(IntHolder h)
4       {
5           System.out.println("methodOne: h.x == " + h.getX());
6           methodTwo(h);
7           System.out.println("methodOne: h.x == " + h.getX());
8       }
9
10      public void methodTwo(IntHolder h)
11      {
12          System.out.println("methodTwo: h.x == " + h.getX());
13          h.setX(500);
14          System.out.println("methodTwo: h.x == " + h.getX());
15      }
16
17      public static void main(String[] args)
18      {
19          PassByRefTest test = new PassByRefTest();
20          IntHolder h = new IntHolder();
```

```
20            test.methodOne(h);
21      }
22 }
```

Here is the output from running this code. Take a look at it, and then I will explain.

```
methodOne: h.x == 100
methodTwo: h.x == 100
methodTwo: h.x == 500
methodOne: h.x == 500
```

The first two printouts on lines 5 and 7 should not be surprising because this code did not change the original value of x inside the IntHolder object. Line 6 calls methodTwo(), passing the IntHolder object as a parameter. methodTwo() (on line 10) then changes the value of x by calling the setX() method and passing 500. methodTwo() (on line 14) prints this new value correctly.

What might seem strange is that the final methodOne() (back on line 7) does not print the original 100; instead, it prints the new value of 500 set in methodTwo(). This is because you are passing an object reference, not a primitive value. The value of h is not 100, 500, or any integral value; the value of h is the object reference that the JVM assigned when the IntHolder object was created. In a sense, when you pass an object by reference, all its current state is passed along with it. Because the state of the object h was changed in methodTwo() on line 13, you see the new value of h.x on the last line of methodOne().

The key here is that when you pass an object, you are passing the entire reference to the object. Any state that the object holds is the same for everyone who sees that reference. In the PassByValueTest and PassByValueTest2 code, a primitive was copied to another method, and the changes that took place did *not* reflect the original caller. In the PassByRefTest code, an object is passed to another method, and the value *is* reflected.

TIP

The truth is that *everything*—both objects and primitive types—is passed by value. For a primitive type, the value is whatever was assigned to the primitive before it was passed. For an object, the value is the actual object reference. All object references in the JVM are just 32-bit integers that the JVM maps to memory addresses.

In the LampWithBulbTest code, a LightBulb object was passed to the Lamp object via the setLightBulb() method. This LightBulb object was passed by reference. The LampWithBulb object then queried the state of the LightBulb object via the isLit() method, which returned a boolean that was passed by value.

The *this* Keyword

Another keyword that you may find useful when it comes to objects is the this keyword. You use this to refer to the specific instance that is currently active.

Think of how you refer to yourself. If you are telling me that you are a Java programmer, you probably do not use your name in the sentence. Instead, you say something like, "I am a Java programmer." Your use of the word "I" means you are talking about yourself, not some other person. I may say in response to you, "A Java programmer? Me too!" In that response, the word "me" refers specifically to, well, *me*. In a sentence like that, you have no doubts about whom I am referring to.

That is exactly what this means to an object. You use the this reference to refer to the current object. For the most part, you can use this just as you would use any other object reference.

You cannot try to assign a new value to this. The compiler will not allow this to appear on the left side of an assignment expression.

WARNING

Take the following code as an example. The first version looks like something you may have written in this book already. The second version adds the this keyword everywhere it makes sense. The important point to keep in mind right now is that the two classes are identical in functionality.

```
public class ClassWithoutThis
{
    private int x;
    private float f;

    public void first()
    {
        x = 100;
        f = 10.0F;
    }

    public void second()
    {
        float z = x + f;
        z += 100;
    }
}

public class ClassWithThis
{
```

```
        private int x;
        private float f;

        public void first()
        {
            this.x = 100;
            this.f = 10.0F;
        }

        public void second()
        {
            float z = this.x + this.f;
            z += 100;
        }
    }
```

The functionality is exactly the same, but the second version of the class adds the this keyword whenever it uses the instance variables *x* and *f*. Whenever you use this, you are accessing instance members (either a variable or a method). Notice that in the second() method, the variable *z* is local, so using the this keyword on the second line would result in a compiler error because there is no instance variable named *z*.

Bypassing Local Variables Using *this*

You use the this keyword in the body of your instance methods to refer to the current object. That "current object" is the actual object in which the method is contained. However, you might be wondering what the point is in the first place. After all, if the two classes defined previously are exactly the same, why use this confusing keyword at all?

The answer is that sometimes you need to ensure that you are talking to the current instance's variables or methods. One such case is if you have the same variable name defined both as an instance variable and as a local variable in a method. The most common case in which this happens is when you are using method parameters.

Many developers, myself included, like to name method parameters the same as the instance variables they relate to (if any). This practice is not required by any means, but I find that it adds to the "self-documenting" function of my code. It is easy for me to look at a method that I defined months or years ago and see that a particular method has some relation to an instance variable because I used the exact same name.

If you define a variable named *fred* as an instance variable, and you also define a variable with the same name inside a method of that class, the scoping rules of the Java language kick in. If you simply say *fred* inside the method, the local variable is used, and the instance variable is "hidden." However, if you say `this.fred`, you are definitely accessing the instance variable.

Here is an example. In the following class, the `main()` method instantiates an instance of the class and then calls a method to perform an addition. The sum of this addition is stored in the instance variable of the object and is eventually retrieved when all the calculations are complete. Notice that the method parameters have the same names as the two instance variables. Because of this, I use the `this` keyword to set the value of my instance variables. If I did not, I would be setting the value of the *local* variables of the same name, which would mean the sum of all the calculations would always be zero (the default value of the instance variables).

```
1  public class SumItUp
2  {
3        private int x;
4        private int y;
5
6        public void addToX(int x)
7        {
8            this.x += x;
9        }
10
11       public void addToY(int y)
12       {
13           this.y += y;
14       }
15
16       public int getSum()
17       {
18           return this.x + this.y;
19           // could use return x + y here!
20       }
21
22       public static void main(String[] args)
23       {
24           SumItUp sum = new SumItUp();
25           sum.addToX(100);
26           sum.addToY(50);
27           sum.addToX(35);
28           sum.addToY(15);
29           System.out.println("Sum: " + sum.getSum());
30       }
31 }
```

The final printout on line 29 will be 200 because every time you add a value, it is stored in the corresponding instance variable. Because the parameter to each method is the same name as an instance variable, the this keyword ensures that you are talking to the instance variables when you should be.

Passing a Reference Using *this*

You can also use the this keyword to pass a reference to an object from within that object. Just like any other object reference, you can pass this as a parameter or return type from any method. It is not at all uncommon to return this from a method to simplify multiple method calls on the same object.

The following class takes a starting value and then provides a method to double that value every time it is called. Notice that the implementation of the doubleIt() method returns an instance of itself.

```java
public class Doubler
{
    private int number;

    public void setNumber(int number)
    {
        this.number = number;
    }

    public int getNumber()
    {
        return number;
    }

    public Doubler doubleIt()
    {
        number *= 2;
        return this;
    }

    public static void main(String[] args)
    {
        Doubler d = new Doubler();
        d.setNumber(10);
        d.doubleIt().doubleIt().doubleIt();
        System.out.println("The value is " + d.getNumber());
    }
}
```

Because the `doubleIt()` method returns a reference to the object itself, you can repeat the method call multiple times on the same line. This is because the syntax for dot notation with instance method calls is `objectReference.methodName()`. Because the return of the `doubleIt()` method is in fact the object reference itself, the method can be called again. If the `doubleIt()` method returned an `int` (which could be the actual doubled value of `number`), you could not make these multiple method calls on a single line like this. If you tried, you would get a compiler error because you would be attempting to invoke an instance method on a primitive type. That is simply not possible.

As mentioned, you can also pass `this` as a parameter to a method. This creates a callback situation that allows the invoked method to access the instance methods of the object parameter.

———— *TIP* ————

Static Methods Have No *this* Reference

You have seen a couple of cases in this chapter in which the `main()` method actually instantiated an object of the class in which the `main()` method is defined. For example, this was true in the previous example, the `Doubler` class. This is often confusing for new Java developers, so let's take a look at the reason this is required.

All instance methods essentially have a hidden parameter named `this` that is always the same type as the object itself. That is why you can use the `this` reference any time you want inside an instance method. However, `static` methods have no such concept. If you think about it, that makes complete sense. Remember that a `static` method does not require an object to be invoked; normally, `static` methods are invoked using the `ClassName.staticMethodName()` syntax. Because a `static` method can be invoked with no object instance whatsoever, how could there be a `this` reference?

The rule is that `static` methods (like the `main()` method) can never access instance methods or instance variables; `static` methods can invoke only *other* `static` class members directly. Another way to say this is that you cannot invoke an instance method or access an instance variable without an object instance.

The following code example will not even compile because you are attempting to access an instance variable from the `main()` method.

```java
public class Test
{
    private int value;

    public static void main(String[] args)
    {
        value = 10; // no object reference!!!
```

```
        }
    }
```

The only way to make this work is to change the code like this:

```
    public class Test
    {
        private int value;

        public static void main(String[] args)
        {
            Test t = new Test(); // create object reference
            t.value = 10; // access variable via reference
        }
    }
```

The best way to keep this straight as it relates to the main() method is to think of the main() method as having no concept of the class in which it actually resides. This is not technically true, but because most of the classes that you create will be based on instance members, creating a little mental separation like this may help you understand what is happening. The only way that the main() method can invoke instance methods is to have an object reference, so you have no choice but to create that object right inside the method itself.

I don't want to belabor the point, but if you are still confused about this, here is a final thought that might help. The rule in the Java language is that *no* method can access an instance method or a variable without an object reference, whether that method is static or not. The trick is that all your instance methods automatically have the this reference associated with any instance members you specify that are not otherwise hidden by local variables. However, as you just learned, static methods do not have the benefit of the automatic this reference. As a result, you have to create the object reference yourself.

TIP

Although static methods cannot access instance members, instance methods *can* access static members. However, it is good practice to always access your static members using the ClassName.staticMemberName() syntax, even if an object exists at the time. This helps to make your code more understandable. If you see that syntax, there is no doubt in your mind that the accessed member is static.

Constructors

constructor
A special method that is automatically executed when a new instance of a class is created. A constructor is used to initialize an object to a desired state.

You will learn a whole lot more about constructors in Chapter 7, "Advanced Object-Oriented Programming," but this section gets you started on the right foot. A *constructor* is a special method that allows an object to initialize itself before the reference is ready to be used. When you instantiate an object, all the instance variables are automatically set to their default values. If you provide a constructor, it is called as part of the instantiation process, and you can initialize these variables to the specific values you want.

The term "constructor" is really a misnomer. A constructor has nothing at all to do with the actual construction of an object but is used solely to initialize an object's state. When you create a new object, the JVM sets aside the required memory and then initializes all the instance variables to their default values. Only after these two steps (when the object is already "constructed") is the constructor called. However, you cannot have a valid object reference until the constructor completes. In short, a constructor guarantees that your object is in a specific state before it can actually be used.

Constructors syntactically look a lot like normal instance methods. However, constructors cannot have a return type. Remember, that is not the same thing as saying that they return `void`. Constructors simply have no return type. In addition, constructors always have the same name as the class in which they reside. For a class named `HelloWorld`, a valid constructor could look like this:

```
public HelloWorld()
{
    // do initialization
}
```

You have already instantiated some objects in this chapter and have seen the syntax of `new ClassName()`. The parentheses following the class name actually signify a call to a constructor. You can create constructors that take zero or more parameters. If your constructor does take parameters, you pass them within those same parentheses that follow the class name.

NOTE

You may be wondering how your objects have successfully instantiated in this chapter so far because you have not provided any constructors in your classes. Your code has worked so far because, if you provide no constructors of your own, the compiler automatically add a default constructor to all classes. We'll look at this process more closely in Chapter 7.

Let's create a constructor to see what all the fuss is about, shall we? The following class is a reworked version of the `LampWithBulb` class. In the previous version of this code, you had to create a `LightBulb` object, create a `LampWithBulb` object, and then pass the `LightBulb` to the `LampWithBulb` via the `setLightBulb()` method. This time a constructor is provided that takes a `LightBulb` as a parameter. This makes more sense because it ensures that all `LampWithBulb` references have a `LightBulb` associated with them before they can be used.

```
1  public class LampWithBulb2
2  {
```

```
3      LightBulb bulb;
4
5      public LampWithBulb2(LightBulb bulb)
6      {
7          this.bulb = bulb;
8      }
9
10     public void turnOn()
11     {
12         if (bulb.isLit())
13         {
14             System.out.println("The lamp is already on!");
15         }
16         else
17         {
18             bulb.setLit(true);
19             System.out.println("The lamp is on.");
20         }
21     }
22
23     public void turnOff()
24     {
25         if(!bulb.isLit())
26         {
27             System.out.println("The bulb is already
off!");
28         }
29         else
30         {
31             bulb.setLit(false);
32             System.out.println("The lamp is off.");
33         }
34     }
35 }
```

Lines 5–8 form the constructor for this class. The name of the constructor is exactly the same as the class, and it returns nothing. In this case, the constructor actually takes a parameter, namely the LightBulb object that will be associated with this lamp during its lifetime. You should also notice changes in both the turnOn() and turnOff() methods because a check is no longer made in either of them to be sure that bulb is not null. I removed this code because there is no way the bulb can be null once it has been set in the constructor.

Truthfully, bulb could be null still if that is the value passed into the constructor in the first place. You will learn how to control situations like this when you learn more about exceptions in Chapter 8, "Exception Handling."

Here is the class that demonstrates how the new LampWithBulb2 class works.

```
1  public class LampWithBulb2Test
2  {
3      public static void main(String[] args)
4      {
5          LightBulb bulb = new LightBulb();
6          LampWithBulb2 lamp = new LampWithBulb2(bulb);
7          lamp.turnOn();
8          lamp.turnOn();
9          lamp.turnOn();
10         lamp.turnOff();
11     }
12 }
```

The lamp reference on line 6 cannot even be created unless the bulb object was passed to the constructor. In the previous version of this code, you created the lamp object by saying:

```
LampWithBulb lamp = new LampWithBulb();
```

If you try to create the lamp this time with the empty parentheses, the compiler will tell you that there is no such constructor. This is true because the constructor takes a LightBulb object as a parameter and is now the *only* way to instantiate a LampWithBulb2 object.

Multiple Constructors

You are not limited to a single constructor in your classes, however. In fact, it is much more common to have multiple constructors so that you have more flexibility when you create objects. If you provide more than one constructor, each will have a different set of parameters. The different parameters are the only way that constructors can be uniquely defined because the rest of their signature is always the same (the class name and no return type).

Providing a constructor that takes zero parameters along with any other constructors you create is usually a good idea. Note that this is not a requirement, just a good idea most of the time. Essentially, by providing a standard, no-argument constructor all the time, you allow your classes to be instantiated in some default manner.

Before we add a new constructor to the LampWithBulb2 class, let's look at a new version of the LightBulb class called ColoredLightBulb. The only change is a new String instance variable that holds the desired color and a method for setting this value.

```
1   public class ColoredLightBulb
2   {
3       private boolean lit;
4       private String color = "white";
5
6       public ColoredLightBulb(String color)
7       {
8           this.color=color;
9       }
10
11      public void setLit(boolean param)
12        {
13          if(lit && param)
14          {
15              System.out.println("The bulb is already lit!");
16          }
17          else if(!lit && !param)
18          {
19              System.out.println("The bulb is already unlit!");
20          }
21          else
22          {
23              lit = param;
24              String str = lit ? "lit" : "unlit";
25              System.out.print("The bulb is " + str);
26              System.out.println(" and the bulb is  + color
                      + ".");
27          }
28        }
29
30      public boolean isLit()
31      {
32          return lit;
33      }
34
35      public void setColor(String color)
```

```
36        {
37            this.color = color;
38        }
39 }
```

When you instantiate a `ColoredLightBulb`, you can either accept the default value of white or pass a color of your own choosing to the constructor (shown on line 6). The printout on line 26 now includes the lightbulb color as well.

Now let's add a standard, no-argument constructor to the `LampWithBulb2` class along with the already-existing constructor. The new class will be called `LampWithBulb3`. Adding this new constructor allows you to create `LampWith-Bulb3` objects without passing in a `LightBulb` object. The benefits of this are discussed after you take a look at the new version of the code.

```
1  public class LampWithBulb3
2  {
3        ColoredLightBulb bulb;
4
5        public LampWithBulb3(ColoredLightBulb bulb)
6        {
7            this.bulb = bulb;
8        }
9
10       public LampWithBulb3()
11       {
12           bulb = new ColoredLightBulb();
13       }
14
15       public void turnOn()
16       {
17           if (bulb.isLit())
18           {
19               System.out.println("The lamp is already on!");
20           }
21           else
22           {
23               bulb.setLit(true);
24               System.out.println("The lamp is on.");
25           }
26       }
27
28       public void turnOff()
```

```
29      {
30          if(!bulb.isLit())
31          {
32              System.out.println("The bulb is already off!");
33          }
34          else
35          {
36              bulb.setLit(false);
37              System.out.println("The lamp is off.");
38          }
39      }
40 }
```

Lines 10–13 define the added constructor. Now you can create a new
LampWithBulb3 object, and it automatically creates a new ColoredLightBulb
for you instead of your having to pass it in manually. The logic is that most lamps
have white lightbulbs, so the no-argument constructor creates one for you. In the
special cases in which you want a different colored lightbulb, you can use the second constructor that takes the ColoredLightBulb parameter.

Finally, here is the code that demonstrates how these constructors can be used.

```
1  public class LampWithBulb3Test
2  {
3      public static void main(String[] args)
4      {
5          ColoredLightBulb bulb = new ColoredLightBulb();
6          bulb.setColor("red");
7          LampWithBulb3 lampOne = new LampWithBulb3(bulb);
8          LampWithBulb3 lampTwo = new LampWithBulb3();
9          lampOne.turnOn();
10         lampTwo.turnOn();
11         lampOne.turnOff();
12         lampTwo.turnOff();
13     }
14 }
```

Line 5 creates a new ColoredLightBulb object, and line 6 sets the color to
red. This object is then passed to the constructor on line 7 to create the lampOne
object. The lampTwo object is created on line 8 when you call the no-argument
constructor, resulting in a white LightBulb object being created for you. Executing this code results in the following output:

```
The bulb is lit and the color is red.
```

```
The lamp is on.
The bulb is lit and the color is white.
The lamp is on.
The bulb is unlit and the color is red.
The lamp is off.
The bulb is unlit and the color is white.
The lamp is off.
```

Constructor Chaining

Another technique that you can use with constructors is a process called *constructor chaining*. This basically translates to invoking a constructor from within another constructor. You chain constructors with the `this` keyword.

Calling a constructor directly by name is illegal, but you can use the `this` keyword to manually invoke another constructor. Normally, you invoke a constructor as an implicit part of the call to new, but with constructor chaining, you can have one or more constructors called automatically for you. This can make your code much simpler to write and maintain because it produces a logical flow to the construction process.

If you think about it, you should always create an object the same way. Though you might not yet know all the possible values for instance variables, the process of creating objects is really the same. The Java language provides a special syntax using the `this` keyword that allows you to avoid duplicating behavior in multiple constructors. Instead, all constructors can end up calling an ultimate constructor that does the initialization work every time.

As an example, let's modify the `ColoredLightBulb` class a bit. In the current version, no constructors are provided. However, including constructors makes some sense because the *color* instance variable should always be set. The code works fine as it is written now, but you can improve it by making the color selection part of the instantiation process.

It is probably best that I show you this constructor chaining in action before we discuss this, so here is the revised `ColoredLightBulb2` class:

```
1   public class ColoredLightBulb2
2   {
3       private boolean lit;
4       private String color;
5
6       public ColoredLightBulb2()
7       {
8           this("white");
9       }
```

constructor chaining
Constructors can be "chained" together, allowing one constructor to invoke another and so on until an "ultimate constructor" executes. To chain constructors, you use the `this` keyword to represent the constructor invocation.

```
10
11        public ColoredLightBulb2(String color)
12        {
13            this.color = color;
14        }
15
16        public void setLit(boolean param)
17        {
18            if(lit && param)
19            {
20                System.out.println("The bulb is already
                    lit!");
21            }
22            else if(!lit && !param)
23            {
24                System.out.println("The bulb is already
                    unlit!");
25            }
26            else
27            {
28                lit = param;
29                String str = lit ? "lit" : "unlit";
30                System.out.print("The bulb is " + str);
31                System.out.println(" and the bulb is " +
                    color + ".");
32            }
33        }
34 }
```

Line 8 shows the special constructor-chaining syntax. Because you can never invoke a constructor by its name, you use this as a placeholder for the constructor name. After this, you provide the parameters to the constructor that you want to call. Whether you create a ColoredLightBulb2 object with or without a parameter to the constructor, the second constructor on lines 11–14 *always* executes.

You can provide as many constructors as you want in your classes, and you can use constructor chaining to ensure a logical and convenient construction process. However, keep in mind two important rules. First, if you do invoke another constructor in this fashion, that invocation *must* come on the first line of your constructor. It would be illegal to provide a constructor like this:

```
public ColoredLightBulb2()
{
```

```
    System.out.println("In constructor");
    this("white");
}
```

The second rule of constructor chaining is that you can explicitly call only *one* constructor from within another constructor. It is illegal to call another constructor more than once. You could expand the first rule to say that you can invoke another constructor only on the first line and never again in the same constructor body.

The reasons for these rules are explained in full in Chapter 7 when you begin learning about inheritance and how it affects your constructors.

You can use this special syntax only inside a constructor. It is illegal to associate parentheses with `this` anywhere but in a constructor.

WARNING

Terms to Know

accessor method	messaging
constructor	mutator method
constructor chaining	object reference
delegation	pass by reference
instance method	pass by value

Review Questions

1. Is the following line of code legal?

   ```
   double d = new double(10);
   ```

2. How many objects exist after the following code completes?

   ```
   Lamp lampOne = new Lamp();
   Lamp lampTwo = new Lamp();
   Lamp lampThree = lampOne;
   lampTwo = lampOne;
   ```

3. Why can the main() method not directly access instance methods and variables?

4. Why should instance variables normally be private?

5. What composes the interface of an object?

6. What is the return type of a constructor?

7. Will the following line of code compile correctly?

   ```
   this = new Lamp();
   ```

8. If you have multiple constructors, what differentiates them from one another in your class?

9. What is the keyword used to invoke another constructor in the same class from within an existing constructor?

10. Assume that you are in the constructor for a class that takes no parameters. Write the line of code that invokes another constructor in your class that takes an int parameter, and give this parameter a value of 100.

Chapter 7

Advanced Object-Oriented Programming

In the previous chapter, you learned about classes and objects at a basic level. In this chapter, it is time to investigate more fully the power that object-oriented programming can bring to you. Just because this chapter is called an "advanced" look at object-oriented programming, do not think that it is optional material. The additional aspects discussed in this chapter will prove vital to your code.

Claiming Your Inheritance

In the previous chapter, you were introduced to the process of defining classes and instantiating objects based on those classes. It is now time to up the stakes a little and introduce inheritance. Inheritance is a feature of object-oriented programming that allows you to reuse existing programs. Instead of always creating a completely new class to capture a specific type, you can define a class that is based on an existing class. This allows variables and methods of the existing class to become part of the newly defined class automatically.

Inheritance basically means that you can make the nonprivate methods and variables defined in one class available to another class. You do so by defining a relationship between the classes. The class that already contains the methods and variables you want to share is called the superclass, and the new class is called the subclass. Generally, the subclass provides additional methods that are specific to its needs or that alter the behavior of existing methods in the superclass.

In the previous chapter, you defined the Lamp class, which had a couple of methods that could be used to turn it on and off. If you think about it, all lamps have this ability, right? However, there are different kinds of lamps. You might have a reading lamp by your chair, a heat lamp by your shower, and a pair of headlights on your car. All these are types of lamps, but each of them possess their own specific characteristics. The reading lamp really only emits light, the heat lamp is designed to provide heat, and the car's headlights have high-beam functionality. In this case, the lamp is a generalized concept, and the various types of lamps are specializations of that concept.

This chapter expands on this lamp concept so that it includes other electrical machines. In your home, you probably have several electrical machines—a television, a toaster, and a computer, as well as others. All these are based on the same concept of turning on and turning off, but all of them obviously have different specific functions. As you continue through this chapter, you will model various machines in your code.

Let's jump right in by defining a new class called Machine that contains the basic functionality required for all the electrical machines you will model. This is a basic class that contains methods for setting and getting a name for the machine, methods for turning on and off the machine, and a method for querying the state of the machine.

```
public class Machine
{
    private String name;
    private boolean on;

    public void setName(String name)
    {
```

```java
        this.name = name;
    }

    public String getName()
    {
        return name;
    }

    public void turnOn()
    {
        if(!on)
        {
            on = true;
            System.out.println(name + " is on.");
        }
    }

    public void turnOff()
    {
        if(on)
        {
            on = false;
            System.out.println(name + " is off.");
        }
    }

    public boolean isOn()
    {
        return on;
    }
}
```

You could instantiate this class, but logically that does not really make a lot of sense. Think about it. Do you wake up in the morning and put bread into a machine? It is more accurate to say that you put that bread into a toaster, which is a *type* of machine. In other words, you do not own anything that is simply called *machine*; instead, you own various items that are all machines by nature. This is another way of saying that all your machines share the same basic traits.

Because a Machine object is not useful by itself, why create it? Because of the power of inheritance. You can reuse this base Machine class and expand on it to model specific types of machines. To do so, you use another Java keyword, extends.

Using the *extends* Keyword

The extends keyword is the secret to inheritance in Java classes. When you declare a class to extend another class, you are creating the superclass-subclass relationship. Following is a version of the Lamp class that extends from the generic Machine class.

```
public class Lamp extends Machine
{
    public Lamp()
    {
        this("Lamp");
    }

    public Lamp(String name)
    {
        setName(name);
    }
}
```

Wait a minute! This class has nothing in it except two constructors; so what is the use? Though it may appear that no functionality is defined in this class, it is not really devoid of content. By extending Machine, you inherit the four methods defined in that class. It is as if you took the contents of Machine and pasted them right into the Lamp class. This is code reuse in action!

Also, take a look at the two constructors that are provided. The first is the default constructor that takes no parameters. It simply calls the second constructor, which takes a String parameter that should be a name describing this object. You might pass items such as "Reading Lamp" or "Kitchen Light." If you choose to use the default constructor, the simple name "Lamp" is passed. The second constructor actually invokes a method named setName(), which is defined in Machine, the superclass in this relationship. Remember that even though you did not redefine the setName() method in the Lamp class, it *is* available because you extend Machine.

As a quick proof of this concept, here is a little class that creates a Lamp object and calls some of the methods on it.

```
public class LampTest
{
    public static void main(String[] args)
    {
        Lamp lamp = new Lamp();
        lamp.turnOn();
        lamp.turnOff();
    }
}
```

When you run the `LampTest` code, you see the following output:

```
Lamp is on.
Lamp is off.
```

The value "Lamp" is stored because the `Machine` class takes care of that for us. The `Lamp` class need not maintain its own copy of the name because the super-class handles those details for us.

The relationship a subclass has with its superclass is often referred to as an "is a" relationship. This is because it is always valid to say that a `Lamp` *is a* `Machine`. However, this is only a one-way a relationship. It is not correct to say that a `Machine` is a `Lamp` because not all `Machine` objects are actually `Lamp` objects.

The Rules of Inheritance

You must follow several inheritance rules in the Java language. As long as you follow these rules, you can extend any class.

Only one class can be extended.   In object-oriented languages, there are two types of inheritance: single and multiple. With single inheritance, only one class can be extended. With multiple inheritance, one or more classes can be extended. The Java language allows only single inheritance. This is largely because multiple inheritance is fairly complex for a language to implement, and quite honestly, it is not a feature that is as useful as you might think. It can be confusing to maintain code that derives functionality from multiple classes, so sticking with a single inheritance model makes a great deal of sense. Because of this rule, you can have only one class name following the `extends` keyword.

The Java language does support multiple inheritance when you are using interfaces, a special form of class that you will learn about later in this chapter in the "Interfaces" section.

NOTE

You cannot extend a *final* class.   You can use the `final` keyword with classes, methods, and variables. In all three cases, you cannot change the corresponding entity when you use `final`. Basically, if a class is declared to be `final`, the class cannot be subclassed. An example of a `final` class is the standard `java.lang.String` class. If you try to extend `String`, you receive a compiler error. If you want to create a class that can never be altered with subclassing, make it `final` with a declaration such as `public final class MyClass`. You will learn more about `final` methods later in this chapter when I discuss method overriding.

Not all members are inherited.   When you extend a class, the only methods and variables that you inherit are nonprivate, nonfinal instance methods and variables. These inherited members always include any explicitly declared as `public` or `protected`. However, these members might also include members that have no specified access modifier provided, which is the indicator of default or "package private" access control.

There are four access modifiers, and you automatically inherit any members declared as `public` or `protected`. When you assign the `protected` modifier to a method or a variable, other methods in the class, any subclasses, and any other classes in the same package can access that variable or method. When you do not provide an access modifier, the member is considered "package private," meaning that the class and other classes in the same package can access the member. This does not necessarily mean subclasses can access a "package private" method; you can extend a class that belongs to one package and have the subclass exist in a completely different package.

Table 7.1 details the access rules for each of the four levels of access available to you.

Table 7.1   Access Modifier Rules

Modifier	Class	Package	Subclass	Anything
public	Yes	Yes	Yes	Yes
protected	Yes	Yes	Yes	No
"default"	Yes	Yes	No*	No
private	Yes	No	No	No

* Subclasses are not guaranteed access unless they are in the same package.

Members with the same name are not inherited.   If you define a variable in your subclass with the same name as a variable in your superclass, the superclass variable is hidden. This can lead to hard-to-find errors, so be careful about doing this. The JVM always uses the variable that is the "most local" to the object. If a variable x is defined in both the superclass and the subclass, a subclass instance "sees" only its own variable.

WARNING

Hiding variables can lead to some interesting bugs. You learn more about how variable inheritance works in the section "Reference Types versus Runtime Types."

Methods work effectively the same way. If you define a method with the same name and parameters in both the superclass and subclass, the subclass "sees" only its own method. However, having the same exact method signature in both the superclass and the subclass is a common practice called method overriding that is discussed in detail later in this chapter.

TIP

You can actually force access to the superclass member by using the `super` keyword, which is discussed later in this chapter in the section "The `super` Keyword."

Reference Types versus Runtime Types

Now check out the following code. In this version, the type of the lamp variable is the generic `Machine` instead of the more specific `Lamp`. What do you think happens when you run this code?

```
public class LampTest2
{
    public static void main(String[] args)
    {
        Machine lamp = new Lamp();
        lamp.turnOn();
        lamp.turnOff();
    }
}
```

What happens is exactly the same thing as what happened in the previous `LampTest` example. This may seem a bit strange to you, so let me define some useful terms. The first line of the `main()` method creates a new `Lamp` object using the `new` keyword and assigns this reference to a variable of type `Machine`. The portion to the right of the assignment operator is called the *runtime type*. The runtime type is the actual class that is instantiated when the code executes. In this case, the runtime type is a `Lamp` object. The portion of this statement to the left of the assignment operator is called the *reference type*. The reference type is a class that is either the same as the runtime type or a superclass of the runtime type. In this example, the reference type is `Machine`, which is valid because `Machine` is a superclass of the runtime type, `Lamp`. It is just like saying, "A lamp is a machine." In that statement, you are "assigning" the specific concept of a lamp to the generic concept of a machine.

By now, you are probably asking why on earth you would ever confuse the matter like this. Why not just make the reference type always the same as the runtime type? To demonstrate the power that this separation of types can bring you, let's add a new class called `Toaster`.

runtime type
The actual instance type stored in memory. The runtime type need not be the same type as the variable that refers to it; it can be a subclass of the reference type instead. The runtime type is the "real" type of an object reference.

reference type
The class name of the variable in which an object reference is stored. The reference type must be either the same as the runtime type or a superclass.

```
public class Toaster extends Machine
{
    public Toaster()
    {
        this("Toaster");
    }
```

```
public Toaster(String name)
{
    setName(name);
}
}
```

Like the Lamp class, the Toaster class defines only two constructors, opting to simply inherit all its functionality from the superclass. Because Toaster also extends Machine, it can pick up the same usage of reference type and runtime type.

All right, now for the payoff. The AllMachines code that you will see shortly defines an array that is meant to hold all the machines owned by a person. This would include anything that could be considered a machine. For our purposes, only two specific machines are defined, but that is enough to work with.

Think about what you learned about arrays earlier in this book. An array must always contain elements of the *same* type. I think it is fair to say that a Lamp is not a Toaster, so initially it would seem that there is no way to store both types of objects in the same array. However, because both Lamp and Toaster inherit from the Machine class, there is a way to store them after all. The array can only hold elements that share the same *reference* type; the *runtime* type does not have to be the same. This is just like what happens when you have an array of int primitives, if you think about it. Although you are guaranteeing that such arrays can hold only legal int values, those values certainly do not all have to be the same. For arrays of objects, the reference type stored in an array simply dictates the base type of each element; the element values (their runtime type) can be different.

The following code is an example of a generic array of Machine elements that actually holds two Lamp objects and one Toaster object. Once the array is populated, each element is turned on and off to show you that everything is working just as you would expect.

```
public class AllMachines
{
    public static void main(String[] args)
    {
        Machine [] machs = new Machine[3];
        Machine machOne = new Lamp("Reading lamp");
        Machine machTwo = new Toaster("4-slice Toaster");
        Machine machThree = new Lamp("Kitchen light");
        machs[0] = machOne;
        machs[1] = machTwo;
        machs[2] = machThree;

        for(int i = 0; i < machs.length; i++)
```

```
      {
          machs[i].turnOn();
          machs[i].turnOff();
      }
    }
  }
```

As far as the machs array is concerned, everything that it holds is of type Machine. It really does not care if the element is a Lamp or a Toaster, only that both classes are extensions of the base Machine class. However, all three objects still encapsulate their own state, so the output from this code is as follows:

```
Reading lamp is on.
Reading lamp is off.
4-slice Toaster is on.
4-slice Toaster is off.
Kitchen light is on.
Kitchen light is off.
```

What is happening here is something called *virtual method invocation*. This complex-sounding term really means that the JVM decides which specific version of a method to call at runtime. This is essential because of the difference between a reference type and a runtime type. The JVM always invokes the instance method of the runtime type, no matter the actual reference type. Thus, in the previous example, the turnOff() method is invoked on the runtime type of each element in the array, not on the Machine class itself.

WARNING

Only instance methods are involved with virtual method invocation. Any static methods you create are always bound to the reference type. Because static methods are class methods, this is logical.

Variables Are Bound to the Reference Type

Although methods can take advantage of virtual method invocation, variables cannot. Variables are always bound to the reference type. This is important to understand if you provide the same variable name in both a superclass and a subclass.

The best way to see what I mean is to look at a short example. It is not typical to define public variables, but in this case, it should hammer the point home nicely. Both of following two classes define a String variable named s. When you execute the subclass's main() method, though, you see the value of the String in the printed superclass printed, not in the subclass, as you might expect.

```
public class SuperVariableDemo
{
```

virtual method invocation
The JVM uses this process to ensure that the method definition closest to the runtime type is called. This is sometimes referred to as "late binding" because the instance methods are not linked at compile time. Instead, a virtual method table is created in memory for each object instance, and the JVM selects the appropriate version of a method at runtime.

```
        public String str = "Superclass";
    }

    public class SubVariableDemo extends SuperVariableDemo
    {
        public String str = "Subclass";

        public static void main(String[] args)
        {
            SuperVariableDemo sd = new SubVariableDemo();
            System.out.println(sd.str);
        }
    }
}
```

The output will always be Superclass even though the runtime type is SubVariableDemo. Remember that instance methods are always bound to the runtime type, and instance variables are always bound to the reference type. If you commit this to memory right now, you will avoid some strange and pesky bugs in the future!

NOTE   **Of course, if the reference type in the previous example was** SubVariableDemo, Subclass **would have been printed.** Superclass **was printed only because the reference type was a superclass.**

Expanding the Subclasses

So far, you have simply inherited all the code you needed in the two subclasses, Lamp and Toaster. However, it is much more common for subclasses to provide functionality beyond the basic methods captured in the superclass. For example, a toaster does not just turn on and off; it also heats up, cools down, and has a temperature. You can capture these toaster-specific characteristics by expanding the Toaster class as shown in the following new Toaster2 class.

```
    public class Toaster2 extends Machine
    {
        private int temp;
        private int maxTemp = 280;
        private int minTemp = 70;

        public Toaster2()
        {
            this("Toaster");
```

```java
    }

    public Toaster2(String name)
    {
        this(name, 70, 280);
    }

    public Toaster2(String name, int minTemp, int maxTemp)
    {
        setName(name);
        this.minTemp = minTemp;
        this.maxTemp = maxTemp;
        this.temp = this.minTemp;
    }

    public void heatUp()
    {
        System.out.println(getName() + " is heating up.");
        while(temp != maxTemp && isOn())
        {
            System.out.println(getName() + " is now " +
                            temp + " degrees.");
            temp += 35;
        }
        System.out.println(getName() + " heated to " +
                            temp + " degrees.");
    }

    public void coolDown()
    {
        System.out.println(getName() + " is cooling down.");
        while(temp != minTemp)
        {
            System.out.println(getName() + " is now " +
                            temp + " degrees.");
            temp -= 35;
        }
        System.out.println(getName() + " cooled to " +
                            temp + " degrees.");
    }
}
```

A third constructor is added to this class that accepts a minimum and maximum temperature. These variables are stored in each object so that you can have various temperature ranges if you desire. This adds to the flexibility of the Toaster2 class and also demonstrates how a subclass can maintain state beyond what is stored in the superclass.

This class inherits the turnOn() and turnOff() methods from the Machine class, but it then adds two methods of its own. The heatUp() method adds 35 degrees to the temperature until it reaches the maximum temperature. The coolDown() method reduces the temperature by 35 degrees until it reaches the minimum temperature, whether the toaster is on or off.

NOTE

A more realistic model of a toaster would probably not hardcode the temperature increment of 35. It would be better to capture this as a variable as well. This was not done in this example to keep the example short.

The following code uses a Toaster2 object by calling methods of the superclass as well as those defined inside the Toaster2 class itself.

```
public class Toaster2Test
{
    public static void main(String[] args)
    {
        Toaster2 t = new Toaster2();
        t.turnOn(); // defined in Machine
        t.heatUp(); // defined in Toaster2
        t.coolDown(); // defined in Toaster2
        t.turnOff(); // defined in Machine
    }
}
```

When you run this code, you see the following output:

```
Toaster is on.
Toaster is heating up.
Toaster is now 70 degrees.
Toaster is now 105 degrees.
Toaster is now 140 degrees.
Toaster is now 175 degrees.
Toaster is now 210 degrees.
Toaster is now 245 degrees.
Toaster heated to 280 degrees.
Toaster is cooling down.
Toaster is now 280 degrees.
```

```
Toaster is now 245 degrees.
Toaster is now 210 degrees.
Toaster is now 175 degrees.
Toaster is now 140 degrees.
Toaster is now 105 degrees.
Toaster cooled to 70 degrees.
Toaster is off.
```

Once the `Toaster2` object is created, the `turnOn()` method is invoked, and then the `heatUp()` method is called. This is followed by the `coolDown()` method, and finally the toaster is turned off via the `turnOff()` method.

The calls to `turnOn()` and `turnOff()` are possible because they are defined in the `Machine` superclass. The other two method invocations are possible only because they are defined in the `Toaster2` class itself. The result is that the `Toaster2` class is more detailed than the `Machine` superclass. This makes sense because the concept of a "toaster" is much more detailed than the concept of a "machine."

The Class Hierarchy

When you are inheriting from classes, it is a good idea to picture the resulting relationships in a treelike hierarchy. In this chapter, you have already created some classes, including `Machine`, `Lamp`, and `Toaster2`. These classes form a hierarchy, as shown here:

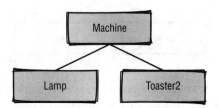

The diagram clearly shows that `Lamp` and `Toaster2` are lower in the hierarchy than the `Machine` class. This is a visual representation of the superclass-subclass relationship. By looking at this diagram, you can draw some specific conclusions such as the following, even if you could not see the source code itself.

- A `Lamp` is always a `Machine`.
- A `Toaster2` is always a `Machine`.
- A `Machine` is *not* a `Lamp` or a `Toaster2`.
- A `Lamp` is *not* a `Toaster2` (thank goodness!).

There is no relationship between the `Lamp` and `Toaster2` classes except that they are siblings in the hierarchy. Siblings in a hierarchy always share a common superclass, as shown in this diagram. When you have a large collection of classes defined, it is often useful to create a diagram such as this so that you can readily identify superclasses and subclasses.

Up to now, your subclasses have had only a single class above them in the hierarchy. However, this is not an enforced limitation. You can extend from a class that extends from another and so on. The result is a larger hierarchy.

WARNING

The more superclasses you have, the more memory you will need when you instantiate your object. This is because the instance members of every class above yours in a hierarchy must be initialized by the JVM. The amount of memory required is not typically a problem, but keep this in mind when you create class hierarchies.

The *Object* Class

The previous hierarchy diagram is not really complete, however. Another class is involved here that you did not define yourself—the java.lang.Object class. Every class eventually extends the Object class; Object is the ultimate class in every object hierarchy. Here is a more complete view of the diagram.

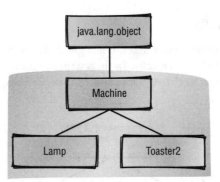

You did not extend the Object class when you defined Machine, so how can it be the superclass of Machine? Well, the truth is that *all* classes you define directly extend Object unless you explicitly provide your own extends clause (as you did for both Lamp and Toaster2). The *only* class you will ever see in the Java language that does not extend from another class is the ultimate class, Object.

So the following two class declarations are equivalent:

```
public class Machine
public class Machine extends Object
```

Because the Object class is always part of your class hierarchy, you can always use Object as a reference type. For instance, you can create a generic array that holds any type of object with the following code.

```
Object [] anyObjects = new Object[10];
```

The anyObjects array can hold any combination of objects you choose because *every* object descends from the Object class. The only elements that you cannot add to this array are primitive types.

Remember that classes called wrapper classes map to each of the primitive types. If you want to store a primitive int in the anyObjects array, you can simply use the Integer class. Chapter 9, "Common Java API Classes," shows examples of how to use these wrapper classes.

TIP

You will learn more about the Object class and how it can be used later in this chapter when you learn about method overriding.

The Reference Type Rule for Methods

A few pages ago, you learned that the reference type of an object does not have to be the same as the runtime type. The reference type can be the same as the runtime class, or it can be a superclass. Although this ability to refer to an object via the superclass can be useful, I have left out an important detail until now that imposes limits on the methods you can directly invoke. The rule is that if you try to call a method via an object reference, that method must be defined in the class of the reference type to begin with. You simply cannot directly call a method solely defined in a subclass if you reference that object with the superclass type.

In the Toaster2 class, four methods are defined only in the subclass. Thus, if you try to do the following, what will happen?

```
Machine mach = new Toaster2();
mach.turnOn();
mach.heatUp();
```

If you said the second method call will not work, you are right. This code would not even compile because the compiler sees that no heatUp() method is defined in the Machine class. It does not matter that the method exists in the subclass because the reference type is not Toaster2. The first method call to turnOn() is fine, though, because that method is defined in the Machine class.

If you look back at the AllMachines code in which an array of Machine objects was created, you will quickly conclude that you are severely limited in the methods that you can call. Although it is possible to call turnOn() on both a Lamp and Toaster2 object, it would be impossible to actually use the Toaster2 object fully.

Obviously, there has to be a way to "talk" to the runtime type directly even if it is originally referenced by a superclass. This is accomplished with the instanceof operator and a process called object casting, which we will look at in the next section.

The *instanceof* Operator and Object Casting

Okay, it is time once again to introduce a new operator (please hold your applause). The instanceof operator is a special operator that you can use only with objects. It is conceptually similar to the == operator that you might use to check the value of an int or float, but instead of checking for a specific value, it checks for a specific runtime type. By using this operator, you can verify the runtime type of an object, no matter what the reference type happens to be.

The following code demonstrates how you can use the instanceof operator with the Lamp and Toaster2 class. Once again, an array is created that holds Machine types, but then inside the for loop, a check is made using an if statement to determine the runtime type of each object in the array. For now, a simple printout shows you which runtime type was found.

```java
public class InstanceChecker
{
    public static void main(String[] args)
    {
        Machine [] machs = new Machine[4];
        machs[0] = new Lamp();
        machs[1] = new Toaster2();
        machs[2] = new Toaster2();
        machs[3] = new Lamp();

        for(int i = 0; i < machs.length; i++)
        {
            System.out.print("Element " + i + " is a ");
            if(machs[i] instanceof Lamp)
            {
                System.out.println("Lamp object.");
            }
            else if(machs[i] instanceof Toaster2)
            {
                System.out.println("Toaster2 object.");
            }
        }
    }
}
```

Once the code creates the array and populates it with the four objects, the for loop processes each element. The instanceof expressions return either true or false, so they are commonly found as the conditions of an if statement. This code queries each element for its runtime type and prints an appropriate message to tell you what type is found. You will see the following output if you run this code:

```
Element 0 is a Lamp object.
Element 1 is a Toaster2 object.
Element 2 is a Toaster2 object.
Element 3 is a Lamp object.
```

Object Casting

Earlier in this book, you learned how to cast primitive types. For example, to cast a float variable named x to an int, you wrote code such as the following:

```
int y = (int)x;
```

This code narrows the floating-point number to a whole integer, effectively chopping off everything after the decimal point. You always have to use the cast operator for primitives if you are downcasting.

You can also perform casting on objects in a similar fashion. The concept is the same. If you have a reference to a Machine but the runtime type is actually Toaster2, you can use casting to gain access to the Toaster2-specific methods. Just like the situation with primitive casting, you must perform a cast if you are narrowing from a superclass to a subclass. You do not ever have to explicitly cast if you are widening from a subclass to a superclass.

The following code shows you what I mean. Only the first statement actually works without generating an error.

```
Machine m = new Toaster2(); // upcasting, works fine
Toaster2 t = new Machine(); // downcasting, fails
```

The first line works fine because you are upcasting from a Toaster2 to the Machine superclass. This works because all Toaster2 objects are Machine objects as well. However, the second line fails because you are trying to shove a Machine object into a Toaster2 reference. This is not possible because not all Machine objects are Toaster2 objects.

The rule is that you can always assign a subclass object to a superclass reference, but you cannot do the opposite unless you perform an explicit cast.

The syntax for casting objects is the same as for casting primitives. You simply put the reference type inside the parentheses and place this right before the object you want to cast. The following revised code now works in both cases.

```
Machine m = new Toaster2(); // upcasting, works fine
Toaster2 t = (Toaster2)m; // casting makes this work now
```

You have to be careful when you cast objects like this, however. The compiler cannot catch all possible errors, so your code may compile fine but generate an exception at runtime. If you try to cast an object and it is not actually that type, you get a `ClassCastException` at runtime.

The compiler cannot always trap potential `ClassCastExceptions` because it might be *possible* that the object is the type you are trying to cast it to; there is often no way for the compiler to be sure. For example, trying to cast a `Machine` to a `String` causes a compiler error because it is impossible for `Machine` to be a subclass of `String`; the `String` class is a `final` class and cannot be extended. However, if you try to cast a `Machine` reference to a `Toaster2` reference, it is possible for it to work. This is because there is an inheritance relationship between the two classes; `Toaster2` is a subclass of `Machine`. The compiler has no choice but to let the cast attempt go and leave it up to the JVM to report any runtime casting errors.

When you are performing object casting, the best practice is to incorporate the `instanceof` operator into your code. First, use `instanceof` to be sure that the target object is the type you expect; only then should you perform the cast. This ensures that you are never trying to cast an object illegally, and you can be sure to avoid those pesky runtime errors.

The following code is a full example of casting that uses the `instanceof` operator to ensure that only legal casting is attempted.

```java
public class Casting
{
    public static void main(String[] args)
    {
        Machine [] machs = new Machine[4];
        machs[0] = new Lamp();
        machs[1] = new Toaster2();
        machs[2] = new Lamp();
        machs[3] = new Toaster2();

        for(int i = 0; i < machs.length; i++)
        {
            machs[i].turnOn();

            if(machs[i] instanceof Toaster2)
            {
                Toaster2 t = (Toaster2)machs[i];
                t.heatUp();
                t.coolDown();
            }
```

```
            machs[i].turnOff();
        }
    }
}
```

The for loop turns on any Machine element it finds, but then it checks to see if the element is actually a Toaster2 object. If it is, an object cast is performed to convert the generic Machine into a more specific Toaster2 reference. This allows you to successfully invoke the heatUp() and coolDown() methods because you are now working with the correct object reference. Once this section of code completes, the Machine element (whether it is a Lamp or Toaster2) is turned off.

The output from running this code is not given here because it is fairly long. Go ahead and run the code and be sure that you understand the output you see.

Introducing Polymorphism

Polymorphism literally means "being able to assume different forms." When you are talking about object-oriented programming, polymorphism is the ability to process objects in a hierarchy differently depending on their actual class type. You have already seen a bit of polymorphism at work between the Machine, Lamp, and Toaster2 classes. When you create an array of Machine elements and then execute methods on each of those elements, polymorphism is the feature that allows the variation of runtime types from the base reference type.

Polymorphism is an important and powerful concept in object-oriented programming. Because of polymorphism, you can easily create extensible classes. You can look at an object as a Machine (one form) or a Toaster2 (another form).

When you extend a class, you inherit a group of methods automatically. This allows you to reuse code defined in a single class instead of having to constantly copy and paste. However, two powerful polymorphic concepts are often useful when you define a class: method overloading and method overriding.

polymorphism
The ability to have many forms of the same object. An object can always be referred to by its own class type or any of its superclasses. This allows the reference type and the runtime type to be separated. The instance methods of a runtime type that are also defined in the reference type will always be invoked because of virtual method invocation.

Method Overloading

In the Java language, a method is uniquely identified by its name and a list of parameters. Therefore, it is perfectly legal to define two methods with the exact same name, but with different parameters. *Method overloading* allows you to reuse the same method name repeatedly, but with varying parameters and results.

Method overloading is actually not limited to use with inheritance. You can overload methods in the same class, and you can overload methods defined in a superclass. You have been calling an overloaded method since the early chapters of this book. The println() method you call via the *System.out* variable is an overloaded method. Ten versions of this method are defined, each with a different parameter type. There is a println() method for six primitive types (char,

method overloading
A convenience in object-oriented programming that allows multiple methods with the same name to exist. These methods must have different parameter lists and might also have different return types. It is not enough to only have variance in return type, however; the parameter lists must be different for a method to be overloaded.

int, long, float, double, and boolean), one for a char [], one for a String, one for generic objects, and one that takes no parameters at all. Every version of the println() method prints the parameter that you pass to it and adds a carriage return to the end. The method always works the same, but it handles the different parameters uniquely.

The alternative to this approach is to define a method for each possible type. A printString(), printInt(), and printChar() method can be defined. Do you see the benefit of method overloading now? Without it, you would have to memorize all those methods to print data. However, because overloading does exist, you do not have to know the specific type that you are passing; you can just call println() and pass anything you wish, and some output will appear.

——— **WARNING** ——— **For the versions of this method that print generic objects, the output is the encoded reference itself. This is not particularly useful, but you will learn how to handle this problem when I discuss the java.lang.Object class in detail in the next section, "Method Overriding."**

You will find method overloading useful when you want to create a collection of methods that perform essentially the same function, but work under varying conditions. Those conditions are typically embodied in the parameters passed to each version of the method. The following class has three methods defined; all of them are overloaded versions of one another.

```java
public class Overloaded
{
    public void sayHello()
    {
        System.out.println("Hello");
    }

    public void sayHello(String name)
    {
        System.out.println("Hello " + name);
    }

    public void sayHello(String name, int count)
    {
        for(int i = 0; i < count; i++)
        {
            sayHello(name);
        }
    }
}
```

All three methods have the same name, sayHello(), but each of them takes a different set of parameters. This lets you call any one of them and still get some output. If you call the first one with no parameters, a simple "Hello" message prints. If you call the second version, passing your name, a friendlier greeting prints that includes your name. Calling the third method and passing your name and an integer greets you as many times as you indicated. This third method actually calls the second version of the method instead of redefining that logic. This is yet another example of reusing existing logic instead of always redefining it.

The three methods effectively do the same thing (issue a greeting), but all of them work with different parameters. Here are the important facts concerning overloaded methods.

♦ When you overload a method, the name must be exactly the same, and the parameter list must be different. There is no escaping this rule.

♦ Although you can have a different return type, it is not enough to *only* have a different return type.

♦ Keep in mind that you can overload methods defined in the same class or any superclass.

♦ A final method can be overloaded.

♦ A static method can be overloaded.

Method Overriding

Method overriding is used only between a subclass and a superclass. You have already learned that when you extend a class, you inherit the nonprivate methods defined in that class. It is often useful to alter the behavior of these inherited methods to suit the needs of your subclass, however. Being able to modify the behavior of an inherited method is the purpose of method overriding.

As you learned earlier, the JVM uses a process called virtual method invocation, which makes method overriding possible. Virtual method invocation guarantees that the version of an instance method closest to the runtime type in the hierarchy is invoked. In other words, if a method is never overridden, the original version executes because it is inherited. If it is overridden in a superclass, that version is inherited and executed. If it is overridden in the subclass, that version is invoked. Don't forget that virtual method invocation guarantees that the instance method of the runtime type executes, no matter the reference type.

Overloading is another form of polymorphism, but there are some major differences between this process and method overloading.

♦ An overridden method must have exactly the same name, parameter list, and return type as the method in the superclass. If the parameter list differs, you are performing method overloading, not method overriding.

method overriding
An object-oriented concept that allows a method in a superclass to be redefined completely in a subclass. The return type, name, and parameter list must be exactly the same in the two classes for overriding to work. If the parameter list is different, you are overloading the method, not overriding it. If the return type is the only thing different, you will get a compiler error. Overriding allows polymorphism to exist in your classes because you can provide refined functionality for a method throughout an object hierarchy.

- Because the name and parameter list must be the same, a class can have only one version of an overridden method; it is not legal to define a method with the same name and parameter list in the same class definition.

- In essence, an overridden method replaces the method defined in a superclass. If you have a method named go() in your superclass and redefine this method in a subclass, any calls to go() on an object of the subclass type execute the subclass's method only.

- You can override any inherited method from any of the classes above it in the hierarchy, all the way up to Object.

- An overridden method cannot have more restricted accessibility than the method defined in the superclass. In other words, a public method in the superclass cannot be redefined as protected in the subclass. However, you can make a method less restrictive if you desire.

- You can override only instance methods that you inherit. Because you never inherit private methods, they cannot be overridden.

- A final method cannot be overridden even though it is inherited.

Overriding Methods in *Object*

referential equality

If two object variables contain the exact same reference (and thus point to the same object in memory), they are considered to have referential equality. You can always test references for equality by using the == operator.

To demonstrate how method overriding works, let's revisit the Object class that you learned about earlier in this chapter. You will often use two key methods in this class in your own code: public boolean equals(Object o) and public String toString().

> *public boolean equals(Object o)*   To check the value of a primitive type, you use the equivalency operator (==); the result will be either true or false. Often it is also necessary for you to determine if two object references are equivalent. You can do this in two ways, but there is an important difference between the two approaches.

The first way to test object equivalency is with the same operator that you use for primitive types. You use the == operator to test for *referential equality*. (You learned how this operator works back in Chapter 3, "Keywords and Operators.") If two references point to the same object in memory, they have referential equality.

logical equality

The equals() method is defined in the Object class and can therefore be overridden in any subclass. Overridden versions of this method can return true to indicate that two objects are logically the same even if they are not physically the same object reference. For example, the two String objects "Hello" and "Hello" are logically equivalent, but might not actually have the same reference in memory.

The second way to test object equivalency is to use the equals() method inherited from the Object class. This method takes a single parameter of type Object. The Object parameter can be checked against the object being called. By default, this method works exactly the same way as the == operator. However, this is a full-blown method and can therefore be overridden in your own classes. This allows you to alter what equivalency means for your own objects. As a result, the equals() method can be overridden to test for *logical equality*. For example, the Integer class overrides this method to return true if two Integer objects contain exactly the same primitive value, even if they are not physically the same object in memory.

public String toString()   The toString() method is extremely useful for controlling what is output when an object is passed to the System.out .println() method. By default, the output is rather strange looking. This is actually the reference code used by the JVM. It would be much nicer if you could output something meaningful to the user of your code.

The Object **class has more than just these two methods, but these are so commonly overridden that this section concentrates on these two.**   *NOTE*

Here is a class named Record that contains some basic information about an individual. It contains variables for the first name, the last name, and the account number. Perhaps a utility company would use Record objects to maintain their accounts.

```
public class Record
{
    private String first;
    private String last;
    private String acctNum;

    public Record(String first, String last, String acctNum)
    {
        this.first = first;
        this.last = last;
        this.acctNum = acctNum;
    }

    public String getName()
    {
        return first + " " + last;
    }

    public String getAcctNum()
    {
        return acctNum;
    }

    public boolean equals(Object o)
    {
```

```
        if(o instanceof Record)
        {
            Record r = (Record)o;
            return getName().equals(r.getName()) &&
acctNum.equals(r.getAcctNum());
        }

    return false;
    }

    public String toString()
    {
        String s =  "Account: " + acctNum + "\n" + getName();
        return s;
    }
}
```

The "\n" is a special code that allows you to manually insert a carriage return within a String.

This basic class accepts three parameters in the constructor and provides two methods for reading this information. The remaining two methods are the overridden methods from the Object class.

First, the equals() method checks to see if the parameter is in fact a Record object. If it is, you cast the parameter to a Record so the accessor methods can be called. If all three variables match exactly, the two objects are considered equal. This is logical equality, not referential equality. In this case, you provide the definition of what equality means for the Record object.

Notice that the logic of the equals() method actually involves calling the equals() method defined in the String class for the name and account number. The String class also overrides the equals() method and provides logic to determine if two String objects have exactly the same characters in the same order and with the same case. If they do, then the two String objects are considered equal.

Second, you override the toString() method to allow a useful output for the System.out.println() method. You then create a String that includes the account number and the name, formatted nicely for readability.

To see how these two overridden methods can be used, execute the following RecordChecker class. This class expects you to pass in a first name, a last name, and an account number as command-line arguments. When you do, these values are wrapped into a new Record object. An array of Record objects is created that holds three unique instances, and then a check is made to see if the arguments that you passed and any of the array elements match; this is done when you call the equals() method. If there is a match, the matched record is printed, which automatically invokes the toString() method.

```
public class RecordChecker
{
    public static void main(String[] args)
    {
        if(args.length != 3)
        {
            System.err.println
                ("Usage: java Record <first> <last>
<acctnum");
                System.exit(1);
        }

        Record one = new Record("Ella", "Mentary", "12345");
        Record two = new Record("Sue", "Nami", "94586");
        Record three = new Record("Frank", "Enstein",
"48735");
        Record [] recs = {one, two, three};
        Record rec = new Record(args[0], args[1], args[2]);

        boolean matched = false;
        for(int i = 0; i < recs.length; i++)
        {
            if(rec.equals(recs[i]))
            {
                matched = true;
                System.out.println("Found a match:");
                System.out.println(recs[i]);
            }
        }

        if(!matched)
        {
            System.out.println("No matches found.");
        }
    }
}
```

If you execute this code, you will see the corresponding output:

```
java RecordChecker Ella Mentary 12345
Found a match:
Account: 12345
Ella Mentary
```

The *super* Keyword

You use the super keyword when you want to access nonprivate members of a superclass. You can use it much like the this keyword that you were introduced to in Chapter 6, "Introduction to Object-Oriented Programming," but super is meant to represent an object of your superclass type. You use super both to directly access members and to perform chaining within constructors.

By this point, you know that you can inherit nonprivate methods of a superclass and invoke them as if they were defined in the subclass. Now you have also learned how to override these methods to fully redefine their functionality. However, a third option provides you with the ability to augment inherited methods. Sometimes you want to allow a superclass's method to execute and then perform some additional functionality. At other times, you might want to perform additional processing before you even invoke the superclass's method. However, if you override a method, the overridden method is effectively hidden. This is where super comes into play.

You will find a more detailed example of using super in the next section when you learn about overriding constructors, but the following example shows you the basics and uses two simple classes. The first class, SuperPrinter, prints the sum of two variables via the printOut() method. The second class is a subclass of SuperPrinter named, appropriately, SubPrinter, that overrides the printOut() method. The overridden method first invokes the parent method and then prints the results of multiplying the two input numbers.

```java
public class SuperPrinter
{
    public void printOut(int x, int y)
    {
        System.out.println("x + y = " + (x + y));
    }
}

public class SubPrinter extends SuperPrinter
{
    public void printOut(int x, int y)
    {
```

```
        super.printOut(x, y);
        System.out.println("x * y = " + x * y);
    }
}
```

The first line of the subclass's `printOut()` method calls the superclass's `printOut()` method, and the sum of the two numbers prints. It then adds an extra step that prints the results of multiplying the same two numbers. You can see this work with the following code.

```
public class PrintTest
{
    public static void main(String[] args)
    {
        SubPrinter sub = new SubPrinter();
        sub.printOut(10, 20);
    }
}
```

When you execute the `PrintTest` code, you see the following two lines of output.

```
x + y = 30
x * y = 200
```

You can invoke a parent instance method using **super** any time you want. You might perform a conditional check, for example, and if the condition is **true**, you invoke the parent method. If the condition is **false**, you can ignore the parent method logic altogether. Using **super** like this allows you to add to the logic of an existing method and create polymorphic classes.

"Overriding" Constructors

When you learned about the **this** keyword, you learned how to chain your constructors. Whenever the first line of a constructor is **this()**, the corresponding constructor in the *same* class is invoked. The constructor to invoke is determined by parameters passed to the **this()** invocation.

Often you will want to control the initialization of a superclass as well. You can do so by using **super()** in a similar fashion to using **this()**. Whenever **super()** is the first line of a constructor, it calls the corresponding constructor with the same parameters in the superclass. This allows you to chain constructors up the hierarchy as well.

However, constructors are a special form of method. One important difference between a constructor and a normal method is that constructors are never inherited. Thus, you cannot truly override them. If your superclass defines a constructor that takes a `String` but the subclass does not, it is impossible to create an instance of the subclass by passing a `String`. This is demonstrated here:

```java
public class SuperClass
{

    public SuperClass(String s)
    {
        System.out.println("Superclass: " + s);
    }
}


public class SubClass extends SuperClass
{
    public SubClass()
    {
        // do something
    }
}
```

Given these two classes, the following statement would cause a compiler error:

```java
SubClass sc = new SubClass("Hello");
```

This fails because there is no constructor that takes a `String` in `SubClass`. Remember, *constructors are never inherited.*

So what do you do? First, you need to provide a second constructor that takes a `String` in `SubClass`, and then you need to call the corresponding constructor in `SuperClass` by using the `super()` syntax. Here is the correct version of `SubClass`:

```java
public class SubClass
{
    public SubClass()
    {
        this("Default");
    }

    public SubClass(String s)
    {
        super(s);
        System.out.println("Subclass: " + s);
    }
}
```

The following code snippet instantiates a SubClass object

```
SubClass sc = new SubClass("Hello");
```

and then shows you this output:

```
Superclass: Hello
Subclass: Hello
```

As with the `this()` syntax, you must make the `super()` call the first line in your constructor if you provide it at all. With constructor chaining, you can chain several constructors within the same class by using `this()` and then a final constructor that you use to call `super()` with whatever parameters you need.

TIP

Because you are not truly overriding constructors, the parameters list does not have to be the same between the subclass and superclass. The parameters that you pass with the super() invocation determine which parent constructor to invoke. In a sense, this is like overloading a constructor.

The "Automatic" Constructor

Before you see a more elaborate example of using `super` both with constructors and regular instance methods, let me tell you a tiny secret. In the last chapter, you learned about the default constructor, a constructor that takes no parameters. The truth is that if you do not provide any constructors, the compiler sticks one in for you. That's right, no matter what you do, at least one constructor will be in every class you define.

This automatic constructor looks like this:

```
public ClassName()
{
    super();
}
```

Note that this default constructor is added to your code automatically if you do not provide your own constructors. If you provide even one constructor—even if it takes parameters—the compiler does not add a default constructor.

NOTE

If the compiler adds a default constructor, it alters only the `.class` file. The source code does not change.

Wait, I have yet another secret for you! The first line of every constructor *must* call another constructor. If you do not explicitly call another constructor with `this()` or `super()`, he compiler always makes `super()` with no parameters the first line of a constructor. In other words, the following two constructors produce the exact same class files.

```
public ClassName()
{
    System.out.println("Hello!");
}

public ClassName()
{
    super();
    System.out.println("Hello!");
}
```

This happens because it is essential that your superclass be initialized before your subclass. Think about yourself, for instance. You could not exist without your parents existing first. Your parents could not exist without their parents existing first. This same logic applies to objects in the Java language. Eventually, of course, all objects spawn from the ultimate `Object` class that resides at the top of the hierarchy.

TIP

Usually, be sure that your class contains a default constructor. This allows a class to be instantiated in a standard fashion. You are not required to provide such a constructor, but it is not a bad habit to acquire.

The Return of the Toaster

For a more complete example of both method and constructor overriding, let's take a look at the `Toaster2` class once again. When you slip bread into a toaster and hit the switch to turn it on, the heating process begins immediately. You do not turn on the toaster and then flip some switch to begin the heating. Therefore, it would make a lot more sense if you captured that functionality in your software model of a toaster as well.

A subclass of `Toaster2` called `MyToaster` is shown in the following code. To alter the basic functionality provided by the `Machine` class, the two methods `turnOn()` and `turnOff()` are overridden in this version. Also notice that constructor chaining is included in this class between the two classes so that the superclass can maintain the correct values.

```
public class MyToaster extends Toaster2
{
    public MyToaster()
    {
        this("Toaster");
```

```
        }

        public MyToaster(String name)
        {
            super(name);
        }

        public void turnOn()
        {
            super.turnOn();
            heatUp();
        }

        public void turnOff()
        {
            super.turnOff();
            coolDown();
        }
    }
```

The second constructor is always called, and it simply passes the `String`
parameter to the superclass. This allows the `Toaster2` class to maintain this
state for us. You do not need to store the `name` parameter in a new instance variable inside `MyToaster`.

The `MyToaster` class inherits all the methods that it needs, but it overrides the
`turnOn()` and `turnOff()` methods to include extra functionality. When you call
the `turnOn()` method, first the original `turnOn()` method defined in `Toaster2`
is invoked. You then call the `heatUp()` method inherited from `Toaster2`. Similarly, in the `turnOff()` method, you invoke the overridden `turnOff()` method
and then call `coolDown()`.

The following class lets you test the `MyToaster` class. Notice that the output
from executing this class is the same as the original example that used `Toaster2`.
This should not surprise you because you have not changed any of the original
method logic, only how and when those methods are invoked. Because the output is exactly the same, I have not repeated it here.

```
    public class MyToasterTest
    {
        public static void main(String[] args)
        {
            MyToaster mt = new MyToaster();
            mt.turnOn();
```

```
        mt.turnOff();
    }
}
```

This model is much closer to a real-world toaster. Instead of your having to heat it up and cool it down explicitly, the MyToaster class encapsulates those details. Polymorphism is also evident with the turnOn() and turnOff() methods. These methods effectively do the same thing as any Machine (which is still one of our superclasses in the hierarchy, remember), but now they include specific functionality for a toaster.

Abstract Classes and Methods

If you really think about it, the Machine class can never really do anything useful in the turnOn() and turnOff() methods. Sure, all the electrical machines you own do turn on and off, but not all machines do this in the same way. It would be fair to say that all machines must be able to turn on and off, but they do not need to follow a specific routine to do so. For instance, a lamp brightens and dims a bulb, a toaster heats and cools its elements, a car starts and stops its engine, and so on. These examples are all semantically the same procedure, though the specific steps are certainly different. So it would make more sense for the Machine class to ensure that all its subclasses provide this functionality but allow each subclass to define the implementation logic on its own.

Luckily, this is fairly simple. You will need to use a new keyword, the modifier abstract. You can make both classes and methods abstract. An abstract method provides only the method signature and can never have a body. An abstract class is simply a class that contains one or more abstract methods. If you make a method abstract, you are *forcing* any subclasses to override that method before they can be instantiated.

The following is a rewritten version of the Machine class called AbstractMachine. The same five methods are defined as before, but this time the turnOn() and turnOff() methods are declared abstract. Also, this version uses a new method, setOn(), that subclasses will call to change the state as needed. Because this class now contains abstract methods, the AbstractMachine class itself must also be declared as abstract.

```
public abstract class AbstractMachine
{
    private String name;
    private boolean on;

    public void setName(String name)
    {
```

```
            this.name = name;
    }

    public String getName()
    {
        return name;
    }

    public abstract void turnOn();
    public abstract void turnOff();

    public void setOn(boolean on)
    {
        this.on = on;
    }

    public boolean isOn()
    {
        return on;
    }
}
```

As you can see, the syntax for an abstract method should provide the access modifier, the abstract modifier, the return type, the method name, the parameter list, and then a semicolon. The concept is that you define the method signature, but you do not provide any logic at this time. The subclasses that must override the abstract method are responsible for the appropriate logic. In a sense, an abstract method is the exact opposite of a final method. You can *never* override a final method, but you *must* override an abstract method.

Also notice that an abstract class can contain fully defined methods as well. These methods are inherited as normal, but they do not have to be overridden (though they still can be, of course). This lets you provide some standard functionality while still forcing subclasses to provide specific logic for any abstract methods.

It might help your understanding to contrast two types of classes. A normal class that provides no abstract methods can be called a concrete class. A class that provides one or more abstract methods is an abstract class. A concrete class can be instantiated; an abstract class cannot. Therefore, a subclass is responsible for overriding any abstract methods to become a full-fledged, concrete class.

Technically, an abstract class does not have to contain any abstract methods. This is rather unusual, but in such a case, the class simply cannot be instantiated.

NOTE

Here is a new version of the Lamp class called MyLamp. Because this class extends from AbstractMachine, it must provide both the turnOn() and turnOff() methods.

```java
public class MyLamp extends AbstractMachine
{
    public MyLamp()
    {
        this("Lamp");
    }

    public MyLamp(String name)
    {
        setName(name);
    }

    public void turnOn()
    {
        if(!isOn())
        {
            setOn(true);
            System.out.println(getName() + " is on.");
        }
    }

    public void turnOff()
    {
        if(isOn())
        {
            setOn(false);
            System.out.println(getName() + " is off.");
        }
    }
}
```

The MyLamp class correctly overrides both abstract methods it inherited from AbstractMachine, so it is a concrete class and can be instantiated. If you created a subclass of AbstractMachine named MotorCycle, you would again override these two methods to provide the specific logic required for that class.

If the MyLamp class did not override both methods, it also must be declared an abstract class. If you try to compile the MyLamp class without overriding both `abstract` methods, the compiler alerts you to this and tells you to either override them or declare this class `abstract` as well.

Here is a summary of the important points about `abstract` methods and classes:

- An `abstract` method provides no body whatsoever.
- An `abstract` method is designed to be overridden by one or more subclasses.
- Any class that contains one or more `abstract` methods must be declared an `abstract` class.
- An `abstract` class can never be instantiated.
- No `abstract` methods can be declared as `private`, `final`, or `static`.

Interfaces

An *interface* is a special type of construct. You can think of an interface as a "pure" abstract class because it can contain only methods that are both `public` and `abstract`. No implemented methods are allowed in an interface. Whereas classes allow you to define type and method functionality, interfaces allow you to define only type and method declarations.

You do not actually have to include `public` **or** `abstract` **in the method declarations of an interface. The compiler automatically adds both modifiers for you in the** `.class` **file.**

TIP

Interfaces are defined much like classes, but instead of using the keyword `class` with them, you use a new keyword, `interface`. Although you use `extends` to inherit from a class, you use `implements` to inherit from an interface. One important difference between interfaces and classes is that you can extend only one class, but you can implement any number of interfaces. Another way of saying this is that you can have multiple inheritance with interfaces, but only single inheritance with classes.

To familiarize you with interfaces, I have provided the following small interface named `LightSource`. I have defined only two methods, `brighten()` and `dim()`.

interface
A completely abstract class that contains only abstract methods. An interface is a construct that captures the `public` methods of a type. All the methods defined in an interface are abstract and must be overridden by implementing classes.

```
public interface LightSource
{
    public abstract void brighten();
    public abstract void dim();
}
```

When you compile an interface, the extension will still be `.class`.

NOTE

Of course, by itself, this interface is not particularly useful because it, like an abstract class, cannot be instantiated. But you can now implement this interface. When you implement an interface, once again you must override the abstract methods provided in the interface. Here is a new class named MyLamp2 that extends MyLamp and implements the LightSource interface.

```
public class MyLamp2 extends MyLamp
                             implements LightSource
{
    public MyLamp2()
    {
        this("Lamp");
    }

    public MyLamp2(String name)
    {
        super(name);
    }

    public void brighten()
    {
        System.out.println(getName() + " is brightened.");
    }

    public void dim()
    {
        System.out.println(getName() + " is dimmed.");
    }
}
```

Granted, the MyLamp2 class does not really do anything interesting in the brighten() and dim() methods, but you can add whatever logic you want. The point is that the MyLamp2 class successfully implements the LightSource interface because it overrides the two methods defined in that interface.

Before we continue, let's talk a bit about the type that an interface brings to your classes. The MyLamp2 class can actually be referenced by no less than five types! The following five lines of code are all completely valid.

```
MyLamp2 lamp = new MyLamp2();
MyLamp lamp = new MyLamp2();
AbstractMachine lamp = new MyLamp2();
Object lamp = new MyLamp2();
LightSource lamp = new MyLamp2();
```

The first four lines all have classes as the reference type and are given in increasing order of the hierarchy. The last line uses the LightSource interface itself as the reference type. You cannot instantiate an interface, but you can certainly use it as a reference type. The advantages to this are the same as if you used a superclass as the reference type. You can refer to any class that implements an interface by that interface name. It all depends on how specific you want your reference type.

Of course, as with classes, the only methods that you can call on the resulting lamp variable are brighten() and dim(); for example, you cannot call the turnOn() method because the LightSource reference knows nothing about this method. As before, though, you can always cast the reference to a more specific reference when necessary.

Let's take a look at another interface that could be implemented by a class such as MyToaster. The HeatSource interface actually defines the same two methods originally found in the parent class Toaster2, heatUp() and coolDown().

```
public interface HeatSource
{
    public abstract void heatUp();
    public abstract void coolDown();
}
```

Although you may not see a clear advantage to implementing this interface in the Toaster2 class itself, you will see the real power of interfaces in a brand new class that I am about to show you.

In many people's bathrooms, you will find a heat lamp to keep you warm when you get out of the shower. A heat lamp combines aspects of a lamp, by providing some measure of light, with aspects of a heat source. In a sense, a heat lamp is what would result if you combined a lamp and a toaster! Because you can implement multiple interfaces, you can model a heat lamp with a class such as the following:

```
public class HeatLamp extends AbstractMachine
                      implements LightSource, HeatSource
{



    public HeatLamp()
    {
        this("Heat Lamp");
    }

    public HeatLamp(String name)
    {
```

```java
        super.setName(name);
    }

    /* methods from the AbstractMachine class */
    public void turnOn()
    {
        System.out.println(getName() + " turned on.");
        brighten();
        heatUp();
    }

    public void turnOff()
    {
        dim();
        coolDown();
        System.out.println(getName() + " turned off.");
    }

    /* methods from the LightSource interface */
    public void brighten()
    {
        System.out.println(getName() + " brightened.");
    }

    public void dim()
    {
        System.out.println(getName() + " dimmed.");
    }

    /* methods from the HeatSource interface */
    public void heatUp()
    {
        System.out.println(getName() + " heated up.");
    }

    public void coolDown()
    {
        System.out.println(getName() + " cooled down.");
    }
}
```

The first thing you should notice is that you implement multiple interfaces by simply separating the interface names with commas after the `implements` keyword. As a result of implementing in this fashion, you must provide overridden implementations of all methods found in both interfaces. Again, you are not providing any interesting logic here, but the printouts will show you what is happening. Although it would be impossible to extend two classes to combine behavior like this, such interfaces give you the power to combine types into entirely new classes.

Here is a summary of the important facts about interfaces:

◆ An interface can contain only `public abstract` methods.

◆ An interface can actually contain variables, but they must be both `static` and `final`.

◆ An interface is implemented with the `implements` keyword.

◆ A class can implement multiple interfaces but can extend only a single class.

◆ A class that implements an interface must override all the interface methods or declare itself an `asbtract` class.

◆ Interfaces can never be instantiated, but they can be used as reference types.

Terms to Know

interface	reference type
logical equality	referential equality
method overloading	runtime type
method overriding	virtual method invocation
polymorphism	

Review Questions

1. Which two access modifiers guarantee that a method will always be inherited by a subclass?

2. If you override a method, which keyword do you use to call the superclass method from the subclass?

3. Does the following class have a superclass? If so, name it.

   ```
   public class Vehicle{}
   ```

4. Does the return type have to be the same in the overloaded version of a method?

5. Given the following class declaration

   ```
   public class Car extends Vehicle
   ```

   is the following statement legal?

   ```
   Vehicle v = new Car();
   ```

6. What is the return type of all constructors?

7. Can you instantiate an **abstract** class?

8. What kind of methods does an interface contain?

9. True or False: You can overload methods within the same class or a superclass.

10. True or False: Instance methods are bound to the reference type.

Chapter 8

Exception Handling

In a perfect world, none of your programs would ever result in runtime errors. You would always create wonderfully bug-free code, and users of your programs would never make a mistake. Let's face it though; this is not a perfect world, and errors do happen. These can include incorrect user input, missing resources such as network connections or files, or even just logic errors that remain in your code. The good news is that the Java language provides an excellent way to handle these unexpected errors called exception handling.

In This Chapter

- How to handle exceptions in your code
- How to use `try`/`catch` blocks
- When to use the `finally` keyword
- How to define your own exceptions
- When to use the `throw` and `throws` keywords

The Method Call Stack

Before we venture into all the details of exceptions, it is a good idea to learn some more about how the JVM handles method calls. Although this is not going to be an abundantly technical discussion, I will show you the key concepts of something called the *method call stack*.

Let's begin with the concept of a stack. A stack is a common data structure in programming that represents a last-in-first-out (LIFO) collection of objects. Perhaps the best way to grasp this concept fully is to imagine a stack of dirty dinner plates that you are going to wash. At some point, there was a single plate, then another was placed on top of that one, then another, and so on. In the end, you have a stack of eight plates to wash. Which plate will you wash first? Of course, you're going to grab the plate on top; that only makes sense. This is an example of the LIFO concept. The last plate added to the stack is the first one taken off.

In the Java language, a stack does not hold your dirty dishes but objects. Any number of objects can be stacked on top of each other, and then the topmost object can be removed from the stack when it is needed. When we talk about a stack in this sense, we usually say an object is pushed onto the stack when it is added and popped off of the stack when it is removed.

The JVM uses a stack of objects that hold information about methods during runtime. When you execute a program, you call the main() method. The JVM pushes the main() method onto the method call stack. If the main() method creates an object of type MyClass and thus calls the MyClass constructor, that constructor becomes the next "method" on the stack. If the MyClass constructor calls yet another method named go(), that method is pushed onto the stack. The following diagram shows you a conceptual view of the resulting stack as the JVM would see it.

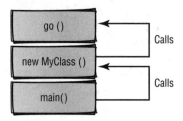

Every time a new method is called, the JVM pushes it onto the stack. Every time a method completes, its information is popped off the stack. By using a stack like this, the JVM knows not only which method is currently being called, but all the method calls that led to it. This ability is important for many reasons; one of those reasons is exception handling.

When a problem occurs during the execution of a particular method, the JVM can report the current information on the stack with something called a *stack trace*. A stack trace allows you to determine the exact process flow at the time of the problem. For example, if a problem was found in the go() method described earlier, the stack trace would contain not just the details of the problem, but also a list of every method currently on the stack. You would be able to determine that the problem is in the go() method, which was called by the MyClass constructor, which in turn was called by the main() method. Stack traces can be extremely useful for debugging your code.

That should be enough information about the method call stack to get you rolling in this chapter. As you learn more about exception handling, you will also see more details about how stacks and stack tracing are used.

stack trace
When an exception or error occurs, the JVM can output the current state of the method call stack. This stack trace includes all the classes, objects, and methods currently active and usually includes the line numbers in the source code where the exception occurred. You can print this stack trace using the inherited method `printStack-Trace()` located in the `Throwable` class.

Exception Noted

In the previous section, the generic term *problem* was used to describe some unexpected condition in a method call. The actual term used in the Java language for a problem of this sort is an *exception*. An exception is an object that is created to indicate a failure of some kind in a program. This failure could be serious (such as running out of memory) or something easily remedied (such as forgetting to enter a username). In this book, you have already come across a few cases in which you were warned that an exception might occur if you do not provide the correct command-line arguments. For example, take a look at the following simple class file.

exception
An object that is used at runtime to indicate that a strange, incorrect result occurred from a method call. A successful method call returns its declared return type, but an unsuccessful method call returns an exception that is usually handled either within the code or by requesting user input.

```
public class Echo
{
    public static void main(String[] args)
    {
        System.out.println(args[0]);
    }
}
```

Here, the Echo class compiles without any problems, but if you fail to pass an argument on the command line, upon execution you will receive a message indicating that an ArrayIndexOutOfBoundsException has occurred. This output will look a lot like the following:

```
Exception in thread "main"
java.lang.ArrayIndexOutOfBoundsException: 0
    at Echo.main(Echo.java:12)
```

This message is an example of a stack trace that indicates a single method existing on the stack. The stack trace tells you that an exception was found in the "main thread," which simply means the process in which your code was running. This is followed by the specific exception name, `ArrayIndexOutOfBoundsException`, which includes the index that is "out of bounds." The value "0" indicates that the exception occurred when you tried to access the first element of the array. That makes sense because you provided no first element in the example. The final portion of the message indicates where in the source code the exception was found.

Now, as you may recall, you have already seen how to prevent this particular exception from happening in the first place. You add an `if` statement that checks the length of the array and then outputs a friendly message informing the user how to execute this code correctly. Whenever possible, ensure that your code does everything it can to prevent exceptions in the first place.

However, in some situations, outside forces (such as the user of your program) may inadvertently cause an exception. A critical exception-handling concept is not only recognizing exceptions, but also deciding what happens *after* they are found. This is where the exception-handling mechanism becomes so useful. You can create robust code that "traps" exceptions as they happen and then handles them any way you see fit. You might prompt the user for input, perform some processing of your own that attempts to correct the problem, or even log the exceptions somewhere. The point is that the exception-handling mechanism puts the control where it belongs—in the developer's hands.

Exceptions are bound to methods only. Any method can have a special clause added to it that indicates the potential exceptions that can occur inside the method body. This includes methods defined in the standard application programming interface (API) as well as your own methods. When a method includes an exception clause, the caller of that method is forced to handle the exception somehow. This is what exception handling really means; you will learn all the ins and outs of this syntax as you forge ahead through this chapter.

The Exception Hierarchy

All exceptions are defined as classes. Four classes define the generic exception types available in Java programs; all these classes are found in the `java.lang` package, and they form the core hierarchy for all exception types. Of course, the highest class in the hierarchy is `java.lang.Object`, so the following diagram actually shows five classes.

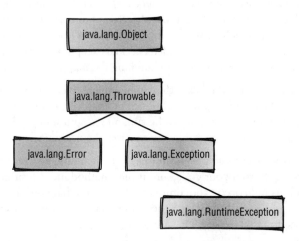

The remaining classes in this hierarchy are discussed next.

java.lang.Throwable   This class contains methods that all exception types will share. The most commonly used method defined in this class is `printStackTrace()`, which prints the exception information to the *standard error*. Another method defined in this class is `getMessage()`, which returns a `String` object that often contains a more "user-friendly" message than the standard stack trace. This class defines two constructors. The first takes no arguments, and the second takes a `String` parameter. The second constructor allows you to set whatever message you want to be returned from the `getMessage()` method.

java.lang.Error   This class (and any subclass) indicates a serious *error* condition that you really cannot do anything about from within your program. This is usually some internal JVM problem. An example of an `Error` subclass is the `java.lang.OutOfMemoryError`, which occurs when no more memory is available for a program to use. Obviously, if you run out of memory, there is not much you can do about it! Normally, when an `Error` is created, the program terminates completely.

java.lang.Exception   You will primarily focus on this class in your own exception handling. This class or subclasses of it indicate logical problems found during code execution. In many cases, your code can recover from an exception either through user intervention or with logic that you include within the code itself. The standard API includes a host of `Exception` subclasses. The occurrence of such an exception does not necessarily mean the program can no longer execute; this is not necessarily a critical problem. As you continue through this chapter, you will learn how to handle exceptions of this type.

standard error

The location where error messages are output. Typically, this is the same as the standard output where normal messages are printed. Sometimes the standard error of a system is a log file or a printer somewhere. Whenever you call the `System.err.println()` method, the provided message will typically be sent to the standard output of the system on which the code is running.

error

An object that indicates that a severe condition has arisen in the JVM. An error is not something that can usually be corrected on the fly at runtime, such as running out of memory.

checked exception

An exception that the compiler forces code to handle. You can usually accomplish this by using a `try/catch` block. All checked exceptions inherit from the `java.lang.Exception` class but do not extend the `java.lang.Runtime-Exception` class.

Such classes are considered *checked exceptions*. This means that you are forced to address them (and typically attempt to correct them!) right in the code. This approach ensures that your code does not let potential problems slip by. These exceptions are called checked exceptions because the compiler "checks" to be sure that you are handling them appropriately in your code.

Checked exceptions indicate that some logical, recoverable failure has occurred during program execution. For example, if a username is required before a program can be run, an exception might be generated that triggers a prompt to the user to enter the username.

How does the compiler perform this trick? It simply analyzes any method that you call from your code, and if that method indicates that a checked exception could occur, the compiler informs you that you have to deal with it. How you actually deal with these potential exceptions is discussed in the next section, "Handling Those Exceptions."

java.lang.RuntimeException   This class is a special subclass of `Exception` that indicates an *unchecked exception*. An unchecked exception does not have to be directly handled in your code, though it certainly can be. Unlike the way it handles checked exceptions, the compiler does not ensure that you are handling these potential exceptions in your code. This type of exception still indicates a logical error that you could potentially handle. An example of this type of exception is the `java.lang.NullPointerException`, which occurs if you attempt to access a member of an object that has not yet been instantiated. Because this could happen almost anywhere in your code, it would be messy to handle a potential `NullPointerException` inside every single method.

Runtime exceptions typically indicate a problem at the source-code level itself. For example, although it is possible that a `NullPointerException` could happen anywhere that an object reference is used, well-written, robust code ensures that this condition never arises.

unchecked exception

Any exception that extends from `RuntimeException` is considered an unchecked exception. Unchecked exceptions do not have to be handled in a `catch` block, though they can be. The compiler never forces you to handle unchecked exceptions.

Handling Those Exceptions

All right, let's get down to it, shall we? You now know that all exceptions are actually objects, but now it is time to learn how to handle them in your code. The first thing we will concentrate on is how to handle some of the standard exceptions defined in the Java API. Once you have mastered these procedures, you will learn how to create your own exception types.

You provide exception handling by using the keywords `try` and `catch` to form `try/catch` blocks. In some cases, you can also use another keyword, `finally`. This section starts with the `try` and `catch` keywords to get you familiar with the most common approach to exception handling and then it adds the `finally` keyword to the mix to complete the discussion.

Using *try* and *catch*

The try and catch keywords are aptly named. The try keyword is used to form a try block. It is inside this block that you call any methods that *could* result in an exception. In other words, a try block tells the JVM, "Try to execute these statements, and if an exception happens, let me know." The code inside a try block is called the *protected code* because the JVM checks any code within such a block at runtime to determine if an exception occurs. Each try block usually has one or more catch blocks associated with it. As the name suggests, a catch block is used to "catch" an exception that was "thrown" in the corresponding try block. In other words, if a statement in the try block results in an exception, the code defined in a catch block is triggered. A catch block is how the JVM lets you know about any generated exceptions.

The general syntax of a try/catch block is shown here.

```
try
{
    // method calls
}
catch(ExceptionClass name)
{
    // code to execute when this exception type is thrown
}
```

Notice that an exception type wrapped in parentheses immediately follows the catch keyword. This can be called the "catch parameter" because it acts much like a parameter passed to a method. Technically, the class specified as the parameter must be a subclass of java.lang.Throwable. However, more often than not, it is a direct subclass of java.lang.Exception. Although this exception can certainly be of the unchecked variety (that is, a class that extends from RuntimeException), it is more common to catch checked exceptions.

Don't forget that the braces ({ }) indicate scope for both the try and catch blocks. Any variable declared inside a try or catch block can be accessed only from within that same block of code.

WARNING

The catch parameter can be referred to anywhere within the scope of the catch block itself. This parameter is a reference to an object of the associated exception type, so any public methods defined or inherited by this class type can be called. The two most common methods called are printStackTrace() and getMessage(), both of which are inherited from java.lang.Throwable.

The process works quite simply. When a method call contained in a try block results in an exception, the JVM takes over the processing and creates a new instance of the particular exception type. The JVM then looks for a matching

protected code
The code inside a try block is considered "protected" because the JVM is monitoring the results of each statement. If an exception occurs, the JVM attempts to find a matching catch block that can process the exception appropriately.

catch block associated with the try block. To be considered a match, a catch block must have a parameter that is the same type as the generated exception object or one of the exception's superclasses.

Let's look at more complete example. Earlier in this book, you used the Integer.parseInt() method to extract a primitive int value from within a String object. At that time, you were told that if the characters in the String object did not actually form a valid integer value, you would receive a java .lang.NumberFormatException. Although NumberFormatException is really a runtime (and therefore unchecked) exception, it is not uncommon for you to provide code as shown here to handle invalid input.

```
1   public class SquareIt
2   {
3       public static void main(String[] args)
4       {
5           if(args.length != 1)
6           {
7               System.err.println("Usage: java SquareIt
                    ➡<number>");
8               System.exit(1);
9           }
10
11          int num;
12          try
13          {
14              num = Integer.parseInt(args[0]);
15          }
16          catch(NumberFormatException nfe)
17          {
18              num = 1;
19          }
20
21          System.out.println(num + " squared is " + (num *
                ➡num));
22      }
23  }
```

The first thing this code does is ensure that an argument was passed on the command line. Note that this is done to avoid any possibility of an Array-IndexOutOfBoundsException. Avoid potential exceptions whenever possible because the exception-handling mechanism does add some overhead to code processing. In simple terms, any code inside a try block executes more slowly than code not contained in a try block because code in a try block has to be closely monitored by the JVM so that any resulting exceptions can be passed to a corresponding `catch` block.

Lines 12–19 form the `try/catch` block that checks to be sure that the supplied argument is a valid integer. If it is, the code in the `try` block executes normally, and the resulting parsed value is stored in the *num* variable. If the argument value is not a valid integer value, a `NumberFormatException` is created and passed to the `catch` block on line 16. The body of this block simply assigns the literal value 1 to the *num* variable. The end result is that whether an exception occurs or not, *num* has a valid value.

Let's go back to the case where an exception did not occur. Obviously, in such a case, you do not need to execute the code contained in the `catch` block. If line 14 works without exception, the next line of code that the interpreter executes is line 21—it prints the squared value of *num*. On the other hand, if line 14 does result in a `NumberFormatException`, the body of the `catch` block executes (line 18), and then the squared result prints (line 21).

The following code shows two examples of executing the `SquareIt` code. The first example executes without exception; the second example causes an exception. However, because you are using a `try/catch` block, the code executes without incident using the value of 1.

```
java SquareIt 10
10 squared is 100

java SquareIt Hello
1 squared is 1
```

How Exceptions Change Process Flow

Now check out the following revised version of the `SquareIt` code. The only difference is an extra printout on line 15 that follows a successful parsing of the supplied argument. This is a key difference, though. If line 14 results in an exception, does line 15 execute?

```
1   public class SquareItAgain
2   {
3       public static void main(String[] args)
4       {
5           if(args.length != 1)
```

```
6           {
7                 System.err.println("Usage: java
    ➥SquareItAgain <number>");
8                 System.exit(1);
9           }
10
11          int num;
12          try
13          {
14              num = Integer.parseInt(args[0]);
15              System.out.println("No problem!");
16          }
17          catch(NumberFormatException nfe)
18          {
19              num = 1;
20          }
21
22          System.out.println(num + " squared is ' + (num *
                ➥num));
23      }
24 }
```

To find the answer, let's run the `SquareItAgain` code. As before, the first execution does not cause an exception, and the second execution does.

```
java SquareItAgain 10
No problem!
10 squared is 100

java SquareItAgain Hello
1 squared is 1
```

As you can see, only the message "No problem!" prints in the first case. This is because of the way processing works in a `try` block. Once an exception occurs, control immediately passes to the `catch` block. Any remaining statements contained in the `try` block are skipped entirely and are not executed again. Instead, the body of the `catch` block executes (line 19, which sets the value of num to 1), and then the next line following the `catch` block executes (line 22, which prints the result).

Adding More *catch* Blocks

Although a `try/catch` block will have only one `try` statement, you can have multiple `catch` blocks. This is an important concept because it is possible that a `try` block can throw more than one exception. You will see a realistic example of this when you learn how to create your own exception types in the "Creating Your Own Exception Type" section later in this chapter, but the general syntax is shown here. Note that the method and exception class names are examples only.

```
try
{
    methodA(); // might generate OneException
    methodB(); // might generate AnotherException
}
catch(OneException oe)
{
    // handle OneException
}
catch(AnotherException ae)
{
    // handle AnotherException
}
```

This pseudocode has two catch blocks associated with the try statement. If the call to methodA() results in the OneException, the first catch block executes. If methodB() results in the AnotherException, the second catch block executes. Only *one* catch block will ever execute when you run this portion of code. Multiple catch blocks cannot execute in this example because only one exception can ever be active. As soon as an exception occurs, that is the end of all the "normal" processing; the exception-handling mechanism kicks in and immediately passes control to the appropriate catch block.

Ordering the Exceptions Correctly

The first catch block that matches a given exception type is the only one that executes. Because both checked and unchecked exceptions extend from the generic Exception class, you have to consider the order in which you place your catch blocks.

Take a look at the following code snippet. Which catch block executes if a OneException is generated by the call to methodA()?

```
try
{
    methodA();
}
catch(Exception ex)
{
    System.err.println(ex.getMessage());
```

```
    }
    catch(OneException oe)
    {
        System.err.println(oe.getMessage());
    }
```

In this example, the first `catch` block *always* executes. In fact, regardless of the actual exception type, the first `catch` block is the only block to execute. This is because the generated exception object is a subclass of the `Exception` class. In Chapter 7, "Advanced Object-Oriented Programming," you learned that an object type is either its actual class type or any of its superclasses. So, because the initial `catch` block traps any class that subclasses `Exception`, it is the only block to execute.

It is not uncommon to have multiple `catch` blocks in your code like this, so you have to remember to order those blocks appropriately. If you change the code as shown in the following example, the code will trap any `OneException` objects in the first `catch` block and any other exceptions in the second.

```
    try
    {
        methodA();
    }
    catch(OneException oe)
    {
        System.err.println(oe.getMessage());
    }
    catch(Exception ex)
    {
        // catches everything except OneException
        System.err.println(ex.getMessage());
    }
```

Always order your `catch` blocks from the most specific to the most generic to ensure that the correct blocks execute when they should. Remember, only one `catch` block ever executes, and it is the one that first matches a given exception type. In the preceding code, if `methodA()` results in a `OneException`, the first `catch` block executes. If `methodA()` throws an `ArrayIndexOutOfBoundsException`, the second `catch` block executes instead.

Using a *finally* Clause

As mentioned at the start of this section, a third keyword can be used in relation to exception handling. If you need to ensure some processing, whether there was an exception or not, you will find a finally clause useful. Most often, you use a finally clause to free some external resource. For example, you might open a file and then attempt to write a few lines of data to the file. This newly written data could work fine, but it could also cause an exception. A finally clause can close the file regardless of whether the new code worked correctly.

Of course, you have not learned how to open and write to files, so it would do you little good to show such code now. Instead, the following SquareIt-Finally code demonstrates how the finally clause works.

```
1  public class SquareItFinally
2  {
3      public static void main(String[] args)
4      {
5          if(args.length != 1)
6          {
7              System.err.println("Usage: java
   ➡SquareItFinally <number>");
8              System.exit(1);
9          }
10
11         int num;
12         try
13         {
14             num = Integer.parseInt(args[0]);
15             System.out.println("No problem!");
16         }
17         catch(NumberFormatException nfe)
18         {
19             num = 1;
20         }
21         finally
22         {
23           System.out.println("This always prints out.");
24         }
25
26         System.out.println(num + " squared is " + (num *
               ➡num));
27     }
28 }
```

If you compile and execute the SquareItFinally code just as you did in the previous two examples, you will see the following output. Notice that the print-out inside the finally block always executes.

```
java SquareItFinally 10
No problem!
This always prints out.
10 squared is 100

java SquareItFinally Hello
This always prints out.
1 squared is 1
```

As you can see, using finally is fairly straightforward. However, there is something special about a finally clause—it *always* executes, no matter what. Look at the following code snippet from the SquareItFinally code; I have altered it to show you an example of what I mean by "always."

```
try
{
    num = Integer.parseInt(args[0]);
    return;
}
catch(NumberFormatException nfe)
{
    num = 1;
}
finally
{
    System.out.println("This always (and I mean always)
prints out!");
}
```

If you add that return statement to the code, you might expect that if the Integer.parseInt() method works successfully, processing immediately returns to the calling method. After all, that is what return does, right? Well, normally, I would say yes, but not this time. In this case, what actually happens is that the integer is parsed, the message in the finally clause is printed, and *then* control is returned to the caller of this code. The same concept applies to break and continue as well.

Bypassing a `return` statement as described here is not common, but you should be sure that you understand the implications of using `finally`, or you could be quite surprised at the results! The only way that a `finally` block will not execute is if a call to `System.exit()` is made; this ends all processing altogether.

NOTE

Creating Your Own Exception Type

Although the Java API provides many exception classes, you can also create your own exceptions. You can create various types of exceptions that indicate specific problems in your code. Luckily for us, creating exceptions is a simple process. All you usually have to do is subclass the `Exception` class and perhaps override a single method.

To see how to create a custom exception type, you will define a new class named `NoSuchEntryException`, which you will then use with a personal phone book application that I introduce in the next section. The concept is that if you search for a particular entry in the phone book and you cannot find it, this exception indicates the failure.

This section defines only the `NoSuchEntryException` class. In the next section, where you learn how to use `throw` and `throws`, you actually use this exception in a complete program.

NOTE

Usually when you define your own exception type, you want it to be a checked exception so that the compiler can ensure that you are handling the exception appropriately. To create a new checked exception, simply subclass the `Exception` class. If you think about it, you are just adding a new exception class to the exception hierarchy that we discussed earlier in this chapter in the section "The Exception Hierarchy."

Whenever you create your own exceptions, you follow some common steps. Although you can certainly add your own methods and variables, it is more common to simply use the inherited methods defined in your superclasses. First, you want to define at least two constructors: a default, no-argument constructor, and a constructor that accepts a `String` object as a parameter. The latter constructor allows you to pass the message that you want this exception type to return from the `getMessage()` method. Normally, all these constructors do is invoke the superclass constructors, located in `Exception`.

The `Exception` class also provides these two forms of constructors; they simply invoke the constructors in its superclass, `Throwable`.

NOTE

Here is the initial version of the `NoSuchElement` class:

```
public class NoSuchEntryException extends Exception
{
```

```
        public NoSuchEntryException()
        {
            super();
        }

        public NoSuchEntryException(String message)
        {
            super(message);
        }
    }
```

Hey, I wasn't kidding when I said it was simple! Remember that your class inherits the key methods `getMessage()` and `printStackTrace()` from the `Throwable` class, so you do not need to redefine them unless you want to add some new functionality.

However, you might often want to augment the existing functionality with your own information. Let's expand this class to make it a bit more useful. Because we are going to use it with a phone book application to indicate a failed search, it might make a lot of sense to include the information being searched for in the output message. To make this happen, you simply override the `getMessage()` method, add a third constructor, and define an instance variable.

Here is the final version of the `NoSuchEntryException` that includes these modifications:

```
    public class NoSuchEntryException extends Exception
    {
        private String searchDetails;

        public NoSuchEntryException()
        {
            super();
        }

        public NoSuchEntryException(String message)
        {
            this(message, "");
        }

        public NoSuchEntryException(String message, String
    searchDetails)
        {
            super(message);
```

```
            this.searchDetails = searchDetails;
        }

        public String getMessage()
        {
            String msg = super.getMessage();
            msg += "\nNo match for: " + searchDetails;
            return msg;
        }
    }
```

The third constructor allows you to pass the details of the search as a single String object. Notice that the message parameter is still passed to the superclass, but the new searchDetails parameter is completely contained within the NoSuchEntryException class. In this code, the getMessage() method has also been overridden. First, this method calls the getMessage() method of the superclass, and then it appends a message that indicates the search details that failed.

Be sure to notice that no "new" methods are defined in the NoSuchEntry-Exception class. The getMessage() method is a standard exception method; you are simply overriding it in this class. This means that users of this exception do not have to learn any new methods; they simply rely on the standard methods they expect to find. This is another example of polymorphism, as discussed in Chapter 6, "Introduction to Object-Oriented Programming," and Chapter 7, "Advanced Object-Oriented Programming."

Now that you have created the exception, go ahead and compile it to be sure that you have no syntax errors. In the next section, you will use this exception in a complete program.

> *TIP*
>
> You can extend from the generic Exception class or any of its subclasses. If an exception class is already defined and you simply want to expand on it, inherit directly from this class instead.

Throwing Exceptions

Up to now, you have learned how to catch any exceptions and how to create your own exception classes. Now it is time to actually throw these exceptions, the final piece of the exception puzzle.

Throwing exceptions involves two aspects. The first is defining your methods so they indicate that they might generate an exception. The second is including logic to determine if an exception should occur and then actually creating it and "throwing" it from within the method.

Using the *throws* Keyword

If you define a method that can generate an exception, you use the `throws` keyword followed by the list of possible exceptions. This can be referred to as a *throws clause.* You place the `throws` clause immediately after the parameter list, as shown here:

```
public void methodA() throws OneException{…}
```

This method declaration adds a `throws` clause that indicates it is possible that a `OneException` could occur as a result of calling this method.

NOTE

Adding a `throws` clause indicates only that a method could generate an exception, not that it actually will. In fact, most of the time, one would hope that no exception occurs.

If you want to throw a checked exception from a method, you must provide a `throws` clause with that exception (or a superclass of it) in the list of exceptions. If a method can throw more than one exception, separate each exception type with a comma. This example shows a method that can throw two exceptions.

```
public void methodB() throws OneException,
AnotherException{…}
```

NOTE

You have to list only the checked exceptions that you might throw from within a method body. Although you can list unchecked exceptions (such as `NullPointerException`), doing so is an uncommon practice. You can throw all unchecked, runtime exceptions from any method without listing those exceptions in the `throws` clause.

The "Declare or Handle" Rule

One result of declaring methods with a `throws` clause that contains checked exceptions is that it forces any code calling this method to deal with the potential exception. The calling method can deal with an exception in two ways: by "handling" the exception, or by "declaring" it.

You handle an exception by providing a `try/catch` block, as you have already seen. This is the most common approach. Declaring an exception is the other option. In this case, you do not provide a `try/catch` block; instead, you add a `throws` clause that lists the same exception type (or types) to the calling method. For example, the following example shows how the "declare" portion of the "declare or handle" rule works.

```
public void testMethod() throws OneException
{
    methodA():
}
```

Because no try/catch block is provided, testMethod() provides a throws clause of its own. The end result is that the caller of testMethod() has to either "declare" or "handle" the exception. Normally, one of the methods that ends up in the call stack provides a try/catch block.

The bottom line is that if you write code that calls a method with a throws clause that includes checked exceptions, the compiler forces you to either declare or handle that exception. This eliminates the possibility of creating code that is ignorant of potential runtime problems.

Remember, only checked exceptions must follow the "declare or handle" rule. You should normally also deal with any unchecked exceptions, of course, but the compiler does not enforce this behavior. If an unchecked exception occurs and is never caught, your program will crash and dump the stack trace to the command prompt.

NOTE

Because you cannot really write a complete version of the phone book code until you read the next section, you will create only an interface at this point. In Chapter 7, you learned that an interface defines all the methods that any implementing class must override. You will implement this interface in the next section.

```
public interface PhoneBook
{
    public void addEntry(String first, String last, String
number);
    public String search(String criteria) throws
NoSuchEntryException;
}
```

The PhoneBook interface defines two methods: The addEntry() method allows new entries to be added to the phone book; you can use the search() method to search the entries based on the criteria provided. The search() method also specifies that it can throw a NoSuchEntryException.

Throwing Exceptions in a Subclass

If you override a method and that method includes a throws clause, you have to follow a simple rule. The overridden version of the method can only throw the same exception types or subclasses of those exceptions as defined in the superclass version of the method. You cannot throw any other exception from an overridden method.

If you recall the discussion about overriding methods and polymorphism, this rule will make complete sense. If a subclass method could throw different exceptions than the overridden superclass method, the JVM could get confused. If you accessed the method via the parent class, that method could generate some set of exceptions. If you accessed the method via the subclass, an entirely different set of exceptions could be thrown. Because this causes confusion, it is a good thing that you simply cannot break this rule!

An overridden method can, however, throw *fewer* exceptions than the method defined in the superclass. The only thing you cannot do is expand the list of exceptions thrown by the overridden method.

The *throw* Keyword

The second aspect of throwing exceptions is to actually do the throwing, of course. You accomplish this by creating a new instance of the exception class, and then you use the throw keyword. Think of the throw keyword as a special form of the return statement that returns only exceptions. Once a throw statement executes, the method stops executing immediately, and the exception object is passed back to the previous method in the call stack. As you just learned, the method receiving the thrown exception object must now either declare it or handle it.

WARNING

Don't confuse the throw and throws **keywords. The** throws **keyword is used right in the method declaration, whereas the** throw **method is used within the method body.**

You can use a conditional expression, usually an if statement, to determine if an exception should be thrown. Here is a pseudocode example of this process:

```
public void methodA() throws OneException
{
    boolean okay = checkSomeCondition();
    if(okay)
    {
        // do whatever processing you like
    }
    else
    {
        // condition failed, throw the exception
        throw new OneException("Oops!");
    }
}
```

Of course, the checkSomeCondition() method call in this code is completely made up, but assume that it performs some test and returns a boolean result. If the result is true, everything is working fine, and whatever processing that needs to be done can continue. However, if the result is false, an exception should be thrown. Notice that an object of the required exception type follows the throw keyword. Once this statement executes, methodA() terminates, and control is immediately passed to the next method in the call stack.

The Complete Phone Book Application

Okay, you have now seen examples of everything you need to write a complete class that generates exceptions and can handle them appropriately. It is time to put together all you have learned in the final phone book application. The phone book application is a little more involved than many of the other examples that you have seen thus far, but if you spend some time reading the code and the descriptions that follow each class, it should be clear.

The first class you will need is the Entry class, which holds the details of a phone book entry. This class is defined as follows:

```
public class Entry
{
    private String first;
    private String last;
    private String number;

    public Entry(String first, String last, String number)
    {
        this.first = first;
        this.last = last;
        this.number = number;
    }

    public String getFirst()
    {
        return first;
    }

    public String getLast()
    {
        return last;
    }

    public String getNumber()
    {
        return number;
    }

    public String getDetails()
    {
        return first + " " + last + " " + number;
    }
}
```

The Entry class contains three instance variables that hold the first name, last name, and phone number. The constructor sets the values of these three variables. The first three methods are accessor methods, one for each variable. The final getDetails() method is a convenience method that returns all the values in a single String object.

Next, the MyPhoneBook class implements the PhoneBook interface that you have already created. Both of the methods in the PhoneBook interface are overridden, and a simple String array is used to store the elements. Note that because an array must have a consistent length, a length is specified in the constructor.

NOTE

It would be a lot more useful if you could store the phone book entries in a structure that could actually change its size rather than in a fixed-size array. In Chapter 9, "Common Java API Classes," you will learn about some different types that allow you to create those kinds of structures. For now, you will stick to using a simple array so that the code remains as clear as possible.

```java
public class MyPhoneBook implements PhoneBook
{
    private Entry [] entries;
    private int index;

    public MyPhoneBook()
    {
        // default to a size of 10
        this(10);
    }

    public MyPhoneBook(int size)
    {
      entries = new Entry[size];
    }

    public void addEntry(String first, String last, String
        ➡number)
    {
        Entry entry = new Entry(first, last, number);
        try
        {
            entries[index++] = entry;
        }
```

```
        catch(ArrayIndexOutOfBoundsException ae)
        {
            System.err.println("Unable to add entry.");
            System.err.println("The phone book is full.");
        }
    }

    public String search(String criteria) throws
        ➥NoSuchEntryException
    {
        String details = "";
        for(int i = 0; i < entries.length; i++)
        {
            Entry entry = entries[i];
            if(entry.getFirst().equalsIgnoreCase(criteria) ||
➥entry.getLast().equalsIgnoreCase(criteria) ||
➥entry.getNumber().equals(criteria))
            {
                details += entry.getDetails() + "\n";
            }
        }

        if(details.equals(""))          {
            throw new NoSuchEntryException("No entry found",
                ➥criteria);
        }
        else
        {
            return details;          }
    }


}
```

Here I have used the constructors to initialize the array of Entry objects, either to the default size of 10 or to the value passed into the second constructor. The addEntry() method attempts to add a new Entry object using the parameter values passed to it. Notice that in this method, I have used a try/catch block to handle an ArrayIndexOutOfBoundsException. In addition, I have used the instance variable *index* to add a new Entry to the array, and then I have incremented the *index* variable by one. So, if you attempt to add an Entry object to the array beyond the fixed size, the catch block will trap the ArrayIndexOutOfBoundsException.

NOTE **The logic of the addEntry() method could be improved a bit. For simplicity, I have not made any checks to ensure that the three parameters actually hold logical values. As a result, once you have completed this code, you might want to tinker with it a bit to validate the input values.**

The search() method iterates through the entries array, checking to see if any of the variables match the given criteria. I achieved this using the "Boolean OR" (||) operator. You will also notice that instead of the standard equals() method, I used the equalsIgnoreCase() method to test the first and last name. The equalsIgnoreCase() method is defined in the String class so that you can compare the two String objects without worrying about case sensitivity.

If a match is found by the search() method, the details of the Entry object are appended to the *details* variable. Once the entire array has been checked, the method reaches the if statement that performs the conditional test to see if any entries were found. If the *details* variable still has its default value of "", no matches were found, and the exception should be triggered. You can accomplish this by using the throws keyword followed by a new NoSuchEntryException object. If the *details* variable holds an actual value, indicating that some matches were found, the *details* variable is returned.

The last class that you need is one that uses a MyPhoneBook object and allows you to search for entries. The TestPhoneBook class that follows expects you to pass an argument that it will use to search the created phone book.

```
public class TestPhoneBook
{
    public static void main(String[] args)
    {
        if(args.length != 1)
        {
            System.err.println
➥("Usage: java TestPhoneBook <criteria>");
            System.exit(1);
        }

        MyPhoneBook book = new MyPhoneBook(4);
        book.addEntry("Joe", "Smith", "999-555-1000");
        book.addEntry("Fred", "Jones", "888-555-2000");
        book.addEntry("Sally", "Cortez", "777-555-3000");
        book.addEntry("Nancy", "Smith", "444-555-4000");

        try
        {
            System.out.println(book.search(args[0]));
```

```
            }
            catch(NoSuchEntryException ne)
            {
                ne.printStackTrace();
            }
        }
    }
```

After ensuring that you passed an argument, the main() method creates a new MyPhoneBook object and adds four entries. Finally, the code searches the phone book using the argument you provided. Because the search() method is defined to throw a NoSuchEntryException, a try/catch block handles this potential exception. If the call to book.search() works without a problem, the entries that were found in the phone book are printed. However, if no matching entries were found, a NoSuchEntryException is passed to the catch block.

The logical thing to do with the catch block is call the standard exception method, printStackTrace(). This outputs a detailed message about the exception that occurred. It first includes the output of the getMessage() method, and then it includes the methods currently in the call stack, usually with the line number where the error occurred.

Let's run this code and see what happens. First, it searches for an entry that exists so that you can see the code work correctly. After all, code that works correctly is usually the idea!

```
java TestPhoneBook Smith
```

The output from this execution is as follows:

```
Joe Smith 999-555-1000
Nancy Smith 444-555-4000
```

Great, everything seems to be working wonderfully. Now it is time to intentionally search for an entry that does not exist.

```
java TestPhoneBook Williams
```

This time the output is the stack trace of the thrown exception:

```
NoSuchEntryException: No entry found
No match for: Williams
    at MyPhoneBook.search(MyPhoneBook.java:54)
    at PhoneBookTest.main(PhoneBookTest.java:26)
```

The first two lines are the results of calling getMessage(). The last two lines contain the stack trace information. The first of these lines indicates the current method in the call stack, which will always be the last method where the exception was thrown. In this case, that is the MyPhoneBook.search method. It includes (in parentheses) the source file and the line number where the exception occurred. If you look at the line number that the exception indicates in the MyPhoneBook source file, you will see that it is the following line:

```
throw new NoSuchEntryException("No entry found", criteria);
```

Well, that sure makes a lot of sense, doesn't it? That is definitely the line where the exception was thrown. Normally, it is the first method listed in the stack trace that is of most concern to you for debugging purposes.

The last line indicates the main() method, which is the last method in the call stack. A line number is given for this method as well:

```
System.out.println(book.search(criteria));
```

Again, this makes sense because it is the call to the search method that generated the exception in the first place.

NOTE Sometimes the output of a stack trace will not have the source file and line number in the parentheses. Instead, it will say "(Compiled code)". This happens if no source file is available.

So what have you learned with this phone book application? You now know how to define your own exception type, which you did with the NoSuchEntry-Exception class. You also learned how to test for an exceptional condition and throw an exception accordingly by implementing the search() method in the MyPhoneBook class. In the TestPhoneBook class, you provided a try/catch block to handle a possible exception. Finally, you learned how to analyze a stack trace to track down a problem in the source code so you can fix it.

Terms to Know

checked exception	stack trace
error	standard error
exception	throws clause
method call stack	unchecked exception
protected code	

Review Questions

1. What type of exception is a `NullPointerException`?

2. From which class do *all* exception and error types inherit?

3. Which method do exception classes use to output the current method call stack information?

4. If a method call results in a user-defined exception that directly extends an `Exception` named `TestException`, is the following catch block legal?

   ```
   catch(Exception ex){}
   ```

5. Which keyword is used to indicate a method that might result in an exception?

6. Which keyword do you use to ensure that certain code always executes whether an exception occurs or not?

7. True or false: A method in a subclass that overrides a method in a superclass that can throw a `TestException` must also throw the `TestException`.

Chapter 9

Common Java API Classes

I have a large toolbox in my basement that has gotten quite full over the years. As different projects around my house come up, I sometimes have to buy special tools to get the jobs done right. Of course, once I am finished with each job, the new tool ends up right in the toolbox so that I can use it again if the need arises. As time has passed, I have made many fewer trips to the hardware store because I know I can reach into my toolbox most of the time and grab the tools that I need.

The Java API is much like a toolbox; it provides a huge number of classes that you can use in specific situations. Instead of having to write the code to do a specific task, you will often find classes in the Java API that you can use instead. In fact, so many classes are provided that there is no way I can cover them all. In this chapter, I will show you some of the common, useful classes that are available.

The *java.lang.String* Class

Let's start with a class that you are already familiar with, the `java.lang` `.String` class. Objects of this class contain an immutable text string, meaning the contents can never be changed. You learned the basics of this immutability back in Chapter 2, "Java Fundamentals." This section provides some more of the hardcore details of this immutability and shows how the JVM uses it to reduce memory usage.

You will find three terms used throughout this section: `String` object, string literal, and text string. These terms are often used interchangeably for discussion purposes.

Up to this point, you have created a reference to a `String` object with code such as the following.

```
String message = "Hello World!";
```

string pool

A special portion of memory set aside by the JVM to store string literals. `String` objects in the string pool can be reused throughout the life of a program, which allows the JVM to conserve memory usage. As always, all `String` objects in the pool are immutable.

This is the typical way to create a text string in the Java language. Let me explain what is really happening in that statement, though. If this line is the first time that the text string "Hello World!" has been assigned to a variable in your code, the JVM adds this text string to the internal *string pool*. If another *String* variable is assigned the exact same text string, the JVM uses the existing text string in the pool. Essentially, this reduces the amount of memory required. After all, because `String` objects are immutable, you don't need copies of the same text string in the pool!

A quick piece of code may better explain what I mean. The `StringDemo` class that follows assigns the same text string to two variables, and then one of those variables is assigned a brand new string. Take a look at the code and then the following explanation. Don't forget, the line numbers are just for reference.

```
1   public class StringDemo
2   {
3       public static void main(String[] args)
4       {
5           String one = "Hello World!";
6           String two = "Hello World!";
7           one = "Goodbye!";
8           System.out.println(one);
9           System.out.println(two);
10      }
11  }
```

Earlier in this book, you saw similar code and were asked how many String objects exist after line 7 executes. The answer is two because of the way the JVM optimizes String object by using the string pool. You do not need to know all the internals of the JVM, but you should reinforce your understanding of how the JVM works with String objects.

Let's start back on line 5. This line adds "Hello World!" to the string pool and stores a reference to it in the *one* variable. When the JVM reaches line 6, it discovers that "Hello World!" already exists in the string pool, so it skips the creation step and simply assigns a reference to it, stored in the variable *two*. At this point, only one String object exists even though there are two references to it. On line 7, a new text string is discovered that does not already exist in the pool. The JVM creates a new String object that contains the text string "Goodbye!" and shoves it into the pool. The JVM also changes the original reference stored in the *one* variable to a new reference to the "Goodbye!" text string.

If you run this code, you will see the following output.

```
Goodbye!
Hello World!
```

The key point here is that the String object referred to by *one* does *not* actually change at all. The JVM is simply reassigning the reference to a new String object.

Common *String* Methods

The String class provides several convenient methods that allow you to transform a string, analyze the contents of a string, and compare two strings. This section introduces you to some of these methods and shows you how to use them with simple code examples. There is not a lot to say about each particular method, so I only briefly explain the methods and how they can be used. As this section progresses, you will see more involved code that accomplishes more interesting results.

This is not a complete list of all the methods in the String class, only the most common and useful ones.

————— *NOTE* —————

Determining the Length of a String

The length() method simply returns the number of characters in a String object. The character count is returned as a primitive int. You will probably not use this method often because normally String objects are just used as is. However, an example of using this method is shown in the following

CharacterCounter code. Just give this program a command-line argument, and it will tell you how many characters it finds.

```
public class CharacterCounter
{
    public static void main(String[] args)
    {
        if(args.length != 1)
        {
            System.err.println("Please give an argument.");
            System.exit(1);
        }

        int count = args[0].length();
        System.out.print("The string " + args [0]);
        System.out.println(" has " + count + " characters.");
    }
}
```

Whatever argument you provide is printed with the total number of characters it contains.

Converting the Case of a String

It is often useful to be able to convert a String object to either all uppercase characters or all lowercase characters. This is something I do quite a lot to gain more control over user input. For example, if I expect a user to enter a command, it is nice if I do not force the user to follow the natural case-sensitivity inherent in String objects. In a recent project I worked on, the user could enter a command named "search". Of course, I have no control over how that user actually enters that command, do I? They could type "search", "Search", "SEARCH", or any number of other combination of case. It would have been painful indeed if I tried to write code that checked for any of the possible inputs.

To solve the problem, I used one of the transformation methods available to me, the toLowerCase() method. This method coverts all the characters of a String object to lowercase characters and returns a new String object. The String class also provides the toUpperCase() method that does just the opposite. These two methods guarantee that a given input is in a specific case, which makes my job of checking for the actual command entered much easier.

The following `StringConverter` class demonstrates how to use both of these transformation methods. Whatever argument you pass is printed as you entered it, and then it prints again in both lowercase and uppercase.

```
public class StringConverter
{
    public static void main(String[] args)
    {
        if(args.length != 1)
        {
            System.err.println("You must enter a string");
            System.exit(1);
        }

        String str = args[0];
        String lower = str.toLowerCase();
        String upper = str.toUpperCase();
        System.out.println("Original: " + str);
        System.out.println("Lowercase: " + lower);
        System.out.println("Uppercase: " + upper);
    }
}
```

Compile and run this code, passing whatever you like as an argument. If you run this code and pass "Hello" as the command-line argument, the output looks like this:

```
Original: Hello
Lowercase: hello
Uppercase: HELLO
```

As you can see, these methods are simple to use. Just remember that both methods actually return an entirely new `String` object.

Removing Unneeded Spaces Around a String

Another transformation method is available to you—the `trim()` method. This method removes all the leading and trailing spaces from a given text string. I have also used this method to handle the user commands in the aforementioned project. If, for some reason, there are extra spaces around a text string, this method removes them automatically and returns a new `String` object.

To see how this method works, check out the following `SpaceTrimmer` code.

```
public class SpaceTrimmer
```

```
    {
        public static void main(String[] args)
        {
            String one = "Hello ";
            String two = " World!";

            System.out.println(one + two);

            one = one.trim();
            two = two.trim();
            System.out.println(one + two);
        }
    }
```

The output from the `SpaceTrimmer` code follows.

```
Hello  World!
HelloWorld!
```

Notice that the first printout has two spaces between "Hello" and "World!" This is because those spaces are explicitly provided in the string literals assigned to the variables *one* and *two*. No surprises there.

The next two lines remove any spaces from around the text strings. In this case, these transformed `String` objects are reassigned to the original variables. Finally, the two `String` objects are printed, but this time the output contains no spaces whatsoever. The `trim()` method removes only the white space around a text string; any spaces contained within a text string are not removed.

Verifying the Prefix and Suffix of a String

A pair of methods allow you to determine the beginning or end of a text string: `startsWith()` and `endsWith()`. Both return a `boolean` to indicate if a match is found. Both methods work in the normal case-sensitive fashion, so you will often find that it helps to convert the characters of a text string to the same case first. The `CheckPrefix` class that follows demonstrates how to use the `startsWith()` method.

```
    public class CheckPrefix
    {
        public static void main(String[] args)
        {
            if(args.length != 1)
            {
                System.out.println("You must give an argument.");
```

```
                System.exit(1);
        }

        String str = args[0].toLowerCase();
        if(str.startsWith("hello"))
        {
                System.out.println("Hello back!");
        }
    }
}
```

If you run this code and pass an argument that begins with "hello" (with any mixing of case you want), you will get a friendly little printed response. Hey, it is not exactly artificial intelligence, but what do you expect in 15 lines of code?

Of course, the endsWith() method works in a similar fashion. I will let you write the code that checks the ending of a text string.

Checking String Equality

Earlier in this book, you learned about the equals() method that all objects inherit from the java.lang.Object class. You learned then that you can override this method to return true to represent logical equality. Specifically, you will find this method handy when you use it to compare two String objects. Remember, comparing two objects using the == operator returns true only if both references point to the exact same object in memory. The equals() method in the String class returns true if the two String objects contain the exact same sequence and case of characters.

Another method in the String class, the equalsIgnoreCase(), also checks for equality. It works exactly the same as the standard equals() method, but (as the method name implies) it ignores case-sensitivity rules. So "Hello" and "HELLO" are considered equal if you use the equalsIgnoreCase() method.

The following StringEquality class demonstrates these equality concepts in action. Pass two arguments, and the code checks them for equality and prints the results.

```
public class StringEquality
{
    public static void main(String[] args)
    {
        if(args.length != 2)
        {
                System.err.println("You must give two
➥arguments to test.");
                System.exit(1);
```

```
                                          }
                        boolean equal = args[0].equals(args[1]);
                        boolean equalNoCase =
               ➥args[0].equalsIgnoreCase(args[1]);
                          System.out.println("Equal? " + equal);
                          System.out.println("Equal (ignore case)? " +
               equalNoCase);
                        }
                      }
```

Searching a String for Content

On another recent project, one of the requirements was to extract the domain name from an e-mail address. This really just meant grabbing all the text following the @ sign. How did I pull off this wonderful feat? Quite easily, actually. After all, one of the mantras among developers is "A lazy developer is a good developer." That does not mean lazing around on the couch munching pretzels is the way to development excellence, of course; it means that a good developer solves a problem the easiest way possible. The Java language is excellent at allowing you to be lazy indeed!

To fulfill the project requirement, I had to do two things. First, I had to locate the @ sign in the text string that contained the e-mail address. Once I found that, I simply had to extract all the text after that point. In this section, I show you how to find the location of a character sequence in a String object, and in the next section, I show you how to extract the *substring*.

Two methods allow you to find the location of a sequence of characters in a string: indexOf() and lastIndexOf(). Four overloaded versions of each method work with various combinations of parameters. The indexOf() method returns the first match (if any), and the lastIndexOf() returns the last match (if any). I am going to concentrate on only one version of indexOf() in this section—the one that takes a primitive char as a parameter.

substring

Any portion of a complete text string can be considered a substring. For example, in the text string "Madam, I am Adam", the phrase "I am Adam" is a substring.

NOTE

The four overloaded versions of each method have the same set of parameter choices. You can pass a single char, a String object, a char and a position to start searching from, or a String and a position to start searching from.

Both methods return a primitive int that is either the index in the text string where the character was found or –1 if the character was not found. As with arrays, the index starts at zero for the first character and increments by one for each character that follows in the text string. Once you have that index, you can use it to extract the substring, as I show in the next section.

Take a look at the following `DomainRipper` code. I will complete this code in the next section to give you a fully working version.

```java
public class DomainRipper
{
    public static void main(String[] args)
    {
        if(args.length != 1)
        {
            System.out.println("Pass an e-mail address.");
            System.exit(1);
        }

        int index = args[0].indexOf('@');
        if(index >= 0)
        {
            System.out.println("Found at index " + index);
        }
        else
        {
            System.out.println("Not found");
        }

        // extract substring in next section

    }
}
```

If you run this code and pass a correctly formatted e-mail address, it prints a message telling you a match has been found. Otherwise, you are told that no match was found.

Now that you can find the index, you are ready to move on and actually extract the domain name as a substring.

Extracting Part of a String

The method you can use to extract part of a `String` object is aptly named `substring()`. There are two overloaded versions of this method. The first takes a single index where the extraction should start. The second version takes two indexes: the point from which to start the extraction and a point at which to end it. First, I will show you how to complete the `DomainRipper` code using the single index, and then I will expand on this a bit.

Here is the DomainRipper code with the actual extraction of the substring that will be the domain name.

```java
public class DomainRipper
{
    public static void main(String[] args)
    {
        if(args.length != 1)
        {
            System.out.println("Pass an e-mail address.");
            System.exit(1);
        }

        int index = args[0].indexOf('@');
        if(index >= 0)
        {
            System.out.println("Found at index " + index);
        }
        else
        {
            System.out.println("Not found");
            System.exit(0);
        }
        // extract the domain name
        String domain = args[0].substring(index + 1);
        System.out.println("Domain Name: " + domain);


    }
}
```

Did you notice that the *index* variable increases by one when it is passed to the substring() method? This is because the substring() method includes the character at the given index by default. Because a domain name does not start with @, you have to be sure to start at the *next* character in the text string.

Run this code, pass your e-mail address, and you should see your domain name printed. For example, you could run the code as follows and see the associated output.

```
java DomainRipper zero@foobar.com
Found at index: 4
Domain Name: foobar.com
```

This code can be refined even more if you want. Instead of just extracting the domain name, it might be handy to simply grab the host name itself. This is something a system administrator might do to track the usage of various hosts in a network. To accomplish this, use the lastIndexOf() method to find the final dot (.) in the domain name. Everything from there on in the text string will be something like ".com" or ".net", so those portions can be removed because they are not part of the host name. Once you have the correct index, all you have to do is make another call to the substring() method.

The DomainHostRipper code works the same as the DomainRipper code, but it adds the logic that you need to extract just the host name as well.

```java
public class DomainHostRipper
{
    public static void main(String[] args)
    {
        if(args.length != 1)
        {
            System.out.println("Pass an e-mail address.");
            System.exit(1);
        }

        int index = args[0].indexOf('@');
        if(index >= 0)
        {
            System.out.println("Found at index " + index);
        }
        else
        {
            System.out.println("Not found");
            System.exit(0);
        }
        // extract the domain name
        String domain = args[0].substring(index + 1);
        System.out.println("Domain Name: " + domain);

        // extract just the host name now
        int lastIndex = domain.lastIndexOf('.');
        String host = domain.substring(0, lastIndex);
        System.out.println("Host Name: " + host);

    }
}
```

Once the code finds the last index, the second version of the `substring()` method is called. This version takes a starting index—0, in this case, because we want to start at the beginning. It also takes an ending index, which is the index found via the call to `lastIndexOf()`. This time, there is no reason to add one to the *lastIndex* variable because the extraction stops at the character just before that index.

So if you run this code:

```
java DomainHostRipper zero@foobar.com
```

you will see this output:

```
Found at index: 4
Domain Name: foobar.com
Host Name: foobar
```

As you can see, combining finding the index of specific characters and extracting substrings is fairly simple. Remember that the `indexOf()` and `lastIndexOf()` methods can also work with more than a single character if you pass a `String` object.

The *java.lang.StringBuffer* Class

By now, I have made it clear that all `String` objects are immutable. If you do not remember that, this might be a good time to take a break to review earlier chapters. However, another class is available to you, `java.lang.StringBuffer`. This class differs from the standard `String` class in that its text string contents can change without a new object being created every time. For example, you might use the `StringBuffer` class to create a text string based on varying user input. As the user provides more input, you can add this new text to an existing `StringBuffer` object. If you tried to do this with a standard `String` object, a new object would be created every time you added the new text.

A `StringBuffer` object does not just have a sequence of characters and a length (as the standard `String` class does); it also has the concept of capacity. When you create a `StringBuffer`, you can specify a maximum size for the text string that it will contain. As long as you do not add more characters than the defined capacity, a new object will not be created. However, a `StringBuffer` will automatically resize itself if you go beyond the capacity. In other words, the capacity is not an enforced limit on the size of the text string; it is a buffer that can grow if needed.

Many of the same methods available in the `String` class are available in `StringBuffer` as well. You will find methods such as `indexOf()`, `lastIndexOf()`, and `length()`. Instead of rehashing those methods, the `StringBufferDemo` method

Take Care with the *StringBuffer*

When you create a StringBuffer, specify a capacity that you think is big enough to handle any text that might be added to it. If you are constantly going beyond the specified capacity, the StringBuffer has to do more work and use more memory to create the space required. This is because the StringBuffer actually contains a char [] and the length of that array is equivalent to the capacity you specified.

For example, if you create a StringBuffer and specify a capacity of 10, a char [] is automatically created with a length of 10. You already know that an array can never change its size once it is created, right? Trying to add an 11th character forces the StringBuffer to create a new array and copy the contents of the original array into it.

A StringBuffer will double in size every time you go beyond the current capacity. For example, if you have a capacity of 10 and you add 11 characters, the new capacity will be 22. Note that the size is based on doubling the total number of characters after the new characters are added.

that follows uses some new methods found only in the StringBuffer class. Check out the code itself, and then read on for all the details.

```
1  public class StringBufferDemo
2  {
3      public static void main(String[] args)
4      {
5          StringBuffer buffer = new StringBuffer(10);
6          buffer.append("help world");
7          showInfo(buffer);
8
9          buffer.append("?");
10         showInfo(buffer);
11
12         buffer.insert(3, "lo");
13         showInfo(buffer);
14
15         int index = buffer.indexOf("?");
16         int length = buffer.length();
17
18         buffer.replace(index, length, "!");
19         showInfo(buffer);
20
```

```
21          buffer.delete(5, 6);
22          showInfo(buffer);
23
24          buffer.reverse();
25          showInfo(buffer);
26   }
27
28   public static void showInfo(StringBuffer buffer)
29   {
30      System.out.println(buffer.toString());
31      System.out.println("Capacity: " + buffer.capacity());
32      System.out.println("Length: " + buffer.length());
33   }
34
35 }
```

As you can see, a lot is going on in this code. Let me walk you through it. First, on line 5, a new StringBuffer object is created with an initial capacity of 10. You do not have to pass a capacity if you do not want to. If you do not pass a capacity to this constructor, it defaults to 16. On line 6, the method append() is called, passing the string literal "help world". You use the append() method to add new characters to the StringBuffer, and it always adds those characters to the end of the current contents. Because on line 6 the StringBuffer contains no characters at all, the given text string becomes the entire content.

Line 7 calls a utility method, which is defined on line 28. The showInfo() method prints the details of the StringBuffer object for us. First, the showInfo() method prints the contents of the StringBuffer by calling the toString() method. Remember, a StringBuffer is *not* a String; it only contains one. To get the internal char [] as a String object, you have to call this method. On line 31, the capacity of buffer is printed, and on line 32, the length of buffer is printed. In this case, both the length and the capacity are 10.

Once line 7 executes, the output is as follows:

```
help world
Capacity: 10
Length: 10
```

Line 9 appends "?" to buffer, which will be the 11th character in the text string. This causes the capacity to be exceeded, so the internal array will double in size. Once the showInfo() method is called on line 10, the output is as follows:

```
help world?
Capacity: 22
Length: 11
```

Notice that the capacity has changed and that the length is now 11. In this output, you can clearly see that the capacity is larger than the length. This is the whole beauty of a `StringBuffer`; you could add 11 more characters to `buffer` without a new object being created.

The code continues on line 12 when the `insert()` method is called. This line inserts the text string, "lo", at the third index of the internal `char []`. This effectively pushes the existing characters from index 3 onward up by two. Note that if this ends up exceeding the capacity, the `StringBuffer` doubles the capacity again. The results of the call to `showInfo()` are shown here:

```
hellop world?
Capacity: 22
Length: 13
```

On lines 15 and 16, the index of the '?' character is found, as is the total length of `buffer`. The `indexOf()` method returns the index of the character if it is found or −1 if it is not found.

The values found on lines 15 and 16 are used on line 18 to replace the ? with the ! character. This is done using the appropriately named `replace()` method, which takes a starting index, an ending index, and the new text string with which to replace the existing content. The output of the call to `showInfo()` looks like this:

```
hellop world!
Capacity: 22
Length: 13
```

That text string does not make much sense right now, so the code continues on line 21 with a call to the `delete()` method. This method also takes a starting and an ending index. The characters from the starting index to one less than the ending index are deleted. The call to `showInfo()` results in this output:

```
hello world!
Capacity: 22
Length: 12
```

If you give a negative index or an index that is beyond the final character in the text string to the `insert()`, `replace()`, **or** `delete()` **methods, you receive a** `StringIndexOutOfBoundsException`.

WARNING

My, that output looks familiar, doesn't it? However, with the call to `reverse()` on line 24, our friendly greeting gets completely messed up. As you can probably guess, this method just reverses the entire text string. You can see the results in the corresponding call to `showInfo()`.

```
!dlrow olleh
```

```
Capacity: 22
Length: 12
```

The whole point of a StringBuffer is that all the manipulation of buffer is done on the same object. This reduces memory usage and allows you to complete some more interesting manipulation than is readily available in the standard String class. However, keep in mind that you have to explicitly call toString() when you want to extract the String object itself. It bears repeating—a StringBuffer contains a String but is not a String itself.

The *java.lang.Math* Class

It is not just a coincidence that a typical computer science class involves a lot of math. After all, when you get down to it, programming is basically just a bunch of mathematical functions that make GUIs display, websites appear in browsers, and all those cool games that keep you up late at night. Conveniently, the Java API includes a useful class named java.lang.Math. This class includes a slew of methods that you can use to calculate various results. In this section, I show you many of these methods and how to use them.

The Math class contains only static methods, so you never actually make an instance of this class. In fact, it is impossible to create a Math object because the constructor is declared private. This means that it is not even accessible for you to call it! Instead, you use the Math class by giving the class name followed by the method you need, as in Math.*methodName()*.

I am not going to turn this into a lecture on mathematics, so don't worry. All the methods in the Math class are self-explanatory, so I am just going to show you some code that uses many of them. Following the MathDemo code is a brief discussion of the details.

```
1   public class MathDemo
2   {
3       public static void main(String[] args)
4       {
5           double x = 10;
6           double y = 20.5;
7           double z = -30;
8
9           double abs = Math.abs(z); // 30
10          double ceil = Math.ceil(y);
11          double floor = Math.floor(y);
12          double log = Math.log(x);
13          double max = Math.max(x, y);
14          double min = Math.min(x, y);
```

```
15          double pow = Math.pow(x, 2);
16          long round = Math.round(y);
17          double sqrt = Math.sqrt(x);
18          double cos = Math.cos(y);
19          double sin = Math.sin(y);
20          double tan = Math.tan(y);
21
22          System.out.println("Math.abs(z) = " + abs);
23          System.out.println("Math.ceil(y) = " + ceil);
24          System.out.println("Math.floor(y) = " + floor);
25          System.out.println("Math.log(x) = " + log);
26          System.out.println("Math.max(x,y) = " + max);
27          System.out.println("Math.min(x,y) = " + min);
28          System.out.println("Math.pow(x,2) = " + pow);
29          System.out.println("Math.round(y) = " + round);
30          System.out.println("Math.sqrt(x) = " + sqrt);
31          System.out.println("Math.cos(y) = " + cos);
32          System.out.println("Math.sin(y) = " + sin);
33          System.out.println("Math.tan(y) = " + tan);
34      }
35 }
```

The output from running this code follows.

```
Math.abs(z) = 30.0
Math.ceil(y) = 21.0
Math.floor(y) = 20.0
Math.log(x) = 2.302585092994046
Math.max(x,y) = 20.5
Math.min(x,y) = 10.0
Math.pow(x,2) = 100.0
Math.round(y) = 21
Math.sqrt(x) = 3.1622776601683795
Math.cos(y) = -0.07956356727854007
Math.sin(y) = 0.9968297942787993
Math.tan(y) = -12.528721729997956
```

Let me just make some brief comments about this code to eliminate any confusion you might have. Eleven methods are called that perform various mathematical functions. Line 9 returns the absolute value of z. Line 10 returns the ceiling of y, which means it returns the smallest integer value that is not lower than the given parameter. Line 11 returns the floor of y, which does the opposite—it returns the highest integer value that is not greater than the parameter. Line 12 returns the logarithm of x. Line 13 returns the higher of the two parameters, and line 14 returns the lower of the two numbers. When you call `Math.max()` and `Math.min()`, that value is returned if both parameters are equal.

The code continues on line 15 by raising x to the power of 2; this does exponential calculations, in other words. Line 16 rounds y following the normal rules of rounding. (If the decimal is 5 or higher, it rounds up; otherwise, it rounds down.) Note that this is different from just casting a `double` to an `int`; in that case, the decimal places are chopped off with no actual rounding taking place. Line 17 calculates the square root of x.

The next three lines deal with the kind of math that you either loved or hated: trigonometry. I hated it, so I am glad that I can rely on Java to do this work for me! Line 18 calculates the cosine of y, line 19 returns the sine of y, and line 20 calculates the tangent of y.

Calculating a Random Number

One other really interesting method in the `Math` class allows you to create a random number. A call to `Math.random()` returns a number between 0.0 and 1.0. Usually, you will multiply this number by some larger number to create a suitable value for your needs.

Let me show you an example of using `Math.random()` with a program that simulates a simple guessing game. However, to really make this game work right, I first need to show you how to supply input to a program interactively while it is executing. You may find reading input interactively from the command line useful in the future, so learning how to do it sure can't hurt.

Interacting with a Program via the Command Line

Up to this point, any time you needed to pass information to a program, you passed it as a command-line argument. Doing this is fine when you want to pass some information once when you first run a program, but what if you want to give more information to a program while it is executing? Admittedly, most of today's programs use some sort of graphical window to allow you to provide this input, but we do not cover graphics in this book. Therefore, the logical solution is to create an interactive program that receives your input via the command line.

The first thing you have to do to read live input from the command line is import a new package called `java.io`. This package contains all the file *I/O classes*. I/O stands for input/output, and the classes in this package allow you to read and write to files as well as to and from the command line. You have already been using parts of this package every time you call `System.out.println()`. The *out* variable is actually an *output stream*, which is a special data structure that

I/O classes
A set of classes found in the `java.io` package that allows files to be read from and written to. There are I/O classes that read and write both binary and textual data.

output stream
Writes bytes to an output source such as a file. Bytes are passed in via method calls. An output stream is a low-level structure lets you send bytes out from a program.

input stream
Reads bytes from an input source such as a file and returns those bytes via method calls. An input stream is the low-level structure that you need to receive input from an external source into a program.

sends characters to a specific destination. In the case of `System.out.println()`, that destination happens to be the command line.

To input values to a running program, you need just the opposite, an *input stream*. An input stream reads data from some location, such as a file on your local system, a server on the Internet, or the command line. Whereas the `System.out` variable outputs characters to the command line, the `System.in` variable inputs characters from the command line. You will be working with the `System.in` variable to grab input from the command line.

However, there are really two types of input streams in the Java language, binary input streams and character readers. A *binary input stream* contains only 8-bit bytes and is best suited for handling nontext content. A *character reader* is a special type of input stream that can read 16-bit Unicode characters, so it is the best choice for text-based input. Unfortunately, the `System.in` variable is a reference to a binary input stream, not a character reader. Luckily for us, the `java.io` package provides a useful class called `InputStreamReader` that can be used to convert the 8-bit input stream to a 16-bit character reader.

binary input stream

An input stream that allows you to read binary data. This data will typically be received in 8-bit chunks. Although it can be used to read text, it is best suited for nontextual data.

character reader

A special input stream that reads 16-bit, text-based data. All the characters read are Unicode characters, potentially allowing any written language in the world to be read.

The `java.io` package includes a lot of streams, readers, and writers (which are used to output 16-bit characters). None of these are covered in this book. However, as you work more with the Java language, you will find these classes useful. You can learn how to use the various I/O classes by checking out the Java Tutorial at `http://java.sun.com/docs/books/tutorial/essential/io/index.html`.

NOTE

After you create the `InputStreamReader`, you can wrap it inside another I/O class named `BufferedReader`. This class contains a useful method, `readLine()`, that returns the text entered after a carriage return is found. This is perfect for us because we want to be able to type our guess, press Enter, and see if we were right.

The Guessing Game

All right, enough talk, let's see some action, huh? Here is the complete `GuessingGame` code; I will explain its key points immediately following it. This code is involved, so be prepared!

```
1  import java.io.*;
2  public class GuessingGame
3  {
4      public static void main(String[] args)
5      {
6          double random = Math.random() * 10;
7          int number = (int)(random + 1);
```

```
8
9            InputStreamReader isr = new
    ➡InputStreamReader(System.in);
10           BufferedReader input = new BufferedReader(isr);
11           String line = "";
12           int numberOfGuesses = 1;
13           String prompt = "Make a guess: ";
14           System.out.print(prompt);
15           try
16           {
17               while(true)
18               {
19                   line = input.readLine();
20                   int guess = Integer.parseInt(line);
21                   if(guess == number)
22                   {
23                       System.out.println("You got it!");
24                       System.out.println("Number of
    ➡guesses: " + numberOfGuesses);
25                       System.exit(0);
26                   }
27                   else
28                   {
29                       System.out.println("Wrong!");
30                       System.out.print(prompt);
31                       numberOfGuesses++;
32                   }
33
34               }
35           }
36           catch(IOException ex)
37           {
38               ex.printStackTrace();
39           }
40           catch(NumberFormatException ex)
41           {
42               System.err.println("That is not a valid guess.");
43           }
40       }
41 }
```

The `java.io` package is imported on line 1 to allow access to the I/O classes required. On line 6, the `Math.random()` method is called. As mentioned, this method returns a number greater than or equal to 0.0 and less than 1.0. Instead of this program forcing you to guess numbers with decimal points, it makes more sense to convert this to a primitive `int`. However, if you cast a number between 0.0 and 1.0 to an integer type, it will always result in zero. That would make for a pretty easy game! So the results of the call to `Math.random()` are multiplied by 10, ensuring that the result is between 0 and 9.

On line 7, the random `double` is cast to an `int` and increased by one. This ensures that `number` is a value somewhere between 1 and 10. Feel free to increase that range if you want a bigger challenge, of course!

On line 9, the code creates an `InputStreamReader` by passing the `System.in` stream to the constructor. One line 10, this object is passed to the constructor for `BufferedReader`, and the newly created object is stored in the variable *input*. The *input* variable is used in this code to read your guesses in via the command line.

Line 11 creates the `String` object that will be used to hold your inputs. Line 12 defines a variable that will count how many times you had to guess before you got the right number. Line 13 defines a `String` object that will serve as a nice prompt on the command line.

Line 15 opens a `try` block. This is required because the `BufferedReader` method that you will call to accept your guesses is declared to throw an `IOException`. The `IOException` is the standard exception type that many of the I/O class methods can generate if a problem occurs. You can see the matching `catch` block on line 36 that simply prints the stack trace if a problem does occur.

Line 17 might surprise you a bit because it defines an infinite loop. I told you back in Chapter 4, "Flow Control," that you should generally avoid creating infinite loops. Well, that is the beauty of the word "generally"; it leaves you the option of breaking that rule if you have a good reason! In this case, you want to continually allow guesses until the right answer is given. However, jump ahead for a moment to line 25, the call to `System.exit()`. Because this statement terminates the JVM, it obviously also ends the infinite loop. So, though an infinite loop appears to exist, the loop actually ends as soon as you guess correctly.

Okay, let's go back to line 19, which calls `input.readLine()`. You use this method call to read input from the command line. Every time line 19 is reached, the `readLine()` method is called, and this "blocks" the remaining execution. Until you press Enter, the `readLine()` method just sits there, waiting patiently. As soon as you press Enter, the characters you typed are shoved into the *line* variable, and the code continues.

Line 20 parses the `String` object, as you have seen earlier in this book. Note that if you do not input a valid integer, a `NumberFormatException` will be thrown and handled by the `catch` block on line 40. However, no provision is made to ensure that your guess is actually within the range of possible correct guesses. I leave that logic for you to add at another time.

Line 21 checks to see if `guess` is equal to `number`. If it is, you win, and a message prints, telling you the number of guesses that it took you to find the right number. Finally, the program ends with the call on line 25. If the two numbers on line 21 do not match, "Wrong!" prints, the prompt is given again, and `numberOfGuesses` is incremented by one. Because all this is taking place in the `while` loop defined back on line 17, the process starts all over again and continues until you finally win the game.

Whew! After all that, you deserve some playtime. Compile and run this code, and see how long it takes you to guess correctly. When you finally tire of this game (which probably will not take long), you can come back and finish the rest of this chapter.

The Wrapper Classes

In our spare time, a friend and I run a large baseball-oriented website. In addition to looking at the massive number of statistics and essays that the site contains, many people purchase a CD we sell that contains all the statistics for every player in history. As the orders come in, we grab a CD, throw it in a case, and mail it to the purchaser.

But I left out an important step in this description. When we mail that CD, we do not just put it in a case and drop it in the mail. First, we have to put it in an envelope, provide the mailing address and a return address, and attach the proper postage. If we just dropped a CD in the mailbox, it is going to end up in a garbage can somewhere, not in the hands of a baseball fan. The envelope and all its trimmings are the correct way to wrap our CD so that it can be processed correctly. Although the baseball fan did not order an envelope, that is really what we send him. Of course, when the order arrives, the envelope is opened, and the CD is finally delivered completely.

The envelope wraps its contents (the CD) so that it can travel through the mail. This is generally how the wrapper classes in the Java API work (except that you don't have to pay for postage!). Every wrapper class contains a specific primitive type that can be extracted when needed. As you can see in the following, there is a wrapper class that corresponds to every primitive type.

Primitive Type	Wrapper Class
boolean	Boolean
byte	Byte
char	Character
short	Short
int	Integer

Primitive Type	Wrapper Class
long	Long
float	Float
double	Double

The main difference in naming is that the primitive types are all lowercase and the wrapper classes all start with an uppercase letter. Also two primitive types do not match their wrapper class name exactly: char maps to Character, and int maps to Integer.

So why on earth do these classes exist? For two main reasons. First, the wrapper classes allow you to create an object that contains the matching primitive type. This is something that is going to become more important in Chapter 10, "The Collections Framework." However, I will show you an example shortly that demonstrates how you might use wrapper classes such as this with an array.

The other reason wrapper classes are useful is that they provide a variety of methods that allow you to find information about the wrapped primitive. For example, you can use the Character class to easily determine if a primitive char is a letter or a digit. I will show you examples of some methods in each wrapper class as well.

Creating Wrapper Objects

The best way to introduce you to wrapper classes is to show you how to create instances of them. This is because the creation process (shown here) is essentially the same for the eight wrapper classes.

```
1   public class WrapperDemo
2   {
3       public static void main(String[] args)
4       {
5           int myInt = 1000;
6           Integer myIntObject = new Integer(myInt);
7
8           byte myByte = 10;
9           Byte myByteObject = new Byte(myByte);
10
11          short myShort = 50;
12          Short myShortObject = new Short(myShort);
13
14          long myLong = 20000L;
15          Long myLongObject = new Long(myLong);
```

```
16
17            char myChar = 'A';
18            Character myCharObject = new Character(myChar);
19
20            float myFloat = 10.5F;
21            Float myFloatObject = new Float(myFloat);
22
23            double myDouble = 100.5;
24            Double myDoubleObject = new Double(myDouble);
25
26            boolean myBoolean = true;
27            Boolean myBooleanObject = new Boolean(myBoolean);
28      }
29 }
```

As you can see, creating an instance of each wrapper class is quite simple. It is essentially the same process for every class except for the types involved.

You can create seven of these classes in another way, however. Instead of passing the matching primitive type to the constructor, you can pass a String object. This provides you with a handy way to convert a text string to a particular wrapper class type. The only class that you do not have this option with is the Character class; the Character class provides only one constructor, and it takes a primitive char as a parameter.

The following code details how to create the other seven primitive types by passing String objects to the constructors.

```
1  public class WrapperDemoWithStrings
2  {
3      public static void main(String[] args)
4      {
5          Integer myIntObject = new Integer("100");
6
7          Byte myByteObject = new Byte("10");
8
9          Short myShortObject = new Short("50");
10
11         Long myLongObject = new Long("20000");
12
13         Float myFloatObject = new Float("10.5");
14
15         Double myDoubleObject = new Double("100.5");
16
```

```
17          Boolean myBooleanObject = new Boolean("True");
18          Boolean myOtherBooleanObject = new Boolean("Java");
19     }
20 }
```

Lines 5–15 all work the same way. The `String` object passed to the constructor is converted into the matching primitive type and then stored in the object. However, in all six of the examples from lines 5 through 15, a `NumberFormatException` can be thrown. You will receive this exception if the `String` object cannot be converted successfully to the primitive type.

The final two statements (lines 17 and 18) create two `Boolean` objects. This is done to show you a slight difference between the constructor in the `Boolean` class and the other wrapper classes. The `Boolean` constructor accepts any `String` that you want to pass. If that `String` contains the value "True" (ignoring case), the wrapped primitive will also be `true`. Any other `String` passed will result in a primitive with a value of `false` wrapped inside the object.

You do not need to append an F to the end of the text string value when creating a `Float` object, though you certainly can if you want.

NOTE

One important point about wrapper classes: the wrapped values are immutable. Absolutely no methods are provided to change the value of the primitive stored inside a wrapper object.

Common Wrapper Methods

All the wrapper classes define four methods. Though the names of the methods are sometimes different based on the particular class you are using, all four methods work the same way in every class with some minor exceptions, which I will note as they come up.

The *equals()* Method   This method is inherited from the `Object` class and is overridden in each of the wrapper classes. This method returns `true` only if both the value of the wrapped primitive in each object and the class type of each object are the same. The following code shows an example of using this method with two of the wrapper classes:

```
public class WrapperEqualityDemo
{
    public static void main(String[] args)
    {
        Integer intObjectOne = new Integer(10);
        Integer intObjectTwo = new Integer(10);
```

```
        Long longObject = new Long(10);

        boolean equal = intObjectOne.equals(intObjectTwo);
        System.out.println(equal);

        equal = intObjectOne.equals(longObject);
        System.out.println(equal);
    }
}
```

This code outputs two values. The first value is `true` because the primitive values are equivalent and the object types are equivalent. The second value is `false` even though the actual primitive values are the same because the object types are different.

The *toString()* Method   This method is also inherited from the `Object` class and overridden in each of the wrapper classes. When this method is called, the primitive value is returned as a `String` object. As always, this method is called automatically whenever you make a `System.out` `.println()` call. Of course, you can call this method any time you want to grab a text string representation of the wrapped value.

The *valueOf()* Method   This `static` method is defined in each wrapper class (except the `Character` class) to allow you to easily convert a `String` object into a wrapper class object. This is essentially an alternative to passing the `String` to a constructor. Simply pass a `String` object to this method, and an instance of that wrapper type will be constructed. Note that this method can throw a `NumberFormat` exception if the parameter cannot be parsed by this method successfully. Check out the quick example that follows.

```
public class WrapperValueOfDemo
{
    public static void main(String[] args)
    {
        Long longObject = Long.valueOf("1000");
        Float floatObject = Float.valueOf("10.5");
    }
}
```

The important point here is that this is a `static` method, so no instance needs to be created manually. The returned wrapper object looks and feels just like one you created by calling the constructor.

The *parseXXX()* Methods Every wrapper class except `Character` and `Boolean` provides at least one version of a parsing method. Each parsing method takes a `String` object as a parameter and parses it into the appropriate primitive type. These methods always follow the convention of the word "parse" followed by the primitive type the parameter is being parsed into. So, as you have seen earlier in this book, the `Integer` class defines the `parseInt()` method that takes a `String` object and returns a primitive `int`. Along these same lines, the `Double` class defines the `parseDouble()`, the `Byte` class defines `parseByte()`, and so on.

However, some wrapper classes contain more than one version of these parsing methods. Think about a `long` primitive for a moment, and you will see why. A `long` is the largest of the integer types, so it can contain a 64-bit `long` value, a 32-bit `int` value, a 16-bit `short` value, or an 8-bit `byte` value. So the `Long` class defines four parsing methods: `parseLong()`, `parseInt()`, `parseShort()`, and `parseByte()`. The methods available to each wrapper class follow.

Class	Methods
Byte	parseByte()
Short	parseShort()
	parseByte()
Integer	parseInt()
	parseShort()
	parseByte()
Long	parseLong()
	parseInt()
	parseShort()
	parseByte()
Float	parseFloat()
	parseInt()
	parseShort()
	parseByte()
Double	parseDouble()
	parseFloat()

Class	Methods
	parseLong()
	parseInt()
	parseShort()
	parseByte()

You have already seen how to use these methods previously with the `Integer.parseInt()` method, but check out the following `WrapperParsingDemo` code to reinforce your understanding.

```
public class WrapperParsingDemo
{
    public static void main(String[] args)
    {
        int intVal = Integer.parseInt("100");
        float floatVal = Float.parseFloat("100.5");
        byte byteVal = Double.parseByte("70");
        double doubleVal = Double.parseDouble("70.8");
    }
}
```

The first two statements in the `main()` method should not be surprising to you. The third statement parses a `byte` by using the `Double` class. The return from this method call is 70 because the parsing method automatically casts the provided value into a `byte` for you. The final statement parses the same value into a `double` in the normal fashion.

The *Character* Class

Most of the wrapper classes work about the same way, but the `Character` class defines some interesting methods of its own. These methods allow you to readily determine details or alter the case of a primitive `char`. All the methods discussed in this section are `static` methods, so you do not need an instance to perform these queries and conversions. The following `CharacterDemo` class demonstrates how you can use some of these methods:

```
public class CharacterDemo
{
    public static void main(String[] args)
    {
```

```java
char c = 'a';
boolean digit = Character.isDigit(c);
boolean letter = Character.isLetter(c);
boolean either = Character.isLetterOrDigit(c);
boolean upper = Character.isUpperCase(c);
boolean lower = Character.isLowerCase(c);
boolean white = Character.isWhitespace(c);
char d = Character.toUpperCase(c);
char e = Character.toLowerCase(d);

System.out.println("Digit: " + digit);
System.out.println("Letter: " + digit);
System.out.println("Either: " + either);
System.out.println("Uppercase: " + upper);
System.out.println("Lowercase: " + lower);
System.out.println("Whitespace: " + white);
System.out.println("c = " + c);
System.out.println("d = " + d);
System.out.println("e = " + e);
    }
}
```

When you run this code, you will see the following output:

```
Digit: false
Letter: true
Either: true
Uppercase: false
Lowercase: true
Whitespace: false
c = a
d = A
e = a
```

The isDigit() method returns true if the value is a number, which it is not in this example. The isLetter() method returns true if the value is a letter of the alphabet. So, the isLetterOrDigit() method returns true if *either* isDigit() or isLetter() returns true.

Both isUpperCase() and isLowerCase() methods verify the case of the provided char. The isWhitespace() method returns true if the char is a tab, a carriage return, or a space.

The toUpperCase() and toLowerCase() methods obviously alter the case of the supplied primitive char. The returns type from both of these methods is a new char; the original primitive is unchanged. In other words, the value of the original primitive is copied and then converted to the new case.

Wrapping It Up

Here is a summary of the points specific to the wrapper classes that you should remember.

- ◆ Every primitive in the Java language has a corresponding wrapper class.
- ◆ All wrapper classes can be instantiated by passing the corresponding primitive type to a constructor.
- ◆ All the classes except Character can have a String passed instead of the primitive type. For the six numeric-oriented wrapper classes, a NumberFormatException will be thrown if the provided String object does not contain a value that is valid.
- ◆ The wrapped values inside a wrapper class are immutable.
- ◆ You can test two wrapper objects of the same type for equality using the equals() method. Both the object type and wrapped value must match for this method to return true.
- ◆ All the wrapper classes except Boolean and Character provide one or more parsing methods.
- ◆ The Character class provides a bunch of static utility methods that you can use to find the details and change the case of a primitive char.

Terms to Know

binary input stream	output stream
character reader	string pool
I/O classes	substring
input stream	

Review Questions

1. Where does the JVM store most string literals?

2. How do you determine the length of a `String` object stored in a variable named *str*?

3. What is the index of the letter 'a' in the text string, "Staple"?

4. Which method allows you to add content to the end of a `StringBuffer`?

5. Assume that a `StringBuffer` has a capacity of 10 and contains the text string "1234567890". What will the capacity be if you append "A" to the object?

6. Assume that you have a `StringBuffer`, `buffer`, that contains the text string "abde". How would you add the character "c" after the character "b"?

7. What method do you use to calculate the cosine of a number?

8. What is the range of values returned by a call to `Math.random()`?

9. Which wrapper class *cannot* have a `String` passed to a constructor?

10. How do you change the value stored in a wrapper object?

Chapter 10

The Collections Framework

You may often need to group related objects to use them in your programs. For example, you might have a number of AddressBookEntry objects that you want to store in a collection so that you can sort, search, add, remove, and replace those objects over time. The collections framework provides an assortment of classes and interfaces that allow you to create containers for objects that can be either sorted or unsorted in nature.

Defining a Framework

framework

A framework includes a group of classes and interfaces that define the most common behavior. Normally, when you work with a framework, you do not concern yourself with the actual implementation types, only the interfaces that are implemented. This makes it easy to swap different implementations of a framework in and out without changing how you access them.

A simple and correct definition of a *framework* is a set of classes that you can extend to provide specific implementations by overriding methods. A framework typically defines one or more generic classes (usually `abstract` classes), and you can extend these classes to provide customized behavior. The results are a group of classes that share a set of common methods but can still provide specific customization.

Perhaps a real-world example will help clarify this. Think of an omelet recipe as a framework. All omelets contain some basic ingredients—some number of eggs and usually some other ingredients such as cheeses, meats, and vegetables. Obviously a cheese omelet is different from a spinach-and-tomato omelet once it is prepared. However, the basic steps are essentially the same. You crack some eggs into a bowl, whip them with a whisk, and pour the eggs into a hot frying pan. At some point, you add your chosen ingredients and eventually shape the omelet so that it can be put on a plate.

However, there are some major differences between the variety of omelets you might create. For example, if you decide to add ham to an omelet, you might want to dice and cook it before you add it to the eggs in the pan. If you add mushrooms, you might choose to add them raw. In essence, the choices you make represent a difference in the implementation details even though the steps are essentially the same for all omelets.

collection

A generic collection contains elements but imposes no order or constraints on those elements. An array is a simple type of collection. More elaborate collections, such as those you find in this chapter, include methods that let you add, insert, remove, and search elements.

Now that I have got you good and hungry, let's get back to the collections framework. A *collection* is simply a data structure that contains zero or more objects and provides some mechanisms for manipulating those objects. Each of the contained objects is called an element. All the collections in Java serve the same basic purpose: they let you add, remove, replace, sort, and retrieve values from each collection type. The generic collection types define the methods, and the subclasses provide the appropriate implementations of those methods.

The good news is that you will rarely have to provide these method implementations yourself. Not only does the collections framework provide the generic constructs, but it also provides some useful implementations. See, and you were beginning to think you had a lot of work in your future, huh?

For years before Java burst onto the scene, developers had to create their own collection types to order, much like a short-order cook dishing out omelets. Java's huge support for collections is a great benefit for creating powerful programs without cracking quite as many eggs.

list

A specific type of collection that imposes rules guaranteeing some form of logical order to its elements. Lists also do not enforce uniqueness of their elements; in other words, duplicates are allowed. Elements in a list are typically accessed via an index.

The remainder of this chapter shows you many of these collection types and how to use them effectively. And I promise, no more omelet analogies!

The *java.util.Collection* Interface

Several types of collections are available. One type is called a *list*, which allows an ordered sequence of data and allows duplicate elements to exist.

The rules for the ordering of the elements in a list might be controlled by the list itself or by some external mechanism. The most common ordering is based on the natural order that you learned about back in Chapter 5, "Arrays."

NOTE

A more refined version of a list is a *set* that enforces rules that prevent a data type from being added more than once; it does this by preventing duplicate elements from being added. A set also does not usually enforce a specific order on its elements, unlike a list. You could model a poker hand with a set because no hand can ever have two of the exact same card present at one time.

The `java.util.Collection` interface defines the basic framework for the more specific collection types. This interface defines the methods that allow adding, removing, finding, and counting the elements stored in a collection. Both lists and sets require these basic methods, so the `Collection` interface provides a convenient superclass for most of the major collection classes. The `Collection` interface is a representation of a group of objects, and just as with an array, those contained objects are called elements.

Many methods are defined in this interface, all of which relate directly to maintaining a collection. The following are some of the more common methods.

set
A refined form of a collection that imposes no ordering rules. A set makes sure that all its elements are unique by not allowing any duplicates to be added. No indexing of elements is typically done with a set.

public boolean add(Object o)   This method lets you add a new element to a collection. If the specific collection that you are working with allows the `Object` parameter to be added, it is added, and this method returns `true`. On the other hand, if the collection class does not allow the supplied parameter to be added, `false` is returned, and no addition is made to the collection. For instance, if the collection class does not allow duplicates and the parameter that you supply is already contained in the collection, this method returns `false`.

public void clear()   You use this method to remove all the elements in a collection. The size of the collection after this method is called is zero.

public boolean contains(Object o)   Use this method if you need to determine whether a collection contains a specific object. Under the hood, the `Object` parameter is compared with each of the elements in the collection using the standard `equals()` found in the `Object` class. If one or more elements match the supplied parameter, this method returns `true`.

public boolean isEmpty()   This method returns `true` if a particular collection contains no elements.

public boolean remove(Object o)   This method lets you remove a specific element from a collection. If the passed `Object` is found and then removed, this method returns `true`. If there is no matching element (determined again by using the `equals()` method) or if the collection does not allow elements to be removed, this method returns `false`.

public int size()   This method returns a count of the number of elements contained in a collection.

You will come across other methods in this chapter, but these six provide the basic control that most collections provide.

NOTE

Only the isEmpty() and size() methods are guaranteed to be available in all implementations of the Collection interface. The remaining four methods are all considered optional. This simply means that a collection does not have to provide the specified functionality. However, as you will see throughout this chapter, the major collection types provide all these methods. If you call an optional method that has not been implemented, you receive a java.util.UnsupportedOperationException.

The collections framework provides no classes that directly implement the Collection interface. This may seem strange, but there is a good explanation. The Collection interface is extended by some other, more specific interfaces. As always, this means that all the methods defined in Collection are inherited by the subinterfaces, and more specific methods can be provided within those subinterfaces. The two main subinterfaces of Collection are

♦ java.util.List

♦ java.util.Set

As you continue through this chapter, you will learn more about List and Set and will see implementations of them in action. Another collection-oriented interface, Map, does not extend from Collection; you will learn all about the Map interface as well.

Understanding Lists

All lists maintain an ordered collection of elements and allow duplicate elements to exist. A list can contain zero or more null elements along with actual objects. The basic rule for ordering the elements is to simply keep them in the order in which they were added. You might use a list to contain the steps of a recipe, for example.

The *java.util.List* Interface

All the list types in the collections framework implement the java.util.List interface. This interface defines a whole bunch of methods that all lists can use by providing their own implementations. Most of these methods are inherited from the Collection interface, so only the methods specific to List follow.

public void add(int index, Object o)   Adds a new element to a List at the specified index.

public Object get(int index)   Retrieves the element at the specified index. This method always returns a generic Object.

public int lastIndexOf(Object o)   Returns the index of the last occurrence of the specified element or returns −1 if no matching element is found.

public Object remove(int index)   Removes the specified `Object` from a `List` and returns that `Object` if you want to keep a reference to it.

public Object set(int index, Object o)   Replaces the element at the specified index with the new `Object`. The element that was replaced is returned if you want to maintain a reference to it.

The *java.util.ArrayList* Class

To demonstrate how a `List` implementation works, I'll spend some time discussing the details of the `java.util.ArrayList` class. This is a common collection to use, so it is an excellent class to learn more about.

Back in Chapter 5, you learned a lot about arrays. You discovered that an array cannot have its size changed and can contain only elements of the same type. Although this is perfectly fine in many cases, you often want to define an arraylike collection that can actually grow if you need it to and that can contain a variety of elements. Think of a program in which a user enters one or more e-mail addresses to send a message to multiple people in an office building. Having an array to hold these addresses would be convenient, but you have no way of knowing beforehand how many addresses your user might need. This is a good case for using an `ArrayList` instead of a normal array.

The `ArrayList` class implements the `List` interface, so you know its elements are ordered and that it can contain duplicates. An `ArrayList` object contains an `Object []` as the main part of its state. However, the `ArrayList` class brings two important features to the mix that make it different from a simple array. First, an `ArrayList` can grow if you add elements beyond its current length, and it can shrink if elements are removed. Second, because an `ArrayList` can hold any `Object`, you can add anything you want to an `ArrayList` except primitive types.

> Remember all that discussion of the wrapper classes in Chapter 9, "Common Java API Classes"? They become useful when you work with collections because they can represent primitive values that you need to store in a collection such as an `ArrayList`.
>
> *TIP*

Before you get too excited though, let's get something clear right now. The array an `ArrayList` maintains for you is still a normal array that has to follow the basic rules. This means, of course, that the `Object []` an `ArrayList` maintains cannot actually be resized. When you add elements beyond the length of that array, the `ArrayList` is forced to create a brand new array and copy the contents of the original array into the new one. Mechanisms are provided to repeat this resizing as few times as possible, but it is a good idea to remember that every time the array is resized, the JVM must access and use more memory.

All ArrayList objects have a length and a capacity. The length is the number of elements currently stored in the ArrayList. The capacity is the space available for more elements to be added. You can specify an initial capacity when you create an ArrayList, and it will increase the capacity as needed.

Enough talk, let's see it work. The following class is a simple example of creating an ArrayList and manipulating its contents using some of the standard methods.

```
1   import java.util.*;
2   public class ArrayListDemo
3   {
4       public static void main(String[] args)
5       {
6           ArrayList list = new ArrayList();
7           boolean empty = list.isEmpty();
8           System.out.println("Empty: " + empty);
9
10          list.add("One");
11          list.add("Two");
12          list.add("Four");
13          list.add(2, "Three");
14          System.out.println("Size: " + list.size());
15
16          boolean found = list.contains("Four");
17          System.out.println("Found: " + found);
18
19          boolean removed = list.remove("Four");
20          System.out.println("Removed: " + removed);
21          System.out.println("Size: " + list.size());
22
23          Object element = list.get(0);
24          String str = (String)element;
25          System.out.println("Index 0 is " + str);
26
27          list.clear();
28          System.out.println("Size: " + list.size());
29      }
30  }
```

The `ArrayListDemo` class starts on line 6 by creating the `ArrayList`. When you instantiate a new `ArrayList`, you can pass either nothing (as shown in this code) or an `int` that represents the desired starting capacity. If you pass nothing, the capacity defaults to 10. This means that this `ArrayList` does not have to resize itself until you exceed that capacity.

Line 7 calls the `isEmpty()` method, which returns `true` because nothing has been added to the `ArrayList` yet. A quick message is printed to show you the status of `list`.

Lines 10–12 add `String` objects to the `ArrayList`. Remember that you do not have to add the same type of elements; the only requirement is that the elements you add must be objects, not primitives. You will see mixtures of objects in a collection as you progress through this chapter. The `add()` method appends each `String` to the end of the `ArrayList`.

However, line 13 does something a little different. Instead of adding the text string "Three" to the end of the `ArrayList`, this overloaded version of the `add()` method specifies a location in the `ArrayList` where the new element should be inserted. As with arrays, the starting index of a collection is zero. To insert the element "Three" so that it comes before the element "Four", you pass 2 as the first parameter. The second parameter is the element that you want to add.

On line 14, a message prints to show you the current size of the `ArrayList` that was retrieved by the call to the `size()` method. The size of an `ArrayList` is the number of elements that it currently contains.

Line 16 demonstrates the use of the `contains()` method. This method searches the `ArrayList` for the specified object and returns `true` if a matching element is found. Because an element matches the parameter "Four", the printout on line 17 indicates this fact.

Line 19 uses the `remove()` method to delete the "Four" element from the `ArrayList`. This method returns `true` if the delete is successful. The `remove()` method does return `false` is if no such element is found. The printout on line 20 shows you that the "Four" element was indeed deleted.

You can combine the logic of the `contains()` method with the `remove()` method if you want. You first determine if a collection (such as an `ArrayList`) contains a specific element, and, if so, only then call `remove()`.

TIP

Line 21 prints the size of the `ArrayList` again to show how the removal of the "Four" element changed things. The new size at this point is 3.

Line 23 shows you how to retrieve a specific element from the `ArrayList`. The parameter of 0 indicates that the first element should be retrieved. Note that the `get()` method always returns a generic `Object`. If you need to, you can cast this `Object` to its real type with a cast operator as shown in line 24. Line 25 prints the element that was retrieved.

You do not actually have to cast the `Object` to a `String` on line 24. Remember that whenever you pass an object to the `System.out.println()` method, the object's `toString()` method is automatically called. Because of polymorphism, this method is always called on the runtime type of the object, which in this case is a `String`. The cast on line 24 is done simply to show you a step you might need if you want to call methods specific to the object retrieved.

Line 27 empties the entire `ArrayList` by calling the `clear()` method. The results of this call are shown in the printout on line 28 that indicates the `ArrayList` has a size of zero.

Here is the complete output from running this code:

```
Empty: true
Size: 4
Found: true
Removed: true
Size: 3
Index 0 is One
Size: 0
```

The *java.util.Vector* Class

Another collection type, `java.util.Vector`, is the predecessor to the `ArrayList` class, and it works essentially the same way, though in most cases, the `ArrayList` works a bit faster. The methods available in both classes are virtually identical, so you could literally substitute `Vector` for `ArrayList` in the `ArrayListDemo` class, and everything would work the same.

There is no reason to discuss the `Vector` class in this chapter because of its strong similarity to the `ArrayList` class. However, you might find `Vector` used a lot in code you come across that has not been updated to the new `ArrayList`. If you just keep in mind that the two classes work the same, you should have little trouble working with the `Vector` class.

Three More *ArrayList* Methods

The methods that you used in the `ArrayListDemo` class are the major methods you are going to need. However, you won't find three other interesting methods in the `List` interface. These methods are specific to the `ArrayList` class.

public void ensureCapacity(int capacity)   Use this method to force an `ArrayList` to increase its capacity instead of waiting for it to do so itself. This is a good method to call if you know you are going to add a large number of elements in your code. For example, if you know you will be adding 100 elements to an `ArrayList`, it might be a good idea to ensure that the capacity of the `ArrayList` is at least 100. This can limit the number of resizing operations, which in turn reduces memory use.

One thing to remember is that an `ArrayList` cannot have a capacity that is less than its size. That is abundantly logical, as I am sure you will agree. After all, how could an `ArrayList` contain 100 elements but have a capacity of only 50? This means that the parameter you pass to the `ensureCapacity()` method is really a *minimum* capacity. If the size is greater than the capacity you pass, the capacity ends up being equal to the size.

public void trimToSize()   This method trims the capacity to match the current size of an `ArrayList`. This is useful to ensure that the smallest amount of memory is being used. If you have added all your elements and plan to add no more, a quick call to this method never hurts.

public int indexOf(Object o)   This method works much as it does with the `String` and `StringBuffer` classes. Whereas the `contains()` method tells you if an `ArrayList` contains a specific element, the `indexOf()` method actually returns the index of an element if it is found.

The following `ArrayListAgain` class uses some of the other methods available.

```
1   import java.util.*;
2   public class ArrayListAgain
3   {
4       public static void main(String[] args)
5       {
6           ArrayList list = new ArrayList();
7           list.add(new Integer(0));
8           list.add("Hello");
9           list.add(new Integer(20));
10
11          Object replaced = list.set(1, new Integer(10));
12          System.out.println("Replaced " + replaced);
13
14          System.out.println("Size: " + list.size());
15
16          list.ensureCapacity(20);
17          for(int i = 30; i < 100; i+=10)
18          {
19              list.add(new Integer(i));
20          }
21          System.out.println("Size: " + list.size());
```

```
22
23          Integer num = new Integer(50);
24          int index = list.indexOf(num);
25          System.out.println("Found at index " + index);
26
27          Object removed = list.remove(index);
28          System.out.println("Removed " + removed);
29
30          list.trimToSize();
31          System.out.println("Capacity and size are " +
                list.size());
32    }
33 }
```

The ArrayListAgain class kicks off on line 6 with a new ArrayList and then proceeds to add three elements on lines 7–9. Notice that two of these elements are Integer objects and the other is a String object. This proves the point that collections such as an ArrayList can contain any type of object.

On line 11, the String object is replaced, however. The call to the set() method replaces the element at index 1 (the String object) with a new Integer object. The return of the set() method is the object that was replaced. This object is printed on line 12.

Line 14 prints out the size of the ArrayList just to show you where things stand at this point. The size printed is 3.

Line 16 forces the ArrayList to provide enough space for at least 20 objects. If the capacity is less than 20, this call to ensureCapacity() guarantees that the ArrayList ends up with a current capacity of 20. However, if the capacity is already more than 20, no change is made. Remember, the ensureCapacity() method specifies a minimum capacity only.

Lines 17–20 add seven more elements to the end of the ArrayList. These elements are all Integer objects. Notice that the for loop is incrementing by 10 here. This means that each of the resulting Integer objects contain a value between 30 and 90, counting by tens.

Line 21 is another quick printout of the size, which is now 10 because of the new elements added.

Line 23 creates a new Integer object that will be used in a search operation. On line 24, the indexOf() method is called to determine not only if there is a matching element, but the exact location of that element. Because there is an Integer object containing the value 50 in the ArrayList, that index is returned and printed on line 25.

On line 27, an overloaded version of the remove() method takes a specific index as a parameter. See, and I bet you thought that the index you got back on line 24 was never going to be used! This version of the remove() method returns the object that was replaced, and that object is printed on line 28.

On line 30, the trimToSize() method is called, making the capacity and the size equivalent. Again, this is a good method to call if you want to ensure that an ArrayList is only as big as it needs to be. The final printout on line 31 shows you the current size and capacity, both of which equal 9 in this case because one of the elements was deleted.

Summarizing Lists

Before you move on to the next section of this chapter, here is a summary of the important facts about classes that implement the List interface.

◆ The List interface extends from the Collection interface.

◆ A list maintains ordered elements.

◆ A list does not reject duplicates.

◆ Elements can usually be added to the end of a list or at a specific position.

> ArrayList is not the only class that implements List. You will also see the Vector class and the LinkedList class using it. Neither of these classes is covered in this chapter, but if you want to learn more about them, you can check out *Mastering Java 2, J2SE 1.4*, by John Zukowski (Sybex, 2002).
>
> *NOTE*

Understanding Sets

A set is the opposite of a list because it does not have to maintain ordered elements and does not allow duplicates. Because no two elements in a set can be the same, a maximum of one null element is allowed. A set might be useful if you want to hold a unique group of e-mail addresses in memory because the set will never contain duplicate addresses.

The *java.util.Set* Interface

All sets in the collections framework are identified by the java.util.Set interface. The Set interface extends the generic Collection interface and adds no new methods. Just think, no new methods to learn!

However, you need to concern yourself with one major change stipulated in the Set interface. Because a set should not contain duplicates, there are special guidelines for the add() method. The method signature is exactly the same as defined in Collection, but implementations of Set should include logic in their add() method to add an element only if it is not already in the set. In other words, it is the add() method's responsibility to ensure that there are no duplicates.

If you are wondering how an interface can enforce a rule like Set does with the add( ) method, the answer is, it can't. The stipulation made in the Set interface should be followed in any implementations, but there is no way to ensure that the rule is followed. Luckily for us, implementations in the collections framework follow the rule to the letter!

The *java.util.HashSet* Class

To see how a set works, let's look at the java.util.HashSet class. This is the only concrete class in the collections framework that directly implements the Set interface. Because the Set interface does not define any methods beyond those that it inherits from Collection, this is a fairly simple class to demonstrate.

Here is the HashSetDemo class. As you read the source code, notice that an attempt is being made to add a duplicate element. The add( ) method defined in HashSet returns false if you attempt to add an element that it already contains.

```
1   import java.util.*;
2   public class HashSetDemo
3   {
4       public static void main(String[] args)
5       {
6           HashSet set = new HashSet();
7
8           for(int i = 0; i < 10; i++)
9           {
10              set.add("Element " + i);
11          }
12
13          System.out.println("Size: " + set.size());
14
15          boolean added = set.add("Element 5");
16          System.out.println("Added: " + added);
17          System.out.println("Size: " + set.size());
18
19          added = set.add("New Element");
20          System.out.println("Added: " + added);
21          System.out.println("Size: " + set.size());
22
23          set.clear();
24          System.out.println("Size: " + set.size());
25      }
26 }
```

First take a look at the output from executing this class, and then we'll look at the details.

```
Size: 10
Added: false
Size: 10
Added: true
Size: 11
Size: 0
```

Line 6 creates a new HashSet. You can pass a variety of parameters to this constructor, one of which is an initial capacity. A HashSet expands automatically, much like an ArrayList does, though usually more efficiently. If you do not pass an initial capacity, the capacity will be 16.

Lines 8–11 define a for loop that adds some String objects to the HashSet. Because all these String objects are different, all are added without a problem.

Line 13 prints the size, which equals 10.

Line 15 attempts to add an element that already exists. Note that this does not generate an exception even though there is a duplicate String object in the HashSet. If the call to add() cannot complete because a duplicate is found, false is returned. You can see in the printout on line 16 that the addition failed and on line 17 that the size is still 10.

Line 19 plays nice and tries to add an element that does not exist. Obviously, this does not cause a problem, so the printout on line 20 indicates the return was true. Line 21 prints the size, which is now 11 because of the element added on line 19.

Line 23 empties the HashSet with a call to the clear() method. This works just like it does for all collection types. As a result, the final printout on line 24 indicates a size of 0.

As you can see from the HashSetDemo class, using a set is simple. However, there is only one add() method and no way to insert an object at a specific location. Likewise, you cannot remove a specific element by giving an index; there are simply no methods provided in Set that work with a specific index. This is logical because ordering is never guaranteed in a Set.

However, I should mention another interface that exists in the collections framework named java.util.SortedSet. This specialized form of a set includes methods that allow its elements to be ordered while still not allowing duplicates. I am not going to discuss the SortedSet any further, but you can find the details of this interface by firing up your browser and going to http://java.sun.com/j2se/1.4.1/docs/api/java/util/SortedSet.html.

Summarizing Sets

Before you continue to the next section, take a look at the following summary of key details about sets.

- A set usually has no ordering mechanism.
- A set does not allow any duplicates.
- A set does not allow access to elements by index.

Understanding Maps

map
A special type of collection that includes both keys and values. Each key relates to one and only one value. There are no indexes in a map because all access is made via the individual keys. A map is the simplest form of a database.

Recently I had to create an online application that allowed users to log in and view their travel itineraries. To make this work, I realized it would make a lot of sense to somehow bind the username to the itinerary details. In essence, I needed to create a rudimentary database that could relate a unique username to an assortment of outstanding itineraries. To accomplish this, I used a *map* from the collections framework.

A map is a collection that matches keys to values. Every value in a map has a unique key associated with it. In the itinerary application, the key is the username, and the itinerary information is the value. Although there can be no duplicate keys, it is perfectly fine to map duplicate values to other keys. However, each key can refer to a single value at most. Different implementations of a map may allow or deny `null` keys and values.

A map implementation can enforce ordering of its elements, but this is not required. A map can also have its contents extracted into a different collection type such as a set or a generic collection.

The *java.util.Map* Interface

All maps in the collections framework are implementations of the `java.util.Map` interface. This interface does not extend the `Collection` interface, however. This does not mean it is not part of the collection framework, of course. The `Map` interface actually provides a few methods that exactly match methods found in the `Collection` interface, but no others. For this reason, it does not extend `Collection`; it would have been messy to handle all those extraneous methods.

The following list does not contain every method defined in `Map`, but it contains most of them. The first three methods are duplicates of methods in the `Collection` interface, so their descriptions will seem somewhat familiar.

> ***public void clear()***   Removes all the elements in a collection. The size of the collection after this method is called will be zero.

public boolean isEmpty()   Returns `true` if a particular collection contains no elements.

public int size()   Returns a count of the number of elements contained in a collection.

public boolean containsKey(Object key)   Returns `true` if the specified key is found in the `Map`. This is determined by calling the `equals()` method to compare it against each element until a match is found or until there are no more keys to check. There can be at most one key that matches.

public boolean containsValue(Object value)   Returns `true` if the specified value is found in the `Map` by using the `equals()` method for comparison.

public Object get(Object key)   Returns the element that maps to the specified key. The return value could be `null`, but this does not necessarily mean that no matching key was found because a value could itself be `null`. If you need to determine whether a key actually exists, call the `containsKey()` method first.

public Set keySet()   Lets you grab just the keys from a `Map`, returned as a `Set` implementation. Because there can be no duplicate keys, using a `Set` to contain them makes a lot of sense. You can use this `Set` to iterate through the keys. You can even remove keys from the `Set`, and the matching keys are automatically removed from the `Map` itself. How cool is that?

public Object put(Object key, Object value)   Lets you add new entries to a `Map`. If the specified key does not exist, the new mapping is added to the `Map`. If the key does already exist, the currently associated value is replaced with the new value (indicated by the second parameter to this method).

public Object remove(Object key)   Deletes the specified key and the associated value from the `Map`. It returns the value to which the parameter key mapped. If no such key exists, this method returns `null`. Again, if you need to determine whether a key exists, call the `containsKey()` method first.

public Collection values()   Returns all the values in a `Map` as a generic `Collection` object. The actual implementation of this collection is immaterial; just use the methods defined in the `Collection` interface to manipulate these values. Note that no keys are returned by this method, only the values themselves.

As I said, there are some more methods, but this list is plenty to get you started. After all, that is why you are reading this book!

The *java.util.HashMap* Class

Several classes implement the Map interface, but we will concentrate on the
java.util.HashMap class. This class is essentially the same as one of the oldest
classes in the Java API, the java.util.Hashtable. The two classes are practically identical except for one important difference. Whereas a HashMap allows
both a null key and null values, a Hashtable never allows a null key or value.
Just as with the Vector class that I mentioned earlier in this chapter, you will no
doubt come across code that uses a Hashtable instead of the HashMap. Because
both Hashtable and HashMap implement the Map interface, what you learn in
this section (except for those null values!) will work the same with either class.

Let's jump right into it. The HashMapDemo class shows you how to use all the
methods discussed in this section. As always, I discuss everything following the
code listing.

```
1   import java.util.*;
2   public class HashMapDemo
3   {
4       public static void main(String[] args)
5       {
6           HashMap map = new HashMap();
7           map.put("Name", "Todd");
8           map.put("Hair Color", "Brown");
9           map.put("Shoe Size", new Integer(13));
10          map.put("Favorite Author", "Philip Heller");
11
12          System.out.println("Size: " + map.size());
13
14          map.put("Favorite Author", "William Shakespeare");
15          Object author = map.get("Favorite Author");
16          System.out.println("Favorite Author: " + author);
17
18          boolean containsKey = map.containsKey("Shoe Size");
19          System.out.println("Has Key (Shoe Size): " +
                    containsKey);
20          Object removed = map.remove("Shoe Size");
21          System.out.println("Removed: " + removed);
22          System.out.println("Size: " + map.size());
23
24          Set set = map.keySet();
25          System.out.println("Key Set size: " + set.size());
26          boolean removedFromSet = set.remove("Hair Color");
```

```
27          System.out.println("Removed: " + removedFromSet);
28          System.out.println("Size: " + map.size());
29
30          Collection values = map.values();
31          System.out.println("Collection size: " +
               values.size());
32
33     }
34 }
```

The class begins by creating a new `HashMap` object. You can specify an initial
capacity by passing an `int` to the constructor, but if you pass nothing as shown
in line 6, the capacity defaults to 16.

Lines 7–10 add four key-value pairs to the `HashMap`. These values probably
tell you more about me than you really care to know, but they will serve our
needs for now.

Line 12 prints the size, which is 4 at that point.

I regard Philip Heller as a dear friend and an outstanding author, but I am
going to be honest about my favorite author. It is William Shakespeare, by far.
So line 14 replaces the value "Philip Heller" associated with the key "Favorite
Author" with a new value, namely "William Shakespeare". My apologies, Phil!

To prove that this replacement worked, line 15 calls the `get()` method to
retrieve the value mapped to the specified key. This value is then printed to show
you the current value (which is none other than Shakespeare, of course).

On line 18, the `containsKey()` method is called to determine if the key "Shoe
Size" exists in the `HashMap`. The results of this method call are printed on line 19,
which indicates that the key was found.

Because I have embarrassingly large feet, I think I should just erase that from
the record! Now that it has been proven that the key exists, the code can go
ahead and remove the key-value pair entirely. The call to `remove()` deletes the
mapping and returns the value that was there. The message printed on line 21
indicates that the value of 13 was removed. This is the result of calling
`toString()` on the `Integer` object that was stored in the `HashMap`.

Line 22 prints the new size, which is now 3 after the deletion on line 20.

Line 24 shows you how the `keySet()` works. The return of this method is a
`Set` implementation. A message is printed on line 25 that indicates the size,
which equals 3. That makes sense because there should be just as many keys in
the `Set` as key-value pairs in the `HashMap`.

An interesting thing is happening on line 26. Once again, the `remove()`
method is called, but this time it is called on the `Set` containing the keys. As I
mentioned earlier, this results in the same key being removed from the `HashMap`
itself. The printout on line 27 indicates that the element "Shoe Size" was deleted
from the `Set`. On line 28, the size of the `HashMap` prints again. This time, that size
has reduced to 2.

Line 30 calls the `values()` method, which returns a `Collection`. Only the size is printed on line 31 because there is not much we can really do with this `Collection` right now. Later in this chapter when you learn about iterators, I will show you how you might use the collection of values retrieved from a `HashMap`.

Summarizing Maps

Here are the main points that you should keep in mind concerning maps.

+ A map is a collection of key-value pairs.
+ The `Map` interface does not inherit from the `Collection` interface.
+ All keys must be unique in a map.
+ A map can contain duplicate values.
+ There can be at most one value for each key.
+ The key controls all access to a map's values; no indexes are used in a map.

Working with Iterators

So far in this chapter, you have learned how to add, retrieve, remove, and count the contents of a collection. What you have not yet learned is how to iterate over an entire collection instead of retrieving individual elements explicitly. You already performed a simple form of iteration when you worked with arrays back in Chapter 5. You learned then that a common way of iterating through an array involves using a `for` loop and accessing the elements of the array by index.

The collections framework provides a standard and more elaborate mechanism using an *iterator*. Simply put, an iterator is a special data structure that represents the contents of a collection and allows you to walk through that collection. An iterator can optionally let you add, insert, and remove elements. Any elements removed from the iterator will also be removed from the collection that it represents.

Here is a real-world example of an iterator in action. My digital cable service provides me with an online channel guide that I can scroll through to find something to watch. Because I get more than 200 channels, this can take a fair amount of time. When I pop up the channel guide, it always starts on the channel I am currently watching. For example, if the current channel is 57 and I want to see what is on channel 58, I press the Up arrow on my remote. If I want to see what is on channel 56, I press the Down arrow.

Now let's think about the available channels as a collection and the channel guide as an iterator. I have no idea how the details of each channel and upcoming programs are stored in my cable box, and I do not need to know. The channel guide iterator provides me with a simple, standard view of the collection of channels. I can move forward or backward through the channel list, view the details

iterator

A data structure that is associated with a list or a set. You use an iterator to traverse a group of elements in a collection (perhaps all the elements or a subset of the elements). An iterator can always move forward through a sequence of elements but might also provide methods for moving backward.

of each channel, and even remove channels from the display altogether. Those abilities are similar to what an iterator can offer when you are working with the collections framework.

NOTE

Not all iterators provide the same functionality. Some allow you to only move forward through a collection; others might allow you to move bidirectionally. Some will allow you to remove elements; others might even allow you to add new elements. You will learn about two iterators in this section that each provide some set of the possible functionality.

The *java.util.Iterator* Interface

All Collection, List, and Set interfaces define a method named iterator(), which returns an object that implements java.util.Iterator. The Iterator interface actually contains elements from a particular collection, so in that sense, it is a form of a collection itself. However, an Iterator implementation hides the details of the underlying collection. This means that you use all Iterator implementations the same way, no matter the actual collection type. This makes the Iterator interface completely polymorphic.

The Iterator interface defines just three methods:

public boolean hasNext()   Call this method to determine if there are any more elements in the Iterator. If this method returns true, you will normally call the next() method (defined next). Once this method returns false, you know that there are no more elements.

public Object next()   If there are elements remaining in the Iterator, this method returns the next element as a generic Object. You should normally call the hasNext() method first to ensure that at least one more element is available. If you call next() when there are no more elements remaining, you receive a java.util.NoSuchElementException.

NOTE

The NoSuchElementException is a runtime exception, so you are not forced to handle it. If you always precede a call to next() with a call to hasNext(), you should never have this exception thrown.

public void remove()   This method removes the last retrieved element from the collection represented by this Iterator. You can call this method only once following each call of the next() method. If you fail to call next() before each call to remove(), you will receive a java.lang .IllegalStateException.

This method is optional; not all Iterator implementations have to implement this method. If you call remove() on an Iterator that does not implement this method, you will receive a java.lang.UnsupportedOperationException.

As you can see, a standard `Iterator` allows you to only move forward through a series of elements. There are no provisions for moving backward using the standard interface. You will learn about a subinterface named `ListIterator` a bit later in this section. But first, let's look at a code example that uses an `Iterator`.

```
1  import java.util.*;
2  public class IteratorDemo
3  {
4      public static void main(String[] args)
5      {
6          HashSet set = new HashSet();
7          set.add(new Integer(2));
8          set.add(new Integer(4));
9          set.add(new Integer(1));
10
11         System.out.println("Size: " + set.size());
12
13         Iterator iter = set.iterator();
14         while(iter.hasNext())
15         {
16             Object o = iter.next();
17             System.out.println(o);
18             iter.remove();
19         }
20         System.out.println("Size: " + set.size());
21     }
22 }
```

If you execute this code, you will see output similar to this:

```
Size: 3
2
4
1
Size: 0
```

The order of your output may not match exactly because the HashSet is not sorted. This is normal behavior for a set because the order is not guaranteed in any way.

In the `IteratorDemo` class, a `HashSet` is created on line 6 and populated with three `Integer` objects on lines 7–9. Line 11 prints the size once the `HashSet` has been built. (The size is 3 in this case.)

On line 13, an `Iterator` is returned by a call to the `iterator()` method. The `Iterator` provides a view of the collection data without your needing intimate knowledge of the collection itself.

Line 14 uses a `while` loop that loops as long as `iter.hasNext()` returns `true`. You will almost always use a `while` loop when you are iterating over an entire collection like this. Because a `while` loop continues until the associated `boolean` expression returns `false`, this makes a great deal of sense.

The call to `iter.next()` on line 16 returns the next element in the `Iterator` as a generic `Object`. In this simple class, that element is simply printed on line 17. You could of course cast this `Object` to its real type (`Integer`, in this case) and use it any way you see fit.

Line 18 demonstrates how to remove an element from the underlying collection. The call to `remove()` deletes the same element returned in line 16 from the collection. Note that calling `remove()` on the `Iterator` is the only way to remove elements from a collection safely during an iterative process like this. Because `remove()` is called every time the `while` loop executes, all the elements are deleted from the `HashSet`.

Do not remove elements directly from a collection while using an `Iterator`. Always use the `remove()` method defined in the `Iterator` itself. If you break this rule, the results are not guaranteed to work correctly, and you may lose or corrupt your data.

WARNING

Using the `Iterator` interface is not difficult, which is its main benefit. No matter how complex a collection, an `Iterator` will always be simple and provide you with a standard way to process the elements of a collection.

The *java.util.ListIterator* Interface

Remember my channel guide analogy at the start of this section? If you think about it, the standard `Iterator` interface would not be a good choice for implementing my guide. A standard `Iterator` can only move forward through the elements. This would mean that if I were on channel 57 and wanted to get to channel 56, I would have to cycle forward through all the other channels instead of just moving backward one channel. Obviously, that would not be a good system.

The collections framework includes a specialized iterator named `java.util` `.ListIterator`. As you can tell from its name, you use this iterator only with `List` objects. Besides just the `iterator()` method, the `List` interface also defines a method named `listIterator()` that returns a `ListIterator` instance. The

ListIterator inherits the three methods defined in Iterator and adds six new methods that provide more elaborate control over the elements, as shown next.

public void add(Object o)   With this method, you can actually add a new element to the underlying collection via a ListIterator instance. The element is added immediately before the element that is returned by a call to next(). This is an optional method for a ListIterator to implement, and if the method is not implemented, you receive an Unsupported-OperationException.

public void hasPrevious()   This method works just like hasNext(), but in the opposite direction. This method always returns true as long as you are not at the beginning of the list of elements.

public int nextIndex()   Use this method to find the index of the next element in the list. If there are no more elements, this method returns the size of the list itself.

public Object previous()   This method returns the element before your current position in a ListIterator. You should call hasPrevious() beforehand to be sure that an element is actually available. If there is not, you receive a NoSuchElementException.

public int previousIndex()   This method returns the index of the previous element in the list. If you are at the beginning of the list, this method returns −1.

public void set(Object o)   This method replaces the last element returned by either previous() or next() with the Object parameter. You can call this method only once after calling either previous() or next(). Further, you cannot call this method if you have already called either add() or remove(). This is an optional method for a ListIterator to implement, and if the method is not implemented, you receive an Unsupported-OperationException.

Obviously the ListIterator provides more elaborate control when compared with a standard Iterator implementation. The following ListIteratorDemo class shows it in action.

```
1   import java.util.*;
2   public class ListIteratorDemo
3   {
4       public static void main(String[] args)
5       {
6           ArrayList list = new ArrayList();
7           list.add("One");
8           list.add("Two");
```

```
9              list.add("Three");
10
11             System.out.println("Size: " + list.size());
12
13             ListIterator listIter = list.listIterator();
14             while(listIter.hasNext())
15             {
16                 int index = listIter.nextIndex();
17                 Object o = listIter.next();
18                 String str = (String)o;
19                 System.out.println("Index: " + index + " is "
                       + str);
20                 listIter.set(str.toUpperCase());
21             }
22
23         listIter.add("FOUR");
24         System.out.println("Size: " + list.size());
25
26         while(listIter.hasPrevious())
27         {
28             int index = listIter.previousIndex();
29             Object o = listIter.previous();
30             System.out.println("Index: " + index + " is "
                   + o);
31         }
32     }
33 }
```

Here is the output from running this code:

```
Size: 3
Index: 0 is One
Index: 1 is Two
Index: 2 is Three
Size: 4
Index: 3 is FOUR
Index: 2 is THREE
Index: 1 is TWO
Index: 0 is ONE
```

Except for the new ListIterator methods, this code should look familiar to you by now. An ArrayList is created and populated on lines 6–9, followed by a printout of the size at that point (which is 3).

Line 13 grabs the `ListIterator` for this `ArrayList` by calling the `listIterator()` method.

Lines 14–19 define a `while` loop that has an associated call to `listIter` `.hasNext()`. Line 16 extracts the index of the next element via the `nextIndex()` method call. Line 17 calls the `next()` method to get the next element available, and line 18 casts this generic `Object` to a `String`. Line 19 prints the index and value of each element as the loop executes. Line 20 calls the `set()` method defined in the `ListIterator` interface. In this case, every `String` element in the `ArrayList` is replaced with an uppercase version.

Once the `while` loop completes, the call to `add()` on line 23 adds a new element to the underlying `ArrayList`. Because the `ListIterator` has walked through the entire list already, this new element becomes the last element in the `ArrayList`. The printout on line 24 shows you that the new size of the `ArrayList` is 4.

Another `while` loops appears on lines 26–31. This time, the `hasPrevious()` method is called, allowing you to traverse the elements in reverse order. Line 28 gets the index of each element using the `previousIndex()` method (so the first index it returns is 3 and the last is 0). Line 29 calls the `previous()` method to get the previous element, and, finally on line 30, the index and element are printed.

You can move forward and backward through the same `ListIterator` as often as you want. With the standard `Iterator` interface, you can only move forward, so you would have to call your collection's `iterator()` method again to be able to work with elements you have already processed.

Iterators and Maps

The `Map` interface does not define any methods for getting an `Iterator`, so how do you iterate through a `Map`? If you recall, the `Map` interface defines some methods that allow you to grab a `Set` of keys (by calling `keySet()`) or a `Collection` of values (by calling `values()`). As you just learned, both the `Set` and `Collection` interfaces define the `iterator()` method. So once you have grabbed either the keys or the values, you can use a standard `Iterator` to process the data.

NOTE   The `Map` interface also defines a method named `entries()` that also returns a `Set`. Each resulting `Set` element is a special construct that contains both the key and value for each entry in the `Map`.

Let's take a quick look at how you might iterate over a `Map`. Remember that a `Map` is different from other collections because you use keys for all access to the element values. A common situation you may find yourself in is how to grab all the values from a `Map` without having to explicitly provide each key. For example, in the itinerary management application that I discussed earlier in this chapter, it might make sense for someone to see all the upcoming trips for all employees. Instead of forcing the user to enter each employee name manually, it would make a lot more sense to simply grab all the keys and values.

The `MapIterationDemo` class is a simplified version of that itinerary management application. Each username is a key, and the value associated with it is the destination city for the traveler. The code gets the `Set` of keys and processes them using an `Iterator`. As each element in the `Iterator` is found, it is used to get the associated value in the `Map`. Take a look at the logic for this class.

```
1  import java.util.*;
2  public class MapIterationDemo
3  {
4      public static void main(String[] args)
5      {
6          HashMap map = new HashMap();
7          map.put("Todd", "Boston");
8          map.put("Don", "New York City");
9          map.put("Sophie", "Miami");
10         map.put("Bill", "Dallas");
11
12         Set keySet = map.keySet();
13         System.out.println("Number of keys: " +
                 keySet.size());
14
15         Iterator iter = keySet.iterator();
16         while(iter.hasNext())
17         {
18             Object o = iter.next();
19             String user = (String)o;
20             Object city = map.get(user);
21             System.out.println(user + ": " + city);
22         }
23     }
24 }
```

The output from running this code is similar to this:

```
Number of keys: 4
Todd: Boston
Don: New York City
Sophie: Miami
Bill: Dallas
```

NOTE Don't forget that the order may be different because the Set of keys is not sorted.

After the HashMap is created on lines 6–10, the Set of keys is retrieved on line 12. This Set contains all the usernames because those are the keys in the HashMap. Line 13 prints the number of keys, which is just the size of keySet. It should come as no surprise that the size is 4, because that is the size of the HashMap itself.

NOTE The implementation of the Set is hidden from you because you really have no need to know what it is. All access is via the methods defined in the Set interface.

Line 15 calls the iterator() method, which is used with the while loop defined on lines 16–22. This is just the standard Iterator, so you can only move forward through the elements.

Line 18 retrieves the next element, and line 19 casts this into its real type, String. The variable *user* is one of the keys, so you pass this value to the get() method on line 20. Although you already learned that you should never change the contents of a collection when you are iterating, it is perfectly fine to retrieve values from the collection. The call to map.get() returns the value associated with each key in turn.

Finally on line 21, the username (the key) and the destination city (the value) is printed on the command line.

Terms to Know

collection	list
framework	map
iterator	set

Review Questions

1. What is a framework?

2. What is a collection?

3. Which interface is extended by both List and Set?

4. Which of the collection interfaces does not extend the Collection interface?

5. What is a list?

6. What is a set?

7. What is a map?

8. Which method is used to retrieve an Iterator from a Set?

9. Which method is used to retrieve a ListIterator from a List?

10. How many null elements can a Set contain?

Appendix A

Answers to Review Questions

Chapter 1

1. Which two components form the Java platform?

   Answer: The Java Application Programming Interface (Java API) and the Java Virtual Machine (JVM)

2. What was the name of the internal project at Sun Microsystems that produced the first version of the Java programming language?

   Answer: The Green Project

3. What are some types of applications for which Java is suited?

   Answer: Providing dynamic content on the Internet, developing large-scale enterprise applications, creating e-commerce applications, and it can be embedded in many consumer devices.

4. Who is considered the father of Java technology?

   Answer: James Gosling

5. What does it mean for a language such as Java to be strongly typed?

   Answer: Both the compiler and the runtime check the code to ensure that it follows the basic rules of the language, preventing against illegal execution.

6. What does the Java compiler produce from source code?

   Answer: Bytecode

7. What is the engine that allows Java code to be platform independent?

   Answer: The Java Virtual Machine

8. To which of today's development paradigms does the Java language adhere?

   Answer: Object-oriented development

9. What is included in the Java 2 SDK Standard Edition?

   Answer: A compiler, the API libraries, the interpreter, and other tools

10. On which language was Java syntax largely based?

    Answer: C++

Chapter 2

1. Which three types of comments are available when you are writing Java source code?

    Answer: The single-line comment, the block comment, and the documentation comment

2. What is the fundamental component of all Java applications?

    Answer: A class definition

3. How many primitive types are there in the Java language?

    Answer: Eight (`byte`, `short`, `int`, `long`, `float`, `double`, `char`, `boolean`)

4. What is the significance of a semicolon in Java source code?

    Answer: The semicolon is the character that terminates the statement. It essentially tells the interpreter when a statement is complete.

5. Name the two major places where the brace characters must be used in Java source code.

    Answer: You must have opening and closing braces in your class definition and around all of your method bodies.

6. What is the difference between a primitive type and a reference type?

    Answer: A primitive type just holds a single value directly. A reference type holds a memory address that can, in turn, "hold" lots of other types.

7. How do you tell the difference between a `char` and a `String` in source code?

    Answer: A `char` is enclosed in single quotes and is one character in length. A `String` contains zero or more characters in double quotes and usually contains several characters.

8. Why does Java use lazy instantiation of `String` objects?

    Answer: This is mainly because it optimizes memory usage, avoiding many objects being created that may never be used.

9. What are the two primitive types in Java that do *not* hold numeric values?

    Answer: The `char` and `boolean` do not hold numerical values. The `char` type holds Unicode characters and the `boolean` type holds either `true` or `false`.

10. What type is the literal value 3.45?

    Answer: The answer is `double`. Remember that *all* floating-point numbers are considered `double`s unless you append an 'F' or an 'f' to the end of the numeral, making it a `float` instead.

Chapter 3

1. Which of the following is not a Java keyword: `sizeof` or `const`?

    Answer: There is no need for a `sizeof` keyword because all of the sizes of types are predefined in Java. Even though `const` is not used at all in the Java language, it is actually a keyword.

2. What does the new keyword do?

    Answer: It creates a new instance of a class. This is called instantiation and means the JVM will create an object in memory.

3. Which of the following is not a valid name for a variable in Java: licenseNumber, 34jump, $inTheMoney, or _$____?

    Answer: 34jump. A variable cannot start with a digit, though it can contain digits anywhere else in the name. Believe it or not, _$____ is a completely legal name...though a really lousy one!

4. What does making a variable final mean?

    Answer: It means the value of the variable cannot be modified at runtime. It creates a constant.

5. What are the characteristics of a static method?

    Answer: A static method can be accessed directly via the class itself. No object is required, though you can actually call static methods via an object as well.

6. How many interfaces can a class implement?

    Answer: There is no limit to how many interfaces can be implemented by a single class. This is because Java allows multiple inheritance with interfaces.

7. How many classes can a class extend?

    Answer: A class can only extend one other class. This is because Java only allows single inheritance with classes. The class being extended is called the superclass and the inheriting class is called the subclass.

8. Which operator tests equality of primitive types?

    Answer: The == operator tests for equality of primitive types and can also be used to test object reference equivalency.

9. Name the two functions of the parentheses operator, ().

    Answer: Parentheses can be used to *group* expressions together to override default precedence. They can also be used to perform casting of primitive types and objects.

10. If x equals 6, what is the result of !((x < 7) ^ (x == 0))?

    Answer: The answer is false. The ^ operator returns true if the two operands do not match. In this case, the first operand is true while the second is false, so the ^ operator returns true at that point. Then the ! operator returns the opposite value, false.

Chapter 4

1. How do you define scope within a class, method, or flow-control statement?

    Answer: Everything defined with an open brace ({) and closing brace (}) is within a unique scope.

2. What are the decision-making flow-control statements?

    Answer: Both if and switch statements work with conditional tests to allow decision making in your code. The for and while statements are used for looping.

3. What is the rule that you must follow when using `else` statements with an `if` statement?

    Answer: When you add `else` statements to an `if`, every one should match a unique test case. It would make no sense if two `else-if` statements made the same test because only the first one would actually execute.

4. What is the difference between a `while` and a `do/while` loop?

    Answer: A `do/while` loop always executes the statements that it contains at least once, no matter what the test condition evaluates to, because this test is not made until after each iteration of the loop. A `while` loop performs the test first and then executes the body of the loop only if the test returns `true`.

5. What statement is used to handle all other results not already associated with `case` statements?

    Answer: The `default` statement matches all other conditions not already met by defined `case` statements in a `switch`. It is always a good idea to provide a `default` statement.

6. What does the `break` statement do?

    Answer: The `break` statement is used to exit a block of code like any of the looping statements or a `case` statement. The `break` statement by itself exits the code block it is found in and returns control to the next statement following that code block.

7. What does the `continue` statement do?

    Answer: When a `continue` statement is found, all remaining statements are skipped and the enclosing loop moves on to the next step in the iteration.

8. If a method is defined as the following, is `return 1987;` a valid `return` statement?

    ```
    public static int getValue()
    ```

    Answer: Yes. The `return` statement must return the same type indicated in the method signature.

9. What is wrong with the following code?

    ```
    for(int i = 0; i < 10; i++)
    {
      if(i = 5)
      {
        System.out.println("Found a 5!");
      }
    }
    ```

    Answer: The test condition for an `if` statement must return `true` or `false`. What this code is trying to do is check to see if the current value of `i` is 5. This is done with the == equality operator, not the = assignment operator. This is a common error many developers make in their code, so watch out for it! If you do make this mistake, the compiler is nice enough to report it to you.

10. Typically, why should a `break` statement be the last line of all `case` statements?

    Answer: To prevent "falling through" into subsequent `case` statements. You do not have to have a `break` statement in each `case`, but if you do not, it means the next `case` statement is also triggered. Be sure that you understand the process flow you desire and include a `break` statement when you need one.

Chapter 5

1. What is the starting index of all created arrays?

    Answer: All arrays in Java start at index 0 with no exceptions.

2. What is the last index of all created arrays?

    Answer: Because all arrays begin at index 0, the final index is always one less than the length of the array.

3. What is the value at index 2 of the following array?

    ```
    String[] names = new String[10];
    ```

    Answer: Although all primitive array elements default to zero or the equivalent, elements of an object array always default to null.

4. Is the following code snippet legal?

    ```
    int [] points;
    points = new int[900];
    ```

    Answer: Yes. The second line of code creates a new array with a length of 900.

5. Is this a legal array declaration?

    ```
    float f [10];
    ```

    Answer: No, because you cannot specify the length of the array in the declaration.

6. Is the following array created legally?

    ```
    int [][] points = new int[5][];
    ```

    Answer: Although it may seem counterintuitive, you do not have to provide a length for the subarrays in a two-dimensional array like this. This allows you to create a non-rectangular array where the subarrays are of varying lengths.

7. What kind of arrays can you search using the `Arrays.binarySearch()` method?

    Answer: All arrays have access to just the single variable `length` that returns the actual runtime length of the array.

8. Which method should you always call before you use the `Arrays.binarySearch()` method?

    Answer: You must call one of the `Arrays.sort()` methods before performing a binary search.

9. In the following array, what is the length of `points`?

    ```
    int [][] points = new int[10][5];
    ```

    Answer: The `points` array contains 10 subarrays. Each of these subarrays has a length of 5, but the `points` array itself has a length of 10.

Chapter 6

1. Is the following line of code legal?

    ```
    double d = new double(10);
    ```

    Answer: No. All strings are objects and all arrays are objects. The code appears to create an object, but `double` is a reserved word for a primitive type.

2. How many objects exist after the following code completes?

    ```
    Lamp lampOne = new Lamp();
    Lamp lampTwo = new Lamp();
    Lamp lampThree = lampOne;
    lampTwo = lampOne;
    ```

    Answer: The first line creates a new `Lamp` object. The second line also creates a new object. At this point, two objects are available in memory. The third line assigns the reference of `lampOne` to `lampThree`. The fourth line reassigns the `lampTwo` reference to the `lampOne` reference. This essentially eliminates the second object that was created, leaving only one available.

3. Why can the `main()` method not directly access instance methods and variables?

    Answer: Only instance methods have access to the `this` reference, which allows them to directly access other instance members. The main method cannot access any instance members unless a new instance of the class is created inside the main method.

4. Why should instance variables normally be `private`?

    Answer: This aids in achieving encapsulation. Encapsulation is an important part of object-oriented programming because it prevents direct access to variables from outside the object in which they live. This ensures that only the object can change the values, presumably in a logical and legal manner.

5. What composes the interface of an object?

    Answer: The interface for an object is the collection of `public` methods defined in the class the object is based on. Normally, only the `public` instance methods are meant to be invoked by callers.

6. What is the return type of a constructor?

    Answer: Though a constructor looks a lot like a normal instance method, it *never* has a return type.

7. Will the following line of code compile correctly?

    ```
    this = new Lamp();
    ```

    Answer: No, you can never assign a new value to `this`. It is always the reference to the object in which it resides.

8. If you have multiple constructors, what differentiates them from one another in your class?

    Answer: The only thing that differentiates one constructor from another is the list of parameters (sometimes called arguments) associated with it. All constructors have no return type and are always the same name as the class in which they reside.

9. What is the keyword used to invoke another constructor in the same class from within an existing constructor?

    Answer: You invoke another constructor using the `this` keyword.

10. Assume that you are in the constructor for a class that takes no parameters. Write the line of code that invokes another constructor in your class that takes an `int` parameter, and give this parameter a value of 100.

    Answer: `this(100);`. Remember that you can only invoke another constructor by using the `this` keyword. The JVM figures out which constructor you wish to call by the parameter list you provide.

Chapter 7

1. Which two access modifiers guarantee that a method will always be inherited by a subclass?

    Answer: Only `public` and `protected` instance methods are always inherited.

2. If you override a method, which keyword do you use to call the superclass method from the subclass?

    Answer: The `super` keyword references your superclass and can be used to directly invoke nonprivate methods of classes above you in the hierarchy.

3. Does the following class have a superclass? If so, name it.

    ```
    public class Vehicle{}
    ```

    Answer: If you do not explicitly extend another class, you automatically extend from `java.lang.Object`.

4. Does the return type have to be the same in the overloaded version of a method?

    Answer: No. Java identifies methods by name and parameter list. An overloaded method has the same name, but different parameters. Although the return type can be different, it is not enough to only have a different return type. Like an overridden method, an overloaded method can be more accessible than the method in the superclass, but never less accessible.

5. Given the following class declaration

    ```
    public class Car extends Vehicle
    ```

    is the following statement legal?

    ```
    Vehicle v = new Car();
    ```

    Answer: Yes. The reference type is valid, and a `Car` "is a" `Vehicle` and an `Object`, so the statement is legal.

6. What is the return type of all constructors?

    Answer: Constructors return nothing.

7. Can you instantiate an `abstract` class?

    Answer: No.

8. What kind of methods does an interface contain?

   Answer: An interface contains only `abstract` methods. Remember, an interface cannot contain any concrete, implemented methods.

9. True or False: You can overload all methods in the same class or a superclass.

   Answer: False. Methods defined within a class can be overloaded in that same class and nonprivate methods defined in superclasses can be overloaded.

10. True or False: Instance methods are bound to the reference type.

    Answer: False. Because of virtual method invocation, all instance methods are bound to the runtime type. Conversely, all instance variables are resolved based on the actual reference type even if the runtime type defines the same variable.

Chapter 8

1. What type of exception is a `NullPointerException`?

   Answer: `NullPointerException` is an example of an unchecked exception.

2. From which class do *all* exception and error types inherit?

   Answer: Besides the `Object` class, all exception and error types inherit from the `Throwable` class.

3. Which method do exception classes use to output the current method call stack information?

   Answer: Exception classes use the `printStackTrace()` method to output the current call method stack information.

4. If a method call results in a user-defined exception that directly extends an `Exception` named `TestException`, is the following catch block legal?

   ```
   catch(Exception ex){}
   ```

   Answer: Yes. This `catch` statement will match any checked or unchecked exception, including the thrown `TestException`.

5. Which keyword is used to indicate a method that might result in an exception?

   Answer: To indicate a method that might result in an exception, you define a `throws` clause using the `throws` keyword followed by the list of potential exception class names.

6. Which keyword do you use to ensure that certain code always executes whether an exception occurs or not?

   Answer: Use the `finally` keyword. The only way that the code within a `finally` block will not execute is if you shut down the JVM as it would be if you made a call to `System.exit()`.

7. True or false: A method in a subclass that overrides a method in a superclass that can throw a `TestException` must also throw the `TestException`.

   Answer: False. The overridden version of the method can choose to throw no exception or throw `TestException` or a subclass of it.

Chapter 9

1. Where does the JVM store most string literals?

   Answer: The JVM stores most string literals in the string pool.

2. How do you determine the length of a `String` object stored in a variable named *str*?

   Answer: The `str.length()` method returns the length of a `String` object. Don't confuse this with the `length` variable used to determine the length of an array.

3. What is the index of the letter 'a' in the text string, "Staple"?

   Answer: The index of 'a' is 2. Remember, the first index in the text string starts at 0.

4. Which method allows you to add content to the end of a `StringBuffer`?

   Answer: The `append()` method allows you to add content to the end of a `StringBuffer`.

5. Assume that a `StringBuffer` has a capacity of 10 and contains the text string "1234567890". What will the capacity be if you append "A" to the object?

   Answer: The capacity will be 22 because after you add the "A" there are 11 characters in the text string. A `StringBuffer` doubles in size when you exceed capacity and the size is based on the number of characters after the appending takes place.

6. Assume that you have a `StringBuffer`, `buffer`, that contains the text string "abde". How would you add the character "c" after the character "b"?

   Answer: You would use `buffer.insert(2, 'c');`. This will end up changing the contents of the `StringBuffer` to "abcde".

7. What method do you use to calculate the cosine of a number?

   Answer: `Math.cos()` calculates the cosine of a number.

8. What is the range of values returned by a call to `Math.random()`?

   Answer: The value will be equal to or greater than 0.0 and less than 1.0.

9. Which wrapper class *cannot* have a `String` passed to a constructor?

   Answer: The `Character` class does not provide a constructor that accepts a `String` object.

10. How do you change the value stored in a wrapper object?

    Answer: You cannot change the value wrapped in a wrapper object. All such values are immutable.

Chapter 10

1. What is a framework?

   Answer: A framework is a group of related and generic classes (usually `abstract` classes); you can extend these classes to provide the customized behavior you desire.

2. What is a collection?

   Answer: A collection is a data structure that contains zero or more elements and provides methods for manipulating those elements.

3. Which interface is extended by both `List` and `Set`?

   Answer: The `java.util.Collection` interface is extended by both `List` and `Set`. This is the base interface for the common collection types.

4. Which of the collection interfaces does not extend the `Collection` interface?

   Answer: The `java.util.Map` does not extend the `Collection` interface. A map is a special type of collection that stored values mapped to unique keys.

5. What is a list?

   Answer: A list is a collection that maintains an ordered sequence of elements and allows duplicate elements to exist.

6. What is a set?

   Answer: A set is a collection that does not usually maintain order on its elements and does not allow duplicate elements to exist.

7. What is a map?

   Answer: A map is a collection that associates keys with values. Each key must be unique, and there is a one-to-one relationship between a key and a value.

8. Which method is used to retrieve an `Iterator` from a `Set`?

   Answer: The `iterator()` method is used to retrieve an `Iterator` from a `Set`.

9. Which method is used to retrieve a `ListIterator` from a `List`?

   Answer: The `listIterator()` method is used to retrieve a `ListIterator` from a `List`.

10. How many `null` elements can a `Set` contain?

    Answer: One `null` element at the most is allowed. This is because a `Set` cannot contain any duplicates. A set also does not guarantee any specific order of its elements.

Glossary

abstract class   A class that must be extended by a subclass. Typically, an abstract class contains one or more abstract methods. An abstract class must include the `abstract` keyword in the class declaration.

abstract method   A method that has its signature defined but leaves the implementation for subclasses. The method signature must include the `abstract` keyword. Abstract classes are meant to be implemented in one or more subclasses.

access modifier   A special Java keyword that controls the visibility of classes, variables, and methods. There are four access modifiers in the Java language: `public`, `private`, `protected`, and `default`.

accessor method   A method that returns the value that is part of an object's state. This state is typically stored in a `private` instance variable. By convention, accessor method names start with `get` and end with the instance variable name. So if you have an instance variable named `value`, the accessor method should be called `getValue()`. The return type of an accessor method is the same as the type of the instance variable that it returns.

applets   Executable modules that are automatically downloaded to a user's web browser over a network like the Internet. Applets allow deployment to be simple and provide a mechanism to add advanced functionality to web pages.

array   An ordered collection of primitives or objects. When you declare an array, you specify the element type and the resulting array can contain only elements of that type.

array element   Each item stored in an array is considered an element of the array. Each array element must be the same type as the array itself. So an `int` array contains some number of `int` array elements.

array initializer   A special variation to creating an array that does not require you to explicitly set the length. Instead, the contents of the array are put right inside a pair of braces (`{}`) and a comma separates each element. The resulting array's length is equal to the number of elements listed between the braces.

assertion   A special expression that can be used to ensure that a specific condition is met in the code. Assertions are useful for debugging code and can be ignored completely in production code. Assertions should never be used to control program logic, only for testing code and tracking bugs.

behavior   The collection of methods for a particular class. The behavior of your objects typically manipulates their state.

binary input stream   An input stream that allows you to read binary data. This data is received in 8-bit chunks. Although it can be used to read text, it is best suited for nontextual data.

branching statements   Allows a change in the normal flow of a flow control statement. Branching statements can be used to escape from a flow control statement if the need arises.

bytecode   The platform-independent format of compiled Java code that executes in the Java Virtual Machine.

C++   An object-oriented version of the C programming language that gained immense popularity in the early 1990s. C++ can be thought of as a very close cousin to the Java programming language.

casting   Whenever you convert a variable of one type to another type, you are casting. For example, you might convert a `float` value to an `int` value. You can cast primitive number types between each other and you can cast objects back and forth.

Upcasting is converting one type to a bigger type, for example, casting a `byte` to an `int`. Downcasting is converting one type to a smaller type, for example, casting an `int` to a `byte`. The only time you must explicitly cast is if you are downcasting.

character reader   A special input stream that reads 16-bit, text-based data. All of the characters read are Unicode characters, potentially allowing any written language in the world to be read.

checked exception   An exception that the compiler forces code to handle. You can usually accomplish this by using a `try/catch` block. All checked exceptions inherit from the `java.lang.Exception` class but do not extend the `java.lang`
`.RuntimeException` class.

class   The fundamental component of all Java programs. A class is a template for a user-defined type. From a single class, several objects can be created.

class body   Everything between the left and right braces is considered part of the class body (except comments). This includes all variables and methods.

collection   A generic collection contains elements but imposes no order or constraints on the elements it contains. An array is a very simple type of collection. More elaborate collections include methods that allow adding, inserting, removing, and searching of elements.

comments   A special notation that you can add to your source code to describe or explain sections of code. Using comments is an excellent practice because it makes your source code much easier to understand when it is referenced in the future.

Common Gateway Interface (CGI)   A standard for interfacing external applications with HTTP servers on the World Wide Web. CGI solutions are often used to provide functionality to a website like form processing, image creation, and dynamic HTML generation.

compile   The process of converting source code into Java bytecode. The Java compiler creates class files that can be interpreted by any JVM.

compiler   The tool that converts the source code into class files. The compiler reads each line of source code and makes sure that you have followed all the rules. If any problems are found, the compiler reports those errors to you on the command line.

concrete class   A class that has all of its method bodies defined and could be a standalone class, requiring no further extension.

constant   A variable that has a fixed value that cannot be changed at runtime. Typically, constants are shared by many different pieces of code because they are read only.

constructor   A special method that is automatically executed when a new instance of a class is created. A constructor is used to initialize an object to a desired state.

constructor chaining   Constructors can be "chained" together, allowing one constructor to invoke another and so on until an "ultimate constructor" executes. This is accomplished by using the `this` keyword to represent the constructor invocation.

delegation   The process of invoking a method in another object from a method in the current object. This allows complex logic to be handled by separate objects to form the overall logic of your program.

dot-notation   Java uses a system of periods—the dots—to refer to member variables and methods. The syntax `object.method()` is typically how dot-notation is used; this denotes that the object "owns" the method.

encapsulation   An object-oriented concept that protects data from uncontrolled access and modification. The mantra, *private data, public methods*, is concerned with encapsulation.

error   An object that indicates that a severe condition has arisen in the JVM. An error is not something that can usually be corrected on the fly at runtime, like running out of memory.

event handling   The process of handling user interaction with a GUI application. For example, if a user clicks a button, this typically kicks off an event handling mechanism that performs some logic. Without event handling, all those GUIs in the world would not do much of anything!

exception   An object that is used at runtime to indicate that a strange, incorrect result occurred from a method call. A successful method call returns its declared return type, but an unsuccessful method call returns an exception that is usually handled either within the code or by requesting user input.

exception handling   A form of flow control that is used to handle program errors. In many other languages, errors are reported as a code number of some kind that is often cryptic and difficult to work with. Java makes use of exception handling, which provides a more robust method for trapping and recovering from logical errors.

flow control   Special constructs in a language that allow simple or complex algorithms to be defined. Essentially, these form the intelligence of your code.

framework   A framework includes a group of classes and interfaces that define the most common behavior. Normally, when you work with a framework, you do not concern yourself with the actual implementation types, only the interfaces that are implemented. This makes it easy to swap different implementations of a framework in and out without changing how you access them.

fully qualified name   When you include the package name with the class name, it is fully qualified. So java.lang.String is a fully qualified name while just String is not.

garbage collection   Part of the Java Virtual Machine's responsibility is managing memory on your behalf. When memory space that you have used in your code is no longer needed, the garbage collection mechanism kicks in and eventually clears that memory automatically. Because of this automatic procedure, there is not a standard way to manually clear memory from within Java programs. The garbage collection process is a great benefit because it reduces both the amount of code you need to create and, more importantly, dangerous bugs that can creep into your code if you could otherwise mismanage memory.

I/O classes   A set of classes found in the java.io package that allows files to be read from and written to. There are I/O classes that read and write both binary and textual data.

immutable   When a data type is immutable, it cannot be changed at runtime. By default, both String objects and arrays are immutable, but in different ways. A String cannot have its contents changed and an array cannot have its length changed.

infinite loop   A looping construct that has a test condition that always evaluates to true. They can be useful, but are often dangerous bugs.

inheritance   An object-oriented concept that involves a child class deriving structure and data from a parent class. Inheritance is used to create object hierarchies and form complex relationships.

initialization expression   The portion of a for loop that is executed only once when the loop starts. It allows the setup of the starting conditions of the loop.

inner class   A special class that is defined within another class. This allows you to include a class closer to where it is going to be used. Whether or not you ever use inner classes is completely your choice.

input stream   Reads bytes from an input source like a file and returns those bytes via method calls. An input stream is the low-level structure that you need to receive input from an external source into a program.

instance method A method that can only be invoked via an object reference. This is opposed to a `static` method that can be invoked via the class name alone.

instance variable A variable that can be accessed only when an object exists. Instance variables are initialized upon instantiation and each object instance holds its own copies of each variable, independent of any other objects of the same type.

instantiation The process of creating an object. This usually involves using the `new` keyword. Instantiation results in the JVM setting aside memory for the created objects contents. An object's members cannot legally be accessed until it has been instantiated.

interface A completely abstract class that contains only abstract methods. An interface is a construct that captures the `public` methods of a type. All of the methods defined in an interface are abstract and must be overridden by implementing classes.

interpreter An interpreter parses and executes each statement as it is found in a class file. When you execute a Java program, you use the `java` command followed by the class that you wish to execute. This `java` command is the interpreter.

iteration expression The portion of a `for` loop that is executed after the last statement in the loop executes. The value resulting from the iteration is then checked by the corresponding termination expression to determine if the `for` loop should continue.

iterator A data structure that is associated with a list or set. You use an iterator to traverse a group of elements in a collection (perhaps all of the elements or a subset of the elements). An iterator can always move forward through a sequence of elements but might also provide methods for moving backward.

Java HotSpot Virtual Machine (Java HotSpot VM)
The Java HotSpot Virtual Machine is specially tuned to provide optimum performance. It incorporates an adaptive compiler that allows code to be optimized as it executes. This means faster, more efficient code at runtime than past virtual machines have been able to achieve.

Java Virtual Machine (JVM) An abstract computing machine that all Java programs execute in. The JVM is the key to Java's cross-platform nature because it provides the same environment on any platform it actually runs on. The JVM is the intermediary between your Java code and the actual system on which the code executes.

JavaScript A scripting language developed by Netscape to add interactivity to web documents. JavaScript is a programming language but is very simple to learn and use, making it excellent for web content developers who may not have backgrounds with more complex programming languages.

label A special identifier followed by a colon that allows a `continue` or `break` statement to escape to a specific location in the code.

lazy instantiation There are two basic choices when it comes to instantiation. The interpreter could create all the objects you might use before the program even begins executing. or it could delay object creation until it is needed. This latter approach is called lazy instantiation and is the process used by the JVM.

list A specific type of collection that imposes rules guaranteeing some form of logical order to its elements. Lists also do not enforce uniqueness of their elements; in other words, duplicates are allowed. Elements in a list are typically accessed via an index.

literal value Any value that can be assigned directly to a variable. Essentially, a literal value is a "real" value and is not represented by a variable, as in 123 or "Hello".

local variables Any variable whose scope is the body of a method. Local variables are only "active" while their containing method is being invoked.

logical equality   The `equals()` method is defined in the `Object` class and can therefore be overridden in any subclass. Overridden versions of this method can return `true` to indicate that two objects are logically the same even if they are not physically the same object reference. For example, the two `String` objects "Hello" and "Hello" are logically equivalent, but might not actually have the same reference in memory.

map   A special type of collection that includes both keys and values. Each key relates to one and only one value. There are no indexes in a map because all access is made via the individual keys. A map is the simplest form of a database.

member   Something "owned" by a class or object. All variables and methods are called members of their corresponding object or class. Sometimes you will even hear the term "member variable" to differentiate those variables defined directly in the class body from those defined in specific method bodies.

messaging   In object-oriented programming, messaging is how two objects communicate with each other. This messaging is realized by invoking instance methods on objects within a program.

method   A unit of code that performs one or more actions. For example, an object may have a method named `print` that sends a document to a printer. In other languages, methods are sometimes called functions, procedures, and operations.

method call stack   All method calls made during runtime are stored on a stack by the JVM. This allows the JVM to maintain information about all the methods that are currently active in a particular moment of runtime. The information in the method call stack is often reported when an exception or error occurs.

method overloading   A convenience in object-oriented programming that allows multiple methods with the same name to exist. These methods must have different parameter lists and might also have

different return types. It is not enough to only have variance in return type, however; the parameter lists must be different for a method to be overloaded.

method overriding   An object-oriented concept that allows a method in a superclass to be redefined completely in a subclass. The return type, name, and parameter list must be exactly the same in the two classes for overriding to work. If the parameter list is different, you are overloading the method, not overriding it. If the return type is the only thing different, you will get a compiler error. Overriding allows polymorphism to exist in your classes because you can provide refined functionality for a method throughout an object hierarchy.

method signature   That part of a method that must be unique in the scope of a class. Technically, a method signature is the name of the method and its parameter list.

modulus operator   A special arithmetic operator that returns the value of the remainder of division between two numbers. If it returns 0, it means one number is a power of the other.

multidimensional array   An array that contains other arrays as its elements. The most common type of multidimensional array is the two-dimensional array. In Java, all multidimensional arrays are just arrays of arrays.

multiple inheritance   The ability to inherit from more than one parent. Java does not allow inheritance of more than one class, but you can implement more than one interface.

multithreaded   An application that can control individual threads to perform specific actions is considered multithreaded. By divvying up the processing across these threads, an application can appear to be performing multiple actions simultaneously. Java is inherently multithreaded, making the creation of these advanced programs simpler than other languages.

mutator method   A method that sets the value of a portion of an object's state. This state is typically stored in a `private` instance variable. By convention, a mutator method begins with `set` and is followed by the instance variable name. So, for an instance variable named `value`, the mutator method would be called `setValue()`. Mutator methods take a parameter that is the same type as the instance variable with which it is associated. This parameter holds the new value to which the instance variable should be set.

natural ordering   A process used in sorting algorithms to determine how a specific set of data should be ordered. This is normally ascending order for numbers and alphabetical order for characters and strings.

nonrectangular array   A multidimensional array whose subarrays are not all the same length. This type of array requires some special care because you will usually have to determine the length of each subarray before you can process its elements.

object-oriented   A programming methodology that organizes programs following a model of the real world. In the real world, objects are often composed of smaller components. In object-oriented development, this same concept is applied. This paradigm leads to flexible, reusable code.

object reference   Whenever you have a variable that holds an object, its value is actually a reference to that object. The reference essentially equates to a pointer to the memory address of the object. While you use the reference, the JVM is responsible for both assigning it and maintaining it at runtime.

objects   Objects are the runtime versions of classes. Two objects built from the same class are considered the same type, but they are distinct from each other in memory. Changes to one object do not affect the other. Objects make up the key data structure of the Java language.

output stream   Writes bytes to an output source like a file. Bytes are passed in via method calls. An output stream is a low-level structure that lets you send out bytes from a program.

package   A mechanism for grouping related classes together in the same namespace. Packages provide both class organization and inherent protection.

package private   If you give no access modifier whatsoever to a class, method, or variable, it is defined as package private. This means that only classes defined within the same package can gain access to the class, method, or variable so defined.

pass by reference   Instead of copying the values of parameters and return types like you do with primitive types, objects only have their reference passed. This allows one object to be referred to from many different points in an application and ensures that state and behavior are consistent.

pass by value   The pass by value semantics mean that parameters and return types are copied when they are passed to and from methods. All primitive types in Java follow the pass by value rule.

pointers   In languages like C and C++, a pointer represents a specific location in memory that is controlled by the code itself. Pointers can lead to dangerous problems, including data corruption, if they are not used correctly. Java removes the whole notion of managing your own pointers, which removes this often unnecessary complexity.

polymorphism   The ability to have many forms of the same object. An object can always be referred to by its own class type or any of its superclasses. This allows the reference type and the runtime type to be separated. The instance methods of a runtime type that are also defined in the reference type will always be invoked because of virtual method invocation.

precedence   The predefined order in which operators execute, enforced by the rules of Java. Understanding precedence helps you ensure that your operations function exactly as you intended them. Often, parentheses are used to group expressions together to better control the precedence.

procedural code   This code is composed of a series of functions that perform distinct units of work on data passed to them. Procedural code is often difficult to manage and extend, though it is easier than object-oriented code to grasp initially.

promotion   The upcasting of one primitive type to another as the result of a mathematical operation. The biggest type in an expression is how big the result of that expression will be. All of the variables in the expression are promoted to the result type before the operation completes.

protected code   The code inside a `try` block is considered "protected" because the JVM is monitoring the results of each statement. If an exception occurs, the JVM attempts to find a matching `catch` block that can process the exception appropriately.

pseudocode   Code written in a logical, natural language style to express process or flow. Pseudocode cannot be compiled; it is used only to explain the steps required for actual code to work.

reference type   The class name of the variable in which an object reference is stored. The reference type must be either the same as the runtime type or a superclass.

references   Java does not use direct pointers for a variety of good reasons. A reference is really a "pointer to a pointer." This system allows the JVM to manage the memory for you while still allowing you safe access to the objects residing in that memory.

referential equality   If two object variables contain the exact same reference (and thus point to the same object in memory), they are considered to have referential equality. You can always test to references for equality by using the == operator.

reserved words   Keywords that form part of the dictionary of a programming language. Java has 52 reserved keywords defined that can never be used as names in your source code.

runtime type   The actual instance type stored in memory. The runtime type need not be the same type

as the variable that refers to it; it can be a subclass of the reference type instead. The runtime type is the "real" type of an object reference.

scope   Scope refers to the accessibility of a variable within a class. Everything in Java has some form of scope. At the class level, you can identify a scope by a matched pair of braces. Whatever is between the braces is in the same scope and cannot be "seen" outside of those braces. Each new pair of nested braces is yet another level of scope.

set   A refined form of a collection that imposes no ordering rules. A set makes sure all of its elements are unique by denying any duplicates being added. No indexing of elements is typically done with a set.

sockets   An endpoint in network communication. When you connect a client to a server, sockets are the constructs that represent that connection on each system. Sockets include streams so that you can both read and write data across the connection as well.

source code   The "human" language of Java. You write the source code and eventually compile it into the more cryptic bytecode needed by the JVM. Source code is a high-level view of a programming language.

stack trace   When an exception or error occurs, the JVM can output the current state of the method call stack. This stack trace includes all of the classes, objects, and methods currently active and usually includes the line numbers in the source code where the exception occurred. You can print out this stack trace using the inherited method `printStackTrace()` located in the `Throwable` class.

standard error   The location where error messages are output. Typically, this is the same as the standard output where normal messages are printed. Sometimes the standard error of a system might be a log file or a printer somewhere. Whenever you call the `System.err.println()` method, the provided message is typically sent to the standard output of the system that the code is running on.

state   The data of a program or application. For example, the balance of a bank account is a state. Subsequent functions can operate on that state. For example, a method can calculate the interest on the balance passed to the method.

statement   A complete unit of work in a Java program. A statement is always terminated with a semicolon and may span multiple lines in your source code. Every statement is executed in the order in which it is found in the class or method.

string literal   A special form of the literal that contains a string of characters enclosed in double quotes. Note that every string literal is represented as an object in memory.

string pool   A special portion of memory set aside by the JVM to store string literals. `String` objects in the string pool can be reused throughout the life of a program, which allows the JVM to conserve memory usage. As always, all `String` objects in the pool are immutable.

strongly typed   When a language is strongly typed, it means that it imposes strict rules on the declarations made in the code itself. Some languages allow a variable to represent an unknown data type, but languages like Java force you to declare all variables to be a specific type before they can be used.

subclass   Sometimes called a child class or a derived class. If you use the `extends` keyword, you are defining a subclass. A subclass inherits all of the nonprivate members from the extended class.

subscript   The syntax for specifying the element of an array that you wish to access. A subscript is shown as a pair of brackets containing an `int` that represents an index. For example, the statement `names[2]` refers to the third element in the array called `names`.

substring   Any portion of a complete text string can be considered a substring. In the text string "Madam, I am Adam", the phrase "I am Adam" is a substring.

super class   Sometimes called a parent class or a base class. The class listed to the right of an `extends` clause is the super class. The class to the left is the *subclass.*

terminating character   Whatever character or characters are used in a programming language to indicate the end of a statement. In Java, the terminating character is always the semicolon.

termination expression   The portion of a `for` loop that tests the value of the for loop for true or false. If this expression returns false, the `for` loop ends at that point.

threads   Lightweight processes contained within an actual process. Threads are the building blocks of multithreaded programs and provide separate distinct processing.

***throws* clause**   Any method declaration can include the `throws` keyword followed by a list of one or more exceptions that might result from calls to the method. If a method throws any checked exceptions within its body, those exceptions must be listed in the `throws` clause.

unchecked exception   Any exception that extends from `RuntimeException` is considered an unchecked exception. Unchecked exceptions do not have to be handled in a `catch` block, though they can be if you desire. The compiler never forces you to handle unchecked exceptions.

Unicode   A character-encoding scheme that defines a unique number for every character regardless of language or platform.

unsigned   An unsigned data type can only contain values that are zero or higher. In other words, there are no negative numbers allowed as values to an unsigned data type. Java has only one unsigned type, the `char`.

variables   These can be defined in classes and methods and hold values that can often be changed through the course of a program's execution.

Variables in Java are either primitive types or reference types.

virtual method invocation The JVM uses this process to ensure the method definition closest to the runtime type is called. This is sometimes referred to as "late binding" because the instance methods are not linked at compile time. Instead, a virtual method table is created in memory for each object instance and the JVM selects the appropriate version of a method at runtime.

wrapper class Java provided classes that "wrap" around primitive types. For example, the `Integer` class contains a primitive `int`, but provides methods to process or retrieve the "wrapped" primitive. All primitive types have an associated wrapper class.

Index

Note to the reader: Throughout this index **boldfaced** page numbers indicate primary discussions of a topic.

C

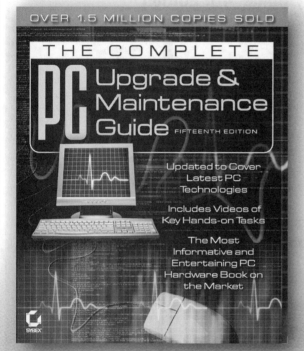

TELL US WHAT YOU THINK!

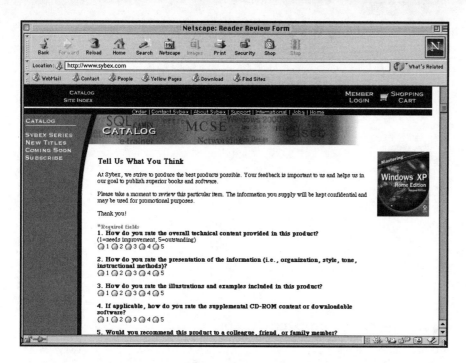

Your feedback is critical to our efforts to provide you with the best books and software on the market. Tell us what you think about the products you've purchased. It's simple:

1. Go to the Sybex website.
2. Find your book by typing the ISBN or title into the Search field.
3. Click on the book title when it appears.
4. Click **Submit a Review.**
5. Fill out the questionnaire and comments.
6. Click **Submit.**

With your feedback, we can continue to publish the highest quality computer books and software products that today's busy IT professionals deserve.

www.sybex.com

SYBEX Inc. • 1151 Marina Village Parkway, Alameda, CA 94501 • 510-523-8233